ATTUNEMENT
THROUGH
THE BODY

ATTUNEMENT THROUGH THE BODY

SHIGENORI NAGATOMO

State University
of New York
Press

Published by
State University of New York Press, Albany

© 1992   State University of New York

All rights reserved

Printed in the United States of America

For information, address State University of New York
Press, State University Plaza, Albany, NY 12246

Library of Congress Cataloging-in-Publication Data

Nagatomo, Shigenori.
        Attunement through the body / Shigenori Nagatomo.
            p.   cm. — (SUNY series on the body)
        Includes bibliographical references and index.
        ISBN 0–7914–1231–8 (hard) . $59.50. — ISBN 0–7914–1232–6 (pbk.) :
    $19.95
        1. Body, Human (Philosophy)—Japan—History. 2. Mind and body-
    -Japan—History. 3. Dōgen, 1200–1253. 4. Body, Human (Philosophy)-
    -History. 5. Mind and body—History. 6. Philosophy, Comparative.
    I. Title. II. Series.
    B5243.H84N34   1992
    128—dc20
                                                        91–39372
                                                           CIP

10 9 8 7 6 5 4 3 2 1

To
Yuasa Yasuo Sensei,
Without Whom Not

CONTENTS

ACKNOWLEDGMENTS

This study is a partial outcome of the dissertation originally submitted to the University of Hawaii, May, 1985. Completing this dissertation was a long and arduous journey for me, since I have not always been convinced that my destiny lies in the direction of academia. Yet, I have a deep longing to pursue knowledge. Perhaps, deep within myself there is compelling need that my thoughts and actions come together. In order to shorten the distance between my thoughts and my actions, I have undertaken the project of writing this work. Yet, as I have travelled this path, I have met many people who have provided me with food for my soul at one time or another. To those who have left indelible marks on my mind, I would like to make the following acknowledgments.

I owe a special debt to Professor and Mrs. Robert O'Dell, the couple who were directly responsible for my introduction into American life and who made it possible for me to attend Central College, Pella, Iowa. This was a major turning point in my life. At Central, I had the good fortune to study philosophy under Dr. William Paul who, a devoted Christian, towered before me as an inspiration, for both philosophy and religion were harmoniously joined in him.

However, as fate would have it, I moved, through the kind effort of Pat Wine, from the cold country of the American midwest to the ever-summer island of Hawaii where I have met numerous friends and teachers. During my first years at the University of Hawaii, Professor T. P. Kasulis with the genius of a first-rate thinker taught me to look at Japanese philosophy from the outside. Monte Hull served as my sounding board with his keen sensitivity. David Shaner, an inspiring friend, guided me on many things American, both academic and nonacademic. Karen Lee has also been a good source of information.

Of all the people I have met during the course of my formal study at the University of Hawaii, Professor Eliot Deutsch stands out as a consummate philosopher who has taught me what philosophy is, and what it is not, especially during our many dinner conversations at his house. I only regret that, in presenting this work to the public, I have not been able to accomplish more. Another equally towering scholar who has been of immeasurable help to me in the preparation of this work is Yuasa *Sensei* of Obirin University in Japan. This study was, in fact, inspired by his numerous works. His timely advice and frequent encouragement have helped me to sustain interest in my inquiry, without which this work couldn't have taken the present shape.

The members of my dissertation committee have read the earlier version of this study and have given me much valuable criticism and many helpful suggestions. My sincere appreciation goes out to Professor K. N. Upadhyaya, Professor Beatrice Yamasaki, Professor Roger T. Ames, and Professor David Chappell. Outside of my committee, I have troubled the following professors; Professor David Hall of the University of Texas, at El Paso and Professor Kimura Kiyotaka at Tokyo University, both of whom gave me encouragement with kind comments. Professor Clifford Ames has revised my prose. Without his skillful hands in repairing my English, part 1 and 2 could not have taken this present shape. Also, Professor Roger Ames kindly proofread part 3. I could not have wished, in the strenuous task of correcting this manuscript, to have anyone better than the Ames brothers.

Outside of my dissertation committee, I have met many people who have been of great help to me. Dr. Motoyama Hiroshi, president of the Institute for Religion and Psychology, often gave me invaluable advice on things spiritual. Professor Okada Takehiko, Professor Emeritus at Kyūshū University, showed me what it means to become a human according to the Confucian tradition. I also want to mention Mr. and Mrs. Larry and Ronnie Shinn, Mr. and Mrs. Donald and Sue Akashi, and Mr. and Mrs. Hideo and Tatsuko Kaneshiro who have been good friends, and who have given me company and welcome relief from my seclusion. Dr. Kubota Susumu, a cardiologist at St. Marianne Hospital, has always given me valuable direction and guidance, and Professor Inoue Yoshiko has been a "great mother." I must thank my natural mother for her constant care and infinite patience.

I wish also to express my gratitude to the editors of the *Phi-*

losophy East and West, the *International Philosophical Quarterly* and *Giving the Body its Due* to incorporate the material that in earlier versions appeared as the following essays: "Ichikawa's View of the Body," (PEW, October, 1986), "An Analysis of Dogen's Casting off Body and Mind" (IPQ, September, 1987) and "An Eastern Concept of the Body: Yuasa's Body-Scheme" (SUNY Press, 1992).

In the last phase of preparing this manuscript, Tom Downey, Gereon Kopf and Elaine Moretti, friends at Temple University, kindly went through it with many constructive insights and criticisms, and Professor Jeff Shore of Hanazono University volunteered to check my English toward the end of this project. Professor Howard Eilberg-Schwartz, the editor of this series, has extended his expertise to shape it into the final version. My sincere appreciation goes to these friends. Last but not the least, I would like to thank the staff of SUNY Press, Ms. Lois Patton, Ms. Susan Geraghty, and Ms. Nancy Ellegate, for their unfailing editorial skills.

INTRODUCTION

The progress in science and technology in modern times shows for the destiny of the genus human two faces like the two-headed God, Janus. One face which science and technology reveal is that of the God of light, who lluminates brightly the future for the genus human, guaranteeing it an affluent and pleasant happiness. The other face is the God of darkness, who betrays a power that could bring a terrifying destruction to the world and mankind. Today, we are confronting the God with these two faces.

———Yuasa Yasuo, from the Preface to
New Age Science and the Science of Ki-Energy

Attunement Through the Body is a personal lyricism cast in a philosophical language. It has arisen as one of my responses to the encounter, in a broad perspective, between East and West, and in a more narrow personal and philosophical sense, between rationality and a-rationality, or between mind and body. What characterizes these encounters is a dualism which has taken a strong hold on our way of life spreading widely in most industrialized nations of the world to the point of being ingrained, as it were, in every cell of our genes although a degree to which the cell is affected may differ from individual to individual and from nation to nation.

The main theme on which *Attunement Through the Body* focuses is the concept of the lived and living human body, or the personal body as it relates to the mind-body issue. It examines from a "Japanese" perspective how we live our personal body in our everyday life (part 1) and how it could be transformed through a process of meditative training (part 2). The everyday mode of living our body and its transformation is theoretically articulated in light of the concept and phenomenon of "attunement" by utilizing the method of "comparative" philosophy (part 3). I should like to explicate, as a way of introducing the work, the following terms, attunement, Japanese perspective, and comparative philosophy so that a clear sense of direction and purpose, along with the organization of the work, will open up within the purview of our inquiry—first, the phrase Japanese perspective, and then the method of comparative philosophy, while relegating the discussion of attunement later when we directly deal with the content of this work.

A most obvious reason that justifies the use of the phrase Japanese perspective for *Attunement Through the Body* is that the first two parts of this three part work, deals directly with the concepts of the body developed by three Japanese thinkers—in part 1 Ichikawa Hiroshi and Yuasa Yasuo, two contemporary Japanese philosophers and in part 2 Dōgen Kigen, a medieval Japanese Zen master. In view of the materials covered in part 1 and 2, therefore, *Attunement Through the Body* unmistakably bears the mark of Japanese.

To be more specific, Ichikawa employs in chapters 1 and 2 phenomenological method, which is Western in origin, to articulate how we live our body in our everyday life, understanding "we" to mean not only "Japanese people" but a collective name for all humans. In chapter 3 Yuasa expands on the concept of body-scheme, originally developed by Henry Head, a British physiologist, to give a comprehensive, conceptual structure to the living and lived body, while incorporating insights gained from his in-depth study of depth-psychology, physiology, Western philosophy and Eastern meditational methods.

Part 2, consisting of four chapters, explores Dōgen, particularly focusing on his philosophy of the body made explicit through meditational training. Insofar as Dōgen is a Japanese religious thinker, his treatment of the body will also bear the mark of Japanese although Dōgen himself may reject such a category, for he firmly believed that what he was teaching was the Buddha way. Nonetheless, when it is examined from a broader context of Buddhist scholarship or scholarship in general, Dōgen's philosophy of the body is the Buddha way that is articulated through Japanese ethos. Even though Dōgen's philosophy of the body carries a Japanese ethos, it does not mean that his articulation of the body in light of Buddhism is, when seen from a broad perspective on human existence, confined to a Japanese view of what the body is. It still carries a universal applicability.

It is a mistake, therefore, to infer from the fact that simply because these three authors are Japanese, the subject matter, the concept of the body, developed in each part, is distinctively and uniquely Japanese. It has a universal applicability to all humans, regardless of the national origin, as the reader will discover in going through *Attunement Through the Body*. In this respect, it is worthwhile to remind ourselves that philosophy knows no national boundary. Each philosopher must learn to go beyond his/her national *karma*, or as Jung might put it, the national collective unconscious. (More on this point later when discussing comparative philosophy.)

We may now explain briefly each of the above mentioned three treatments of the concept of the body to give a sense of the conceptual running thread so that a fuller picture of what is developed in part 1 and 2 will be in our purview.

In dealing with Ichikawa's concept of the body, our primary concern is to learn how we live our body in our everyday life. Can we give a philosophical explication to this question? To respond to this question I shall focus on Ichikawa Hiroshi's book, *Seishin toshite no shintai* (The Body As the Spirit), where he demonstrates, through the skilful use of phenomenological method, the thesis that the body *is* spirit, a counter thesis to the well-known Cartesian dualism. Since the official Cartesian mind-body dualism is fraught with many theoretical and existential problems, Ichikawa's work deserves full attention and exposure as a corrective to Cartesian dualism. Moreover, since Ichikawa uses phenomenological method, that is, his project is to *describe how* we live our body in our everyday existence, his thesis is not a mere "theoretical solution" advanced solely for the sake of logical and theoretical consistency.

In advancing the thesis that the body is spirit, Ichikawa analyzes what he calls "the body as phenomena," that is, the body as it appears to (everyday) consciousness and "the body *qua* structure." This body as phenomena is divided in two categories in our articulation of his phenomenological discussion:[1] the subject-body, that is the body we live immediately and directly from within, and the object-body, that is the body we objectify through our external sense perception. Ichikawa's analysis of the body *qua* structure focuses on the relation of dependence between the subject-body and the object-body and shows that the subject-body is functionally regulated and controlled by the object-body. This analysis is offered in preparation for maintaining his main thesis that the body is spirit, leading us to a phenomenological discovery of the preconscious origin of the concepts of subject-body and object-body. He skillfully describes, by delving into such phenomena as "body-space," "bodily dialogue," and "personalization of lived body," that there is a preconscious, lived body-scheme that *synthesizes* the subject-body and the object-body. He characterizes this phenomenological finding as a lived body-scheme which *unifies* the subject-body and object-body, uncovering the phenomenological fact that underlying this distinction, there is a lived unity or oneness between the subject and the object, between the interior and the exterior. In this manner, Ichikawa shows phenomenologically how to overcome Cartesian dualism, while answering, at the same time, the question of how we live our body in our everyday life. This issue is examined in chapter 1 and 2 of part 1.

Yet, Ichikawa maintains that this unity is an "ambiguous oneness" as well as a "preconscious" operation of the lived body-scheme. The status of oneness thus recognized is rooted in the very fact that Ichikawa restricts his phenomenological analysis to phenomena as they appear to *everyday* consciousness.[2] But, the question arises whether or not this unity, which Ichikawa characterizes as "ambiguous" and preconscious, is a final position achievable by human beings, or put differently, whether or not it may be brought to a higher unity with an exhaustively transparent awareness through the process of transforming everyday consciousness.

This question leads us to Yuasa Yasuo's treatment of the lived body-scheme in chapter 3. He develops his own concept of body-scheme from a contemporary perspective while incorporating a *transformative* dimension into this concept. This will mark a departure from the analysis confined to the body as phenomena appearing within the horizon of everyday consciousness because if transformation can be effected on the lived body of our everyday consciousness, we will see a concept of oneness quite different from Ichikawa's characterization. Yuasa introduces this transformative dimension by bringing into the scope of his analysis the Eastern self-cultivation methods, primarily meditative training.

Yuasa defines his concept of body-scheme primarily as the hierarchical system of multilayered information circuits, which he conceptually divides in four, each circuit correlated, as much as possible, with the neurophysiological structure of the object-body. In so doing, he implicitly assumes that the body-scheme, understood thus as a system of information circuits, is an energy phenomenon.

According to Yuasa, the system of these four circuits is comprised of (1) the "external sensory-motor circuit," (2) the "circuit of coenesthesis," (3) the "emotion-instinct circuit," and (4) the "unconscious quasi-body circuit." He notes that the first two circuits belong to conscious function, that is, we can readily become aware of their functions. We learn from Yuasa that it is these two circuits, particularly the first one, on which a majority of the Western philosophers have cast theoretical speculation in tackling the mind-body issue. The third emotion-instinct circuit borders between conscious and the unconscious. For the incorporation of this circuit within the concept of body-scheme, Yuasa is assisted by his knowledge of depth-psychology and Eastern self-cultivation methods, and this incorporation marks an expansion of the concept of body-scheme in scope and depth, making it more comprehensive than any other treatment of the subject-matter, East or West. The fourth circuit of the unconscious quasi-body is so termed because this circuit remains closed or imperceptible for most of us insofar as we attempt to experience it through our external sensory perception: it exists only as a potential circuit insofar as our everyday awareness is concerned. Therefore, it is called "unconscious." The adjective "quasi" qualifying the body indicates further that it cannot be understood in terms of the materiality of the object-body. Yuasa introduces the concept of unconscious quasi-body primarily in view of the meridians of acupuncture medicine. According to Yuasa, this circuit, however, can become available to our awareness in a deepened state of meditation or in the case of meridian-sensitive persons. This is how and where Yuasa introduces a transformative dimension into his concept of body-scheme, a point which Yuasa benefitted from his study of the Eastern meditative tradition of self-cultivation.

Conceptually, this introduction of a transformative dimension owes its theoretical plausibility in Yuasa's concept of body-

scheme to the fact that the four information circuits are conceived of as forming a hierarchy, with the fourth circuit serving
as the base of this hierarchy while the first is assuming its apex.
This hierarchical conception of Yuasa's body-scheme is proposed
in view of an experiential awareness of these circuits. That is, the
system of multilayered information circuits decreases its transparency, or increases its opacity in terms of their experiential
correlate, as one moves from the first to the last circuit, insofar
as one remains within the everyday, natural standpoint. This
suggests to Yuasa that the mode of existence characteristic of
everyday consciousness is *provisionally dualistic* in character. It
is dualistic because there is a disparity in terms of awareness
between the first two circuits and the last two circuits, and it is
provisional because it is not the permanent status admitting of
no transformation. Yuasa contends, however, that this provisional dualistic stance can be changed into a nondualistic stance
once the transformative process is existentially effected in the
course of Eastern self-cultivation methods. In light of the distinction between the four circuits, this transformation suggests that
both the third emotion-instinct circuit which borders between
conscious and the unconscious, and the fourth unconscious
quasi-body circuit that remains simply potential, become incorporated within the conscious domain. This will be philosophically interpreted then as a transformation from the dualistic stance
of everyday existence to a nondualistic stance.

When Yuasa discusses this transformative dimension in his
concept of body-scheme, he has in mind such phrases as Eisai's
"body-mind oneness," Myōe's "crystal clear body-mind coagula-
tion," and Dōgen's "casting off the body and mind," all expressive of a heightened state of meditative awareness—a dimension
of experience higher than the mere "ambiguous, preconscious
oneness."

In an effort to delve further into Yuasa's idea of transformative dimension, part 2 will focus on Dōgen's philosophy of the
body, particularly on an analysis of the practice of "just sitting,"
which is a somatic modality of the person. This part is concerned
with theoretically articulating the process of bodily transformations vis-à-vis the practice of just sitting while holding in view an
epistemological perspective opening up through such transforma-

tions. Throughout this inquiry two overriding questions are raised, namely, (1) how does the body go through transformations in the process of just sitting, and (2) what epistemological perspective do these transformations bring forth?

In particular, chapter 4 specifies this transformative process to be an existential, practical movement from an "I" to a "who," wherein the personalization of experience is ceased and exchanged with a holistic appropriation of experience. In this connection, the term "samadhic awareness" is introduced to justify this existential and practical movement, where samadhic awareness means to become one with an object of meditation, and a precondition for having samadhic awareness is an absence of I as an ego-consciousness. This translates into effecting the everyday existence to change into samadhic existence. This will be shown as a process of "uncovering" the "accidental dust," that is, as a process of transforming the negative affectivity, associated with the somatic modality of a person's ego-consciousness, to the positive affectivity. When this is examined in light of its experiential correlate, it will be shown that it is reflected in a transformation from the dependence and opposition of *dharmas* to their nondependence and nonopposition. In actuality, this is a further specification of what samadhic awareness means. When samadhic awareness obtains, there is no opposition and dependence among the things experienced, because there obtains a oneness between the experiencer and the experienced. Conversely, when there is opposition and dependence among the things experienced, the things in this modality are not experienced in spontaneity and freedom to their fullest.

Chapter 5 will analyze the *practical* procedure involved in just sitting in order to learn in more concrete terms how the experiential correlate of nondependence and nonopposition is achieved. While discussing this issue in consideration of the preparation, the attitude, and the goal of just sitting, this chapter will examine the experiential meaning of what Dōgen deems to be the highest form of meditation, "immobile sitting," vis-à-vis the samadhic awareness that accompanies it, and this samadhic awareness will be interpreted to be an instance of achieved body-mind oneness. Since this is understood to be an achievement, it will provide us with a theoretical justification for understanding the practical and existential transformation of everyday existence into samadhic existence. Examining this transformation in light of the mind-body problem, it will be shown that it further correlates with the transformation of provisional dualism into nondualism. To demonstrate the validity of this interpretation, this chapter will further discuss Zen's contention that theory and practice must be one, that is to say, the theoretical formulation of Zen experience must be verified first by practical lived experience.

Chapter 6 will delve directly into Dōgen's confirmatory satori experience of enlightenment, which is linguistically expressed as casting off the body and mind, and will argue that an essential meaning of casting off the body and mind is an epistemological reorientation in which the concepts of the mind and the body are radically modified. This modification may alternatively be stated as a change in the experience of body-image. More specifically, the body we objectify through the external sensory apparatus is synthesized or appropriated within the body we live from within, thereby losing its resistance as a material object to the mind. It shows an instance of achievement of oneness between mind and body.

The analysis then moves on to the examination of an experience generative of this modification, which will take us to an examination of the experience of "felt inter-resonance." The term felt inter-resonance designates a lived feeling in meditative awareness where Dōgen claims that there obtains a "subtle mutual assistance" between the meditator and the things engaged through the meditative awareness. Conceptually, the experience of felt inter-resonance, as I interpret it, enables the meditator to locate the object engaged within a complex matrix of conditioned generation-extinction. A contention here is that when this occurs, a complete attunement between the person (or his/her personal body) and the things in the ambiance is engendered. Moreover, it will be argued that this attunement is epistemological in character: since the object no longer epistemologically opposes the subject which experiences it due to the nature of samadhic awareness, there is no dichotomy between the object and subject who knows it. In this connection, it will be pointed out that the mode of judgement operative in the experience of felt inter-resonance is somatic in character in contrast with the act of *cogito* associated with our everyday, ego-consciousness, where we propose to understand "somatic" to mean somatically induced awareness. The attempt to respond to the initial questions, raised in the beginning of this part concerning the epistemological perspective that opens up through the process of bodily transformations, is completed in this chapter through the examination of felt inter-resonance which gives rise to a phenomenon of attunement.

Chapter 7 will take our investigation out of the context of just sitting to see whether or not the above mentioned felt inter-resonance also serves as a basis for the body in action, which we term "samadhic action," in contrast to samadhic awareness. This move is motivated partly to dispel a criticism that whatever obtains experientially in samadhic awareness is an instance of "Oriental Quietism."

This chapter will analyze Dōgen's identification of the mind with objects, where it will be shown that this identification presupposes a samadhic experience of felt inter-resonance. This understanding will guide us to articulate what it means for the body to act vis-à-vis the experience of felt inter-resonance. The chapter will analyze it in light of Dōgen's concept of "true human body," interpreting this concept to mean an achievement wherein understanding and action are correlative with each other—a further specification of Zen's contention that practice and theory are one. When this correlativity is lived, it will be characterized as an actional realization of nonduality.

Next, the samadhic awareness generative of attunement is also shown to be actional in character. It is actional because an epistemological object provides an opportunity for the person in samadhic awareness to "play with" it, wherein "samadhi-at-play" is at work. This will be explained as follows: since the object is located properly within the complex matrix of conditioned generation-extinction, its past and its destiny are disclosed, which gives rise to an opportunity for an object to be played with in the sense of engaging objects unself-consciously.

Part 3 develops a new theory of what we call attunement, while incorporating the fruits of our investigation gathered in the previous two parts. There is, however, a certain discontinuity between the first two parts and this part, because it departs from the conceptual schemes and terminologies employed in the previous two parts. Part 3 is incorporated into this work as an instance of comparative philosophy. Here I would like to give a brief explanation of how this phrase is understood in the present context.

Comparative philosophy is usually understood to be a method of achieving a philosophical clarity or position by contrasting and comparing the terminologies, the ideas, individual thinkers, schools of thought, and/or different philosophical traditions. Such an approach to "comparative philosophy" is necessary at an initial stage of inquiry—in fact, the first two parts of *Attunement Through the Body* have this purpose—for it has a merit of bringing into the open what is seemingly disparate and unintelligible. However, it cannot be taken as its final goal, because such an attitude tends to become a mere pedantic, academic exercise without a clear sense of direction and purpose. In contrast to this usual understanding of the term comparative philosophy, the attitude which *Attunement Through the Body* assumes is to think creatively, particularly in the present context to cast the dualism noted in the beginning of this introduction, in a new outlook across the boundaries of traditions, cultures and philosophies with the vision for preparing a life style conducive to a maximum *eudaimonia* for the coming generations. In this sense, comparative philosophy carries a sense of thought experiment. It calls for a *new* understanding of traditional, philosophical issues while *going beyond* them. When understood in this manner, it is no different from genuine philosophizing. In fact, philosophizing must be comparative in our contemporary age when we witness an increasing exchange among the peoples of different ethnic origins. This situation suggests that we need to embody a deeper understanding of human nature across the traditional boundaries, hoping to achieve "peace among Gods."

The main concern in part 3 is to develop, following the spirit of comparative philosophy mentioned above and based on the study accomplished in parts 1 and 2, a philosophical theory different from the various Western theories such as Idealism, Empiricism, and Materialism. As was mentioned in the foregoing, this position is cast in a theory of what is called attunement. The theory of attunement purports to articulate the mode of engagement obtaining actionally as well as epistemologically between a personal body and his/her living ambiance, both internal and external. The term attunement is used to describe the nature of this relationship. In covering both the epistemological and practical issues together, the theory examines the vital role which our lived body plays in achieving an attunement. Hence, the title *Attunement Through the Body*.

This theory recognizes a provisional dualistic tendency observed in our everyday mode of existence, but it demonstrates that this tendency undergoes a transformation, changing into a nondualistic position. In this process of transformation, the theory perfunctorily introduces an analysis of three different modalities of engagement generative of the attunement—tensionality, de-tensionality and non-tensionality—in order to reflect a degree of attunement obtaining between the personal body and its living ambiance. The difference in the degree of attunement will be analyzed, among other things, in terms of the concept of "feeling-judgement." This judgement consists of two momenta of knowing-that and feeling-that but these two momenta, when judgement is formed, occur spontaneously and immediately with one stroke. What is particularly emphasized throughout the development of the theory of attunement is the focus on the somatic knowledge to counterbalance, if not to change, the emphasis which has been unduly placed in the Western way of learning on cognitive, intellectual knowledge.

A suggestion for reading through *Attunement for the Body* is in order here. Those who are not familiar with Buddhism, particularly that of Dōgen, may read part 1 and part 3 first and after completing part 3, they may go back to part 2 to appreciate the intellectual and conceptual background which informs part 3. Otherwise, the arguments and analyses developed in part 2 may appear too technical and involved to those who are not familiar with Dōgen's general philosophical position, although I have taken some care to avoid this appearance.

We enjoy the great fruits of scientific and technological progress, whose philosophical origin goes back to a dualistic methodology, but we are also increasingly becoming aware of the adverse effects that science and technology have brought on us, threatening the very mode of our personal existence. In cities where technology and science abound, promising "affluent and pleasant happiness," we witness a drastic increase of brutal crimes and inhuman interpersonal relationship. It appears that the more we enjoy the fruits of science and technology, the more we face an increasing process of de-humanization in every aspect of our daily life. We are today standing in the chasm between a material affluence and spiritual impoverishment. I wonder if we could leap out of the dualism by envisioning a conceptual framework of attunement pointing toward a unity or oneness of the dualistic modes of our everyday existence, where we can enjoy a spiritual physicality or physical spirituality.

PART 1

Two Contemporary Japanese Concepts of the Body: Ichikawa Hiroshi and Yuasa Yasuo

CHAPTER 1

Ichikawa's View of the Body

INTRODUCTION

In 1975, Ichikawa Hiroshi published a remarkable book on the concept of the body entitled, *Seishin toshite no Shintai* (The Body As the Spirit)[1] in which he presents systematically his unique understanding of the human body with the philosophical sensitivity always discernible in a first-rate thinker, Eastern or Western. As the title indicates, he attempts to elevate the human body, long degraded within the Western philosophical tradition, to the dignity of the spirit (*seishin*). In this attempt, Ichikawa claims the unity (*gōitsu*) of spirit and body by arguing that the body *is* spirit, a counter thesis to the well-known Cartesian dualism. He arrives at this conclusion not by reducing the body to spirit, but by phenomenologically describing the lived content of the human body. Consequently, his position is different from various "solutions" in response to the Cartesian dualism.

   The phenomenological method through which he argues for, and demonstrates his position is not, however, that envisioned by Husserl, but is closer in spirit to that of Merleau-Ponty as developed in his *Phenomenology of Perception*.[2] Ichikawa follows Husserl in his methodological attitude to perform an "epoché," a suspension of judgment on our "natural attitude" in understanding our body,[3] but he, unlike Husserl, consciously avoids performing a series of "phenomenological transcendental reductions" in order to obtain an "eidetic sphere" of the phenomena of the concretely lived body—the essential structure, Husserl thought, shared by all human beings.[4] In any case, Ichikawa certainly avoids using this terminology and doesn't describe his phenomenological findings by appealing to various "phenomenological reductions" and the "eidetic structure," which is no doubt a result of the fact that he is more influenced

3

by the French phenomenologists, such as Marcel, Sartre and Merleau-Ponty than by the originator of phenomenology, Edmund Husserl. For this reason, Ichikawa's phenomenological method is a descriptive endeavor undertaken with the express purpose of making the concretely lived body intelligible to us.

In the first part of *Seishin*, Ichikawa restricts himself in his discussion of the body strictly to that which lies within the boundaries of the phenomenological: he treats the human body only insofar as it appears to consciousness, arguing for his thesis through an examination of the lived experience of the human body. This part of the book is thus entitled "the body as phenomena" (*genshō toshite no shintai*). In the second part, he moves on to describe and capture *living* structures of the human body under the heading "the body as structure" (*kōzō toshite no shintai*), and thereby he seeks to establish a dependency of *cogito* upon the phenomenologically revealed concept of the lived human body.

THE SUBJECT-BODY

At the beginning of part one of Ichikawa's book *Seishin*, he asserts, before dealing with the body as phenomena, that "Being clothes itself in phantoms, afraid of its exposure to nakedness." In making this statement, Ichikawa does not mean to reiterate the Kantian distinction between noumenon and phenomenon in understanding the human body,[5] but rather seeks to reveal "the nakedness of Being." To properly understand Ichikawa's intention as it is stated in this passage, we might substitute the metaphysically neutral phrase, "the phenomena of concretely living body," for the word "Being." Hence, the statement may be taken to mean that Ichikawa intends to reveal the lived body bare, a metaphorical way of promising to render it intelligible.

Such a project requires that we suspend our judgement with respect to the commonly held notion of the body. The human body is generally regarded as "a material something with various physiological functions such as metabolism, that becomes a tool for the spirit in acting upon a real world, sometimes resisting, and at other times troubling the spirit, or being dominated by it."[6]

But, if we are to comprehend "the living body in its concrete entirety,"[7] we must first of all "forget the concepts of the spirit and the body as understood by our intellect, and attempt to grasp the concrete body that we live as it is in its functioning aspects."[8]

Ichikawa feels that we must suspend our judgement with respect to the commonly understood notion of the body because "both the concepts of spirit and body are kinds of extremes (i.e., concepts abstracted) used as clues for understanding (our) life."[9] Contrary to our ordinary conception of the human body, Ichikawa contends that "our concrete life in its great part is spent within the structure which cannot be reduced either to the spirit or to the body."[10] This being the case, "we should consider this unique structure itself as fundamental, and regard the spirit and the body as aspects abstracted from it."[11] Ichikawa's claim that "the body *is* spirit" must then be understood in light of some "fundamental structure" that allows the possibility of abstracting the contention that the body is the spirit. Consequently, the linking verb, is, grammatically equating the spirit and the body as a unity is maintained at the level of this fundamental structure. As a phenomenologist, Ichikawa is obliged to explicate this fundamental structure. Until this explication has been completed, we cannot hope to understand the sense of unity which, according to him, embraces both the spirit and the body.

Ichikawa's initial phenomenological investigation starts with what he terms the "body *qua* subject" (*shutai toshite no shintai*), or the "subject-body" (*shukan shintai*), phrases which he employs interchangeably throughout his book. It is important to recognize that the expression "subject" as it is used in the above phrase is not a felicitous English rendition of the Japanese term, *shutai*. Far from carrying the sense of a *disembodied* subject with its primary focus on intellect and rationality, shutai carries the sense of the subject being incarnate or embodied, while, nevertheless, simultaneously being an epistemological center of consciousness. When the term "body" is combined with this understanding of the incarnate subject, the body which is thematized here is the concrete human body. If we fail to observe this linguistic point, it might very well appear that Ichikawa's description of the concretely functioning human body is confused, if not completely unintelligible.

Even if we obscure this linguistic clarification, we should be able to sense at least the direction in which the phenomenon of the subject-body points. Insofar as it is a body with the characteristic of a subject, the phenomenon of the subject-body cannot be reduced to the purely physical, no more than it can be identified with the purely mental. If we regard the body in this manner, we seem to have an ambivalent, if not indeterminate articulation: the subject-body is both the physical and the mental or it is neither. By the term, the subject-body, Ichikawa points to a phenomenon which is not capable of reduction to either the physical or the mental, and insofar as it is treated as phenomena, it is within the boundary of "consciousness-of." The subject-body, then, embraces both the physical and the mental. Ichikawa characterizes it as follows:

> Although it is not quite an appropriate expression, we live it from within, grasping it immediately. This body is a basis (*kitai*) for our action, penetrating through a bright horizon of consciousness to an obscure, hazy horizon. It is always present in front of, or rather *with* us. In spite of this, or because of this, it in itself remains without being brought to awareness. In this sense, we should say that we do not *have* the body, but we *are* the body.[12]

There are three points in this characterization which we should take note of in order to understand properly what Ichikawa means by the subject-body. First, the fact that this body is said to be lived from within with its mode of living immediately grasped, suggests that it is foremost my body; where the possessive pronoun "my" indicates that the body belongs to the individual in an *intimate* sense rather than merely being possessed by him/her. This distinction is necessary because the individual is not aware of his/her body most of the time. This understanding, for example, echoes Scheler's concept of the lived body in that it is said to underlie both outer and inner perceptions, functioning as a basis for the perceptual consciousness.[13] Secondly, this body is conceived of as a necessary, but not a sufficient, condition for cogito to function. This second point follows from the first, because the subject-body is that which is grasped immediately, or to use Scheler's terminology, it is grasped through "phenomenological intuition."[14] Moreover, if this subject-body is the basis for perceptual consciousness, perceptual consciousness as a partial meaning of cogito no doubt *requires* the subject-body, in the sense that cogito cannot function without it, that is, it is dependent for its function on this body. This is a radical shift from the standpoint in which the mind and the body are rendered ontologically separate, that is, a disjunctive Cartesian dualism, for there is no dependency of one upon the other in dualism. We will see that Ichikawa elaborates further on this "dependency" when he deals with how perception, feeling, and mood are rooted in "the obscure, hazy horizon of consciousness." For now, let us observe how Ichikawa further characterizes the subject-body. He states:

> This body, which is a precondition for all *cogito* (i.e., "I am conscious"), follows *cogito* around as a horizon upon which *cogito* is established. This horizon enables *cogito* to take root in the world, making it an actual consciousness with a perspective. If this horizon is lost, *cogito* can no longer exist as a concretely functioning *cogito*.[15]

To put it simply, this passage reads that cogito, as it relates itself to the external world, is perspectivally determined by virtue of the fact that it is founded upon the subject-body. Consequently, the loss of this body necessarily entails a loss of the "concretely functioning cogito." In other words, according to Ichikawa, the function of cogito is contingent upon the body in question. Therefore, the subject-body is a necessary condition in order for cogito to function.

From this observation, Ichikawa goes on to make the more radical claim that "the concretely functioning body is a kind of *cogito* or a horizonal *cogito*."[16] This assertion seems at first problematical. Why, for example, is the subject-body "a kind of cogito"? Or what does a "horizonal cogito" mean? These questions are especially difficult to answer if we cling to the view that there is a clear split between the mind and the body. Since the subject-body forms a background for cogito to function, that is, in terms of a perspectival determination, we can understand that the body in question is a horizon for cogito, especially in view of the earlier statement that the subject-body is not brought to a complete awareness. Moreover, recalling that we have translated *shutai* as an incarnate subject, then the body in question is endowed with subjectivity, and although this subjectivity does not clearly surface to awareness, it is, we can surmise, "a kind of cogito." Of course, having made this point, we should be careful not to identify this kind of cogito with a fully developed everyday cogito that can be consciously reflected upon. The cogito which Ichikawa has in mind here is "an obscure, hazy horizon" for consciousness,[17] but it is nonetheless cogito. Consequently, if we use a fully developed, everyday cogito, a bright cogito, as a parameter to characterize the body in question, we can say that the subject-body is a kind of cogito. At any rate, we can see why Ichikawa wants to examine the subject-body: the subject in this phrase refers to the horizonal cogito, or the obscure, hazy horizon upon which the transparent cogito assumes its function and its *raison d'être*. For a point of clarification, we might mention the notion of an "inner" and "outer" horizon. Just as the "externally" perceived object lies in a horizonal field, and is analyzable into a figure and its background, so too the perception comes forth from the horizonal field of the subject-body.[18] To use a spatial metaphor, a transparent cogito is supported from below by its subject-body, and it is reflected through the obscure, hazy horizon below.

A third point concerning Ichikawa's understanding of the subject-body is that if we accept that the subject-body is a necessary condition for all cogito to take place, it follows logically that we *are* the body. As we recall, the subject-body is that which "penetrates through a bright horizon of consciousness to an obscure, hazy horizon." It serves as a horizon upon which cogito can function. If this horizon is lost, as Ichikawa maintains, "cogito can no longer exist as a concretely functioning cogito." In this respect, we cannot arbitrarily decide to have, or not to have a body insofar as the subject-body is concerned.

In this characterization of the subject-body, we already have a glimpse of Ichikawa's contention that the body is the spirit. For if the subject-body is a continuum ranging from a bright, transparent consciousness to an obscure hazy horizon of consciousness, and moreover if we accept that the spirit and the body are intellectual abstractions from this continuum, it follows that both the spirit and the body are aspects of the same continuum.

This, then, is a partial reason that Ichikawa claims that the spirit and the body are abstracted from the *same* continuum.

THE BODY-SPACE

Ichikawa understands that the subject-body is, among other things, "lived from within." This understanding may be regarded as an extrapolation from phenomenological intuition, through which we discovered that his concept of the lived body is the foundation which underlies the perceptual consciousness. However, the meaning of lived from within is not *objectified* by perceptual consciousness, because the subject-body is lived immediately from within. This means that so-called "external" perception is incapable of forming a *definite* shape with respect to the subject-body. Experientially, then, the lived subject-body has for its general "intentional object,"[19] or the background for the perceptual consciousness, a kind of "extension and volume as its fundamental tone."[20] This is a somatic sensation which each of us has with respect to one's bodily condition.[21]

Since the subject-body is not objectified, Ichikawa proposes that the subject-body *does not* have a definite external delimitation.[22] Ichikawa argues that this can be illustrated if we reflect phenomenologically upon how we position a painful spot or an itchy place.[23] If we take the contrary position that the subject-body does have an external delimitation, that is to say, if the extension of the subject-body is demarcated by the surface of the skin, then a distance between a given point and another within the subject-body (or two points on the surface of the skin), could *only* be measured by external perception, and must conform to a *measurable* distance. However, from Ichikawa's perspective, the subject-body is lived from within, immediately, and without reliance upon the external perception. Accordingly, the lived experience of pain, for example, is such that we locate its position *prior* to a visual or tactile replacement. In other words, we do not position localized pain in terms of a measurable external distance that is calculated by our external perceptions.

If this is an accurate way of describing a lived experience of the subject-body, it follows that there must be an internal space that does not conform to the measurability of distance discernible in external space. If, on the other hand, the internal space conforms to the measurability of distance, we are no longer concerned with the lived experience of the internal space nor with the immediacy of the subject-body. In order to make this clear, then, we may designate the space experienced in this way as "body-space" (*shintai kūkan*). The measurement or measurability of distance presupposes the concept of separation of two points *and* that what is measured is divisible into homogeneous units. However, such concepts have no application to a "distance" experienced within the subject-body. One might argue that the use of the word distance in this regard is, to use Ryle's terminology, a "category mistake." But, if it is indeed a category mistake, how are we to account for the fact that we can *position* a painful spot on, and/or within the subject-body, since "positioning" presupposes a separation of two points, that is, the concept of distance? Ichikawa accounts for this by arguing that there is a "qualitative distance," operative in the lived subject-body, as opposed to the measurable quantitative distance. This qualitative distance makes sense only if we assume that the body-space which pertains to the subject-body is nonhomogeneous as opposed to the homogeneity of external space in nature. Although we grasp intuitively a spatial relationship among, for example, the forehead, the leg, the knee and the back, the perspective experienced (the nearness or the remoteness) is special. For example, my finger or my toe is "closer" or more intimate to me in terms of its experiential correlate than a physical object placed right in front of my eyes.[24] This sense of lived space establishes a phenomenological fact that there is a unique body-space with a nonhomogeneous spatiality operative in the lived experience of the subject-body.

What then, Ichikawa asks, determines qualitative distance within this nonhomogeneous body-space lived from within? Varlery points out that among the consciously movable parts of the body, there is an order of distance,[25] which is determined by the mobility of a part and the time it takes for moving it. The order, according to Varlery, is "the eye, the most mobile, fingers,…head, toes, hands, forearms, legs…shoulders." This ordering is approximate and variable, and the reason for this, Ichikawa argues, is that "an *actual* movement in the functioning body leaps beyond this order of distance [set] in terms of mobility."[26] For example, when a person shrugs his/her shoulders, the shoulders as experienced are more intimate than the head. What this means is that the lived space is constantly generated without a definite delimitation. However, this applies only to the movable parts of the body. Beneath this order lies various parts of the body which are characterized by the involuntary movement, and these, because they do not surface to transparent consciousness, constitute the "obscure, hazy horizon of consciousness"—which do not surface to the transparent consciousness.[27]

Accordingly, the body-space of the functioning subject-body has its unique space irreducible to the anatomical structure of the body. Ichikawa likens this indefinitely generated body-space to a mobile, the parts of which intersect with each other, but constantly change direction and distance.[28] In spite of this, there is, says Ichikawa, a more or less constant, sedimented or habituated body-space, though it cannot be identified with the anatomical structure of the body. An example of this is the phenomenon of the so-called phantom leg: even though a leg has been amputated and is thus no longer anatomically present, this "amputated leg" seems to be available to stretch or to stand, and even has a sensation of itchiness or pain, thus preserving the habituated body-space.[29]

Recognizing that the subject-body does not have a definite shape or external delineation, Ichikawa is led to the phenomenological finding that body-space as it pertains to the functioning body cannot be reducible to the anatomical structure. Furthermore, this body-space is constantly generated without fixing determinate boundaries.

On the basis of these findings, Ichikawa now contends that the spread of the lived body *extends beyond* the physical, objectified body by virtue of the phenomenological fact that the body-space is always varying. This is not to suggest, however, that there are no discernible types of this constantly generated body-space. On the contrary, Ichikawa thinks that there are at least three discernible types of body-space functioning in the subject-body. In fact, this observation is a further development of Merleau-Ponty's concept of "habit-body" which is said to create its own space.[30]

The first type of generated body-space called the "innate-body-space" (seitokuteki shintai kūkan) roughly corresponds to the surface boundary of the skin, and is the most stable among the three.[31] Since we are accustomed to identify the delineation of our body in terms of the objectified body, the difference between the surface boundary of an objectified body and that of the innate body-space passes unnoticed, or to be more precise, is grasped preconsciously.[32] For example, when a foreign object threatens to fly into one's eye, the threshold at which one closes his/her eye reflexively indicates the limit of the innate body-space that does not necessarily correspond to the surface boundary of the skin.[33]

In addition to innate body-space, we can discern another type of body-space with a spread greater than that of the innate body-space, though with a duration more unstable in its configuration. Ichikawa designates this body-space the "semi-definite body-space" (junkōseiteki shintai kūkan). Although he delves into two sub-classes of phenomena that fit the above description, it will suffice to mention only one of them here,[34] the body-space that is generated through a mediation by the use of tools. As an example, let us use the fishing pole; one's body-space extends to the end of the line where one "feels" the pull of the bait. Naturally in this subclass, a scope of the body-space varies according to the type of tool employed, and the familiarity that one has with it, that is, to the degree to which one achieves, to use Merleau-Ponty's term, a level of habit-body. For example, a surgical knife in the hands of a skilled surgeon is an "incarnated, secondary finger,"[35] where the tip of the surgeon's fingers extend as far as the end of his/her knife. What this suggests is that a tool which is initially an external supplement can become internalized within the subject-body, and can become "second nature" as one attains a mastery of the implement, consequently taking the individual beyond the boundary of innate body-space.[36]

Innate body-space is more stable than semi-definite body-space, but the extension of body-space stands in an inverse proportion to its stability. Take for example the acquired skill of driving a car through a narrow gate which has little clearance on either side. The driver's feelers extend to the fenders of the body of the car, and once the car passes through the gate, this extension "shrinks" into what Ichikawa calls the innate body-space. This inverse relationship between the stability and the extension of the body-space is similarly true of the third aspect of the body-space, which Ichikawa designates as the "indefinitely varying body-space" (*fukakuteki na kahenteki shintai kūkan*). Its scope of this body-space is said to be "constantly changing, temporary and nonhabitual,"[37] and it is through this body-space that we live our subject-body in the greater part of our everyday life. By indefinitely varying body-space, Ichikawa has in mind body-space generated through perception, primarily visual and the tactile. Because of its mobile activities, he chooses the term, "indefinitely varying body-space," and characterizes it as "constantly changing, temporary and nonhabitual."

In recognition of this characteristic, Ichikawa's claim is that (1) an act of perception extends over into the object perceived and (2) in such a process there is a "bodily dialogue" (*shintai teki taiwa*) with the object perceived.[38] He argues these two points by pointing out that we do not make contact with the world by means of the *surface* of the perceptual organs, nor do we passively receive a given stimulus from the external world; the latter is implied by the phrase bodily dialogue, since a dialogue is by definition a dialogue only when two or more participants are actively engaged. If it were otherwise, we would be unable to detect "depth" in scenery, or would be unable to grasp the shape of a stone.[39]

At first glance, it might seem counter-intuitive that our visual and tactile perceptions fulfill both conditions, namely, (1) that perception extends to the object perceived, and (2) that there is a bodily dialogue between the subject-body and the object of perception. With respect to visual perception, Ichikawa argues that the retina does not directly touch the objects that make up the landscape, for example, but the act of visual perception extends as far as these objects seen, enabling the individual to feel depth in the scenery. Therefore, as visual perception is lived, it extends to the objects seen.[40] In order to understand Ichikawa's claim, we must take "extension" here to mean a *nonhomogeneous, qualitative* space as in the lived experience, for example, of the hands holding the fishing pole.

In explaining the concept of bodily dialogue, Ichikawa uses

the example of an individual looking at the leaning tower of
Pisa, although this is a somewhat atypical example for visual
perception, it is nonetheless effective in disclosing an aspect of
visual perception that otherwise might been overlooked. He says:

> When we look at the tower, our body [has a proclivity] to lean
> toward it in an attempt to assume potentially a posture similar
> to the [leaning] form of the tower. We sketch it and respond to
> it. We feel within our body a tension between the power that
> inclines with the tower and the power which restores it.[41]

According to Ichikawa, then, what makes a visual perception
lived is this mutual participation between the perceiver in the act
of perception and the object perceived. To use Ichikawa's terminology, lived perception is possible only when we presuppose
that there is a bodily dialogue between the perceiver in the act of
perception and the object perceived.

This type of bodily dialogue is similarly the case, he argues,
in tactile perception. He says:

> When we grasp a stone, we sketch its possible shapes and
> respond both to its actual and possible shapes while fondling
> its factual shape. To explain it in reverse, we elicit the stone's
> response by grasping and posing questions to it.[42]

In the above quotation, the contrast between "actual" and "possible" may be translated for our purpose as a contrast between
"actually definite" and "potentially indefinite." Ichikawa's claim
is that when a stone is grasped, its actual shape comes into being
only when there is a *mutual* searching out of the event of grasping the stone; mutual in terms of the hand holding the stone and
the stone that is held. Consequently, what is lived as the actual
shape or hardness of a stone is the result of an *agreement*
reached between an anticipation on the part of the holding hand,
and a response on the part of the stone. Only when this agreement has been reached, then, do the potentially indefinite aspects
of the stone become an actually definite stone with its lived sense
of shape and hardness.[43]

It might seem superfluous to speak of the tactile perception
"extending" to an object, for it is through the contiguity of the
object that tactile perception occurs with its proper effect. But

Ichikawa has already rejected this notion that perception takes place through the direct "contact" with the object. If this were the case, he argued, not only would depth of perceptual experience be lost, but it would also be contrary to the lived experience of perception. Consequently, Ichikawa uses the term extending in dealing with tactile perception to mean a "search for an inner horizon," or alternatively to reach an agreement between the anticipation on the part of the hand grasping the stone, and the response elicited from the stone that is being held. James Gibson discovered that a subject will score a high (95%) in the recognition of objects when he is allowed to touch the objects (active touching) but will score low (45%) when the subject is touched by the objects (passive touching). Taking note of what Gibson calls the "body's active preparedness," Ichikawa argues that "through such an active dialogue, the functioning body intersects with the object and searches for its inner horizon."[44]

It is perhaps needless to say that Ichikawa's description of the characteristics of "indefinitely varying body-space" and bodily dialogue and the perception that extends to an object—does not imply that we are conscious of them at the time of perceiving, but rather that we are preconsciously aware of them. They are the structural elements that constitute perception and that make it lived perception. Moreover, it has only been through a phenomenological reflection upon the act of perception that these characteristics have been revealed.

We may briefly compare Ichikawa's concept of bodily dialogue with Merleau-Ponty's concept of bodily intentionality. Both contend that the lived body creates its own space; in the case of Merleau-Ponty this space is created through the function of habit-body, whereas for Ichikawa this space comes through the function of the subject-body. Merleau-Ponty contends that the body's intentionality *reaches in potentia* its intentional object prior to its actual execution by means of the actual body, and his idea of reaching an intentional object is translated by Ichikawa into the idea that the subject-body extends to its intentional object. What distinguishes Ichikawa from Merleau-Ponty in this respect is that Ichikawa recognizes in the concept of bodily dialogue a contributing factor that issues from the intentional object and must be present in the constitution of a meaning of a perceptual object in order for the perception to be a lived perception. To use Aristotle's terminology, it would seem that Merleau-Ponty has given only a "form" to the structure of perception and motility without providing its "matter." This raises a serious question concerning the validity of the meaning-bestowing activity of intentionality on the part of an epistemological subject. As we shall see shortly, Ichikawa rejects the thesis that meaning can be generated by an epistemological subject alone.

These three aspects of body-space, namely, the innate body-space, the semi-definite body-space, and the indefinitely varying body-space, are said to be synthesized through their overlapping in the actual functioning of the subject-body.[45] Ichikawa's metaphor used to describe this is a "mobile whose parts intersect with each other, constantly changing its direction and distance."

THE OBJECT-BODY

The preceding phenomenological analysis of the body as phenomena has touched upon the aspect of the body as it is lived "from within" or what Ichikawa prefers to call alternatively the body *qua* subject and subject-body. Needless to say, this analysis has not provided an exhaustive description of the lived body. In fact, Ichikawa points out, in addition to the subject-body, there is another aspect of the lived body equally close and intimate to "myself" in its experiential correlate, namely "the body *qua* object" (*kyakutai toshite no shintai*) or "object-body." In contrast to the subject-body, this object-body is said by Ichikawa to be lived "from outside," although he has expressed some discomfort in this expression.[46] The phrase "lived from outside" is translatable as my body objectified through "my looking at or touching it," and this would roughly correspond to Scheler's "thing-body" (*der Körper*). In other words, this is my physical body lived through external perception in respect to myself, although such a body, along with the other's body, can become the object of scientific investigation. However, Ichikawa wants to distinguish the object-body from the body that is the subject of medical science, since the latter does not concern itself with the lived meaning of the body. Consequently, Ichikawa's concern is to describe this lived sense of the body as it appears in our concrete life.

The first point to be noted in our discussion of the object-body is that it has, unlike the subject-body, a definitely delineated shape. By virtue of this fact, it *is placed* among the things in the world. What this suggests is that my body is given an exteriority, and is closed off as an individual physical thing from the other physical things in the world. Consequently, it is separated from them,[47] and I am like "an island floating in the world."[48] However, the exteriority of my body enables me, by virtue of my object-body, to have *access* to and to have *an intimate relation with* the *shaped* things in the world in a way otherwise impossible had I remained as a subject-body. Ichikawa reasons that were we to remain as subject-body, "the world would appear as numerous patterns with qualitative differences,"[49] and this suggests that an access to, and an intimacy with the things in the world would be impossible. But we have de facto access to and an intimate relation with the things in the world. According to Ichikawa, this is partly due to the fact that the object-body has a definitely delineated physical shape. Moreover, Ichikawa wants to argue that the object-body is "one of the momenta which enable us to understand the objectivity of an object." This line of argument, especially what is meant by "the objectivity of objects," is not immediately clear unless we recall that the body-space of the subject-body is characterized as qualitative non-homogeneous space. We will remember that the body-space of the subject-body is grasped from within, and this grasp extends *outward* in an indefinite configuration. The point, then, is that we cannot reach the object by means of the subject-body, since it does not have a definite shape; rather, we require the mediation through the object-body. If this is so, and if one were to remain as the subject-body, then there would be no way of relating the subject-body physically to the shaped things in the world. But since the object-body, by virtue of its physical delineation, enables us to relate ourselves to the world of shaped things, the objectivity of objects can emerge. Consequently, the word "objects" in the phrase the objectivity of objects, has to be understood as "tangible" objects accessible through the object-body. In this regard, tangible objects (or the shaped things in the

world) and the object-body share a common feature in that both
are physically delineated.

Therefore, the objectivity of objects presupposes the existence of the object-body, and it is by means of this object-body
that we experience the world of shaped things through the subject-body's function of living them from within it. Ichikawa gives
a concrete example to illustrate his point:

> The shape, and the hardness or the softness of an object which
> I learn through grasping this object announce and relate to me
> [tugeshiraseru] at the same time the shape, hardness or softness
> of "my" body *qua* object.[50]

Upon reading this passage, one might accuse Ichikawa of anthro-
pomorphizing objects, for it could be contested that a (tangible)
object does not "announce" qualities such as hardness, softness,
or shape. This criticism, of course, stems from the fact that an
object is not sentient. But more importantly, it has at its source
the philosophical assumption that a meaning-bestowing function
can operate only in an intentional subject. From this presupposition, the qualities of an object, such as hardness, softness, and
the shape is a *constituted* meaning. Consequently, an intentional
subject is considered to be an *active* agent. The British empiri-
cists, notably Hume, took the diametrically opposed position
arguing that qualities of objects are considered to be "impressed
upon the mind," and hence the subject is a *passive* recipient of
perception. Ichikawa, however, opposes both of these positions,
maintaining that the living body is an ambiguous "being-in-the-
environment." Thus he rejects the one-sided notion that the living body is either an active agent or a passive recipient. Based
upon the ambiguity of the relationship that obtains between the
living body and its environment, Ichikawa argues that a meaning
is generated out of the mutual dependency that exists between
the living body and its environment.[51] This is a corollary to
Ichikawa's contention that there is a bodily dialogue between the
act of the subject-body and the things engaged by it. Moreover, a
phenomenological reflection reveals that I would not be able to
sense the softness of my hand *without* reference to something
harder than my hand. When I grasp a stone, for example, there is
an ambiguous permeation between my hand and the stone being

held, and through this permeation I can either direct to the surface of the stone, or to the palm of my hand where it makes contact with the stone. As a result, I discover that the lived experience of my hand holding the stone gives me a sense of "difference" that differentiates my hand from the stone. If I felt no difference, and my hand seemed to melt into the stone, I could not be able to distinguish it from the stone, insofar as relative softness or hardness of my hand and the stone is concerned. This would establish an "equilibrium" between the grasping and the grasped. In other words, in order for the softness of my hand to emerge as an aspect of experience, when it is in contact with the hardness of a stone, a mutual dependency must exist between the emergent qualities, for without the relative softness and the hardness of my hand and a stone as points of contact, there can be no sense in talking about softness or hardness in this context.

This *reciprocal* dependency between the grasping and the grasped exemplifies Ichikawa's claim about our accessibility to, and our intimacy with, the physical objects of the world by means of the object-body, for intimacy requires mutual agreement. Furthermore, this dependency also illustrates the earlier claim concerning bodily dialogue in which the subject-body engages itself with its objects of perception. This fact indicates that bodily dialogue with respect to the subject-body, is dependent upon the object-body, or more specifically, upon its definite physical delineation. Moreover, this reciprocal dependency between the grasping and the grasped suggests to Ichikawa that "a deepening of inner understanding with regard to the objectivity of objects is at the same time a deepening of understanding of self." This follows from the earlier observation that the indefinitely varying body-space with respect to the subject-body extends beyond the physical delineation of the objectified body in order to "search for the inner horizon" of a given object engaged by the subject-body.

The second point to be noted with respect to the object-body is that, because it is endowed with a definite exteriority, it makes actual a separation between my body and myself, a separation only potentially present in the subject-body.[52] In the case of the subject-body, my body is not objectified in the same way as the object-body, because the subject-body is lived from within. However, in the case of the object-body, when I touch my hand, I am both the subject that is doing the touching as well as the object that is being touched.[53] Therefore, the subject-object dichotomy is clearly established with respect to the object-body. Moreover, since I am able to turn into an object that is capable of being touched means that I am a thing among the shaped things in the world, and therefore acquire a contingency by virtue of the fact that I *have* the body *qua* object.

Ichikawa points out, moreover, that the way in which my object-body as it appears to me is not the same as the way in which my object-body appears to others. This identification is also made by Sartre, albeit somewhat confusedly in his *Being and Nothingness*.[54] In other words, Ichikawa contends that my object-body, as it appears to me, is essentially different from another's object-body as it appears to me. More simply, he argues that there is a fundamental difference between the appearance of another's body to me, and my object-body as it appears to others. By means of illustration, Ichikawa offers the following example of double sensation.[55] When I touch my foot with my hand, I feel that my hand is touching my foot and, at the same time, I feel that my foot is being touched by my hand. This "double sensation" holds true only with respect to my object-body for myself. Hence, I should be distinguished from my object-body for others as well as another's object-body for myself. "If," on the other hand, "we were deprived of this double sensation, my foot could not have a status different from a stone, and my object-body would no longer be *my* body."[56]

The preceding two points concerning the object-body: (1) that it has a definitely delineated physical boundary, and (2) that it makes actual the separation of my self from my body, establish firmly that the body in question deserves special phenomenological reflection. From here, then, Ichikawa now moves on to *hint* at the phenomenological observation that leads him to assert that the body is the spirit.

According to Ichikawa, the separation for which double sensation is responsible brings forth a fissure, as it were, within "my body."[57] What does he mean by "a fissure within my body"? We can compare the familiar, critical observation that consciousness is split in terms of subject-object or noesis-noema. Why does

Ichikawa contend it is my body instead of consciousness that is divided by this fissure? According to Ichikawa, the fissure splits my body simply because the double sensation is "an externalized reflection." He writes:

> Double sensation is an externalized reflection...The doubling [of sensations] motivates the body to return to the self itself. An external reflection is gradually internalized and opens up the possibility of reaching Cartesian *cogito*, a reflection of *pure* thinking [*junsui shii*] through an infinite regress.[58]

As we have seen, double sensation involves a subject that is touching and an object that is being touched, when both subject and object pertain to one and the same body, namely my body. This will provide an occasion for reflection, for reflection requires precisely that which does the reflecting and that which is reflected upon. Moreover, it can be seen as an "externalized" reflection because the subject-object dichotomy takes place *on the surface* of the clearly delineated physical boundary of my body. It would be meaningless to argue that an object, my foot, for example, appears only as the noematic content of my touching my hand, since the sensation localized is not simply *in* consciousness. Ichikawa goes on to explain why and how this "external reflection" can be internalized and how it subsequently leads to Cartesian cogito. He states:

> Although I am touching myself who is [also] being touched, this doubling of sensations is further internalized to enable me to discover myself who takes note of touching, which invites me to a purification of the thought that "I am touching."[59]

In this passage Ichikawa explains that the factual event of double sensation is preconscious, or at least, it is not a fully transparent consciousness—by "not fully transparency" here, Ichikawa means that one cannot reflect upon and as a consequence distinguish a subject and an object within a factual event of double sensation. On the basis of this understanding of double sensation, we can discern a movement, though its actual functioning is subtle and complex. At the outset, we begin with the factual event of touching, preconsciously grasped. In turn, this preconscious "event" becomes an awareness within which is a clear demarcation of the subject-object, and finally this awareness develops into its "purification" as a consequence of the thought that "I am aware of touching." In this context, the term purification may be interpreted as a progressive elimination of the somatic act of touching and being touched. This movement, then, is a movement into the interiority of self, and simultaneously a movement away from the factual event of double sensation. Ichikawa's description of the process through which "externalized reflection" becomes an "internalized reflection" is an "ontogenesis" of a fully developed cogito, in a manner perhaps similar to Husserl's later "genetic phenomenology."

The preceding characterization of object-body, however, does not take into account the materiality of the object-body, although the very fact of double sensation presupposes it. According to Ichikawa, double sensation brings about a grasp of the body as a material thing at the preconscious level, for he says: "Insofar as it is a being that is being touched upon, (my) body is disclosed to be a material thing, without merely remaining as a subject-body."[60]

If Ichikawa's analysis were to stop here, he would not have provided us with any clear justification for his claim that the body is the spirit. However, he moves on to point out that the subject-object dichotomy involved in double sensation is interchangeable. In other words, the subject that is doing the touching can easily become the object that is being touched. For example, if I simply shift my perspective, my hand touching my foot can become into my foot touching my hand. That is to say, insofar as my body is concerned as it appears to "me," touching means nothing more than being touched, and being touched means nothing more than touching.[61] Underlying this interchangeability is the phenomenological fact that there is an "intuition of identity" (*dōitsusei no chokkan*) between that which does the touching and that which is touched. Logically speaking, then, this interchangeability or, to use a technical term from logic, this substitution presupposes an identity between the two terms, for example X and Y, where X and Y must have the same truth-value. Experientially, this logical identity is *based upon* an intuition of identity; a feeling that one and the same thing is experienced. For instance, when I touch myself I *feel* that I am touching, and at the same time I feel that I am being touched. This feeling is not comprised of two distinctly different feelings, but is one and the same feeling, or the feeling of "mine." Ichikawa observes:

> Double sensation, through the intuition of identity between that which is touching and that which is being touched, links the subject-body with the object-body...and brings them into an interfusion [*yūgō*].[62]

When Ichikawa states that there is an intuition of identity, he is mitigating the active-passive bodily-scheme as a fixed, invariable relation that obtains between touching (active) and touched (passive) as a primary way of understanding the concretely functioning living body. He regards it simply as a tendency. Consequently, the interchangeability of the subject qua touching and the object qua touched forms, to use Merleau-Ponty's terminology, "an ambiguous organization" (*une organisation ambiguë*) between the functions of touching and being touched.[63] According to Ichikawa, this ambiguous organization in double sensation does not mean that both the right and the left hand, when they are joined together, assume respectively the active as well as the passive function at the same time. A *distinct* contrast between touching and being touched in such an instance is impossible, even when one makes a supreme effort to separate the two. Rather, Ichikawa says, one has "a primitive sensation of mutual permeation that is ambiguously spread."[64] This is more clearly exemplified in praying with both hands pressed against the other or simply joined together. He observes:

> In many religions, the reason that one closes his eyes, and joins his hands together when he prays is because he attempts to reach by way of this activity a certain pure state that is without the fissure between activity and passivity, between interiority and exteriority, and between subject and object.[65]

To recapitulate, Ichikawa's concept of an intuition of identity, with respect to double sensation, is based upon the experiential fact of an interchangeability between touching and being touched, and its descriptive characterization is a primitive sensation of mutual permeation which is ambiguously spread.

Up to this point, Ichikawa has concerned himself only with an examination of tactile perception, particularly emphasizing double sensation in order to demonstrate his thesis that the body is the spirit. The question that naturally arises here, is whether or not this thesis can also be maintained at the level of visual perception in the task of phenomenologically disclosing the lived aspect of my body.

In the passage we have just cited, Ichikawa mentions the act of closing the eyes in prayer as an attempt to reach a certain pure state. When a person attempts to reach this "pure state" by closing eyes, he simultaneously closes off "the world in front" and enters into "the world behind."[66] The reason that one closes one's eyes in prayer is that, since visual perception involves a clear distinction between a subject qua seeing and an object qua seen, one blocks out the world in front, by disengaging the organ of visual perception, and thus avoids establishing a dichotomy. Moreover, unlike tactile perception, visual perception does not allow for double sensation to take place. "When I look at my hand, my hand does not *directly* feel being looked at, nor can it become (the organ that does) the seeing. I cannot look at my eyes with my hand"[67] (emphasis added). However, what we ought to pay special attention to in this quotation is that while Ichikawa points out the lack of any clear evidence that double sensation operates in visual perception, he nevertheless suggests that there is a bodily scheme that enables me in some indirect manner to *identify* the hand looked at as mine. Hence, Ichikazwa mounts the argument that "if my hand looked at remains simply being looked at, I would not probably be able to recognize the hand as mine."[68] But de facto when I look at my hand I can identify it as mine, unless of course I suffer from a psychosomatic disorder that would prevent this recognition. According to Ichikawa, the reason I am able to visually identify my hand as mine is that:

> the hand that is looked at is grasped by a more primitive somatic sensation [than visual perception itself], which lurks *at the base of* the active-passive sensory motor scheme, continuous with the primitive somatic sensation at the base of a clear and distinct consciousness [*meiryō ishiki*] of looking at.[69]
> (emphasis added)

At this point, Ichikawa does not specify what he means by "primitive somatic sensation,"[70] but in light of our discussion of the subject-body, we can for now take it to mean that which is issued from an obscure, hazy horizon of consciousness. Ichikawa claims that this obscure, hazy horizon of consciousness is responsible for my ability to recognize the hand looked at as mine. By virtue of the fact that this recognition, a somatic recognition, takes place in an obscure, hazy horizon of consciousnss, the visual perception does not enable us to sense directly an occurrence of double sensation. To put it another way, "a bright consciousness," though continuous with an obscure, hazy horizon of consciousness, overshadows its immediate connection with the latter because visual perception is directed outward to the object-body with a strong sense of discrimination. This does not mean, however, that visual perception so directed is not lived from within, for if it were not lived from within, in looking at my hand, I would not be able to recognize it as mine. This creates a peculiar situation when I am in the act of "looking at my hand," or more generally, it creates a peculiar relationship between my object-body and my subject-body. Insofar as what is looked at is concerned, it pertains to the object-body, but insofar as visual perception as lived perception is concerned, it pertains to the subject-body. In other words, both the object-body and the subject-body, as they pertain to my body, are engaged in the case of "my looking at my hand." But, what is actually lived or experienced can be explained neither in terms of the object-body, nor in terms of the subject-body. To Ichikawa, this implies that both the object-body and the subject-body are "synthesized" (*tōgō*) in the concrete functioning of my lived body. Or, in view of the subject-body, the object-body is "subjectivized" (*shutaika*), thereby enabling us to incorporate it within the subject-body. Both "synthesis" and "subjectivization" capture well the characterization of the lived body: the former points to a factual state of affairs while the latter refers to a phenomenological state of affairs. To substantiate this observation, Ichikawa reports cases of neurotic patients who, in each instance, disclaim the ownership of the subject-body.[71] In light of Ichikawa's interpretation, these case studies indicate the patient's failure to synthesize the object-body and the subject-body. From the point of view of a clinical diagnosis, they represent the failure of subjectivization in the lived experience of the body.

What this suggests to Ichikawa in his phenomenological investigation of the lived body is that both the subject-body and the object-body are united insofar as they pertain to my body. He says:

> My "object-body" and my "subject-body" are inseparably united in *their deeper layer*,[72] and cannot be separated clearly and decisively, except through intellectual abstraction.[73] (emphasis added)

Synthesis or subjectivization is a preconscious operation, and hence the unity asserted in the above quotation takes place in the lived dimension that is neither the subject-body nor the object-body, but rather is a dimension that *underlies* them. This is the reason that Ichikawa recognizes and locates cogito in the obscure, hazy region of our being. Importantly, the distinction between the subject-body and the object-body is not invalidated by this insight. On the contrary, it is only through this distinction that the phenomenon of a unifying function underlying subject-body and object-body has emerged. Ichikawa refers to this unifying function as the "lived bodily scheme" (*ikeru shintai zushiki*), its specific function is to unify through synthesis and subjectivization. Obviously, then, synthesis and subjectivization are the characteristics which describe the lived bodily-scheme from the perspective of an apparent or consciously lived dimension of the body qua phenomenon. But, if the perspective is shifted to that of the lived bodily-scheme underlying both the subject-body and the object-body, the distinction between the subject-body and the object-body amounts to a separation from this unity; hence the term synthesis refers to their origin. Ichikawa seems to hint that this lived bodily scheme is, at least in part, an articulation of what he earlier referred to as the fundamental structure of the concrete functioning of our body.

Ichikawa's phenomenological investigation of the lived body has taken us as far as the lived bodily-scheme which synthesizes both the subject-body and the object-body, as they pertain to my body in the lived dimension that is deeper than my apparent awareness of my body.

Ichikawa's finding may be traced back to Descartes' position which is advanced in his *Principles of Philosophy*.[74] After declaring the reality of two substances namely the thinking substance, and the extended substance, Descartes asserts in principle 48:

> Il y a encore outre cela certaines choses que nous expérimentons en nous-même, qui ne doivent point être attribuées a l'âme seule, ni aussi au corps seul, mais à *l'étroite union* uie est entre eux.[75] (emphasis added)

In Descartes, the close and the intimate union (*l'étroite union*) which is said to exist between the mind and the body does not belong to the two and only two real substances. Aliquié, the editor of the work just cited, refers to this union as "the third primitive notion" (*une troisième notion primitive*).[76] In light of the reality which two substances are said to possess, this third primitive notion does not have a "reality" in Descartes' official ontology. However, the somatic elements which are included in the close and intimate union are the internal passions or affections, such as anger, joy, sadness, and love, the natural appetites such as hunger and thirst, and the sensations pertaining to the five sensory organs. The reason that Aliquié considered that these elements comprise the third primitive notion is that they do not fall within the proper domain of Descartes' official position of his metaphysics or ontology. However, the somatic elements which Descartes mentions as comprising the third primitive notion, nonetheless possess an experiential reality for us. As a consequence, we should be suspicious of the validity of the sharp separation of the mind and the body. Ichikawa has advanced the unity of the mind and the body vis-à-vis the synthetic function of the five sensory organs, although he has relied exclusively on visual and tactile perception to demonstrate it.

As we know, Descartes divides the world into two substances based upon the abstract faculty of our mind, or cogito. For our present consideration, corporeal things, or more specifically the bodies of human beings are conceived of from the perspective of this cogito, or in terms of abstract thinking. Hence, in Descartes' well-known official doctrine, the body is not a concretely lived body as it is in the conceptual model of Ichikawa. It is a *bodyness*. The methodological procedures of Ichikawa and Descartes, the former phenomenological and the latter metaphysical, render their respective concepts of the body fundamentally dissimilar. In spite of these methodological procedures, however, Ichikawa has made great gains in demonstrating the unity of the mind and the body vis-à-vis a phenomenological articulation of the lived body. He has been able to make this progress, primarily because he conceived of the subject-body as a continuum of cogito ranging from the bright consciousness (Descartes' cogito) to its obscure hazy horizon (Descartes' concept of the body). In the next chapter, we shall examine this continuum of the lived body in light of Ichikawa's exposition of its structure.

CHAPTER 2

Ichikawa's Concept of the Body Qua Structure

STRUCTURE AS FUNCTIONING

What does the living body understood as structure mean, and what is the living body's primary function? According to Ichikawa, the primary function which the living body assumes as its structure, is its directionality (*shikōsei*) with respect to its environment or ambiance. This "directionality," to be distinguished from that of the intentionality thesis, is defined as the living body's comporting itself towards its ambiance. Ichikawa claims that it is necessary to understand the primary function of the living body in this manner, since without this primary function of the directionality of a living body, there can be no living body. In other words, the concept of the body otherwise understood is a futile resurrection of a corpse. For example, in order for the living body to maintain its life effectively in its ambiance, it must absorb positive elements into itself, while transforming negative elements into positive or neutral ones. This transformation is effected through *directing* the action of the living body towards the external ambiance by means of perception and behavior, and/or towards the internal ambiance via self-functional activities such as metabolism.

Ichikawa points out that the directionality cast both inwardly and outwardly maintains a complementary relationship. The externally directed activities of the living body directly alter the external ambiance and consequently its meaning, while they are accompanied by changes in the internal ambiance (such as an increase in pulsation and blood pressure, and an expansion of the blood vessels) which set up a condition conducive to actions. Similarly, the internally directed activities change the internal ambiance (such as homeostasis which maintains a bodily temperature despite a decrease or an increase in outside temperature, and maintains the concentration of blood in response to perspiration or to the intake of water) while they directly change the meaning of the external ambiance.[1] Although these self-functional activities are indirect in terms of their influence upon the externally directed activities, if these self-functional activities were to fail, the external ambiance would pose a threat to the living body, and consequently change the meaning of the external ambiance.

The foregoing observations suggest to Ichikawa that the living body *is* already *placed*, or to use Heidegger's terminology, "thrown" into a *meaningful* ambiance or environment. The living body, when it is thrown into an environment, is surrounded by the contingent facts which are prefigured prior to its thrownness by such factors as historicity, temporality and spatiality, and these contingent facts are the basis for the living body to encounter an environment that becomes meaningful. In this sense, the "thrownness" is a "fundamental, radical contingency"[2] for the living body. The living body acts in such an ambiance, directing itself to the various meanings potentially as well as actually present in it. However, this radical contingency does not mean that the living body is determined by the already existing external ambiance, if we understand the latter to be compelling force. Rather, "the living body is relatively free from the ambiance thus understood."[3]

Accordingly, meaning in the broadest sense is generated through the interaction between the ambiance and the living body.[4] Ichikawa says: "Meaning is that which the living body bestows upon the ambiance, and *at the same time* meaning is given to the living body by the ambiance."[5] (emphasis added) The meaning that is generated, then, is dependent upon both the living body and the ambiance, and therefore is ambiguous. Based on this ambiguity of generation of meaning, a certain subjective idealist can insist upon the meaning bestowing activities on the part of an intentional subject, or a certain empiricist can ascribe the passive reception of meaning to an epistemological subject. Both contend partial truths, but the whole truth must take account of the mutual determination of meaning-generation between the living body and the ambiance. Ichikawa points out that once we recognize that the living body is placed in the ambiance and that meaning is ambiguously generated, the living body comes to be seen as a "being-in-the-ambiance" (*kankyōnai sonzai*). In Ichikawa's own words:

> The ambiguity of meaning in this respect indicates the living body's intrinsic belonging to the world, that is, both the living body and the ambiance are mutually inseparable correlates. This means that the living body is a "being-in-the-ambiance."[6]

Ichikawa warns, however, not to identify his being-in-the-ambiance with Heidegger's "being-in-the-world." According to Ichikawa, "*Dasein* (or personal existence) is taken to mean that which *understands* (*Verstand*) its relation to the world and is capable of questioning it."[7] In contrast, Ichikawa's being-in-the-ambiance is more primitive and comprehensive than Heidegger's being-in-the-world: it is more primitive because Ichikawa's concept of the living body with its primary function of directionality is existentially prior to *Dasein's* capacity to understand, which is a cognitive aspect of the living body. In other words, Ichikawa argues that Dasein's being-in-the-world is existentially founded upon the living body's being-in-the-ambiance, for Dasein's capacity to understand is a second order for the mode of being a living body in light of the thrownness of Dasein. Empirically, when the living body is impaired in the lower aspect of the concretely functioning body (e.g., its self-functional activity), or in its higher aspect (e.g., its understanding), it is disclosed to be a being-in-the-ambiance, since living human body cannot act much less think when, for example, its heart is beating faster than normal. The maintenance of the life of the concretely functioning body cannot be sustained if the self-functional activities of the living body fail.

This primitiveness of Ichikawa's being-in-the-ambiance over against Heidegger's being-in-the-world is reflected in Ichikawa's understanding of the living body as subsuming or sustaining Dasein or personal existence, thus rendering the former more comprehensive than Dasein in its characterization. Ichikawa states:

> The body as functioning is nothing other than this ambiguous being of "that which defines and that which is defined," that runs through "being-in-the-ambiance" to "being-in-the-world."[8]

The ambiguity of "that which defines" and "that which is defined" with respect to the concretely functioning body corresponds broadly to two modes of personal existence; its passivity and activity. Ichikawa seems to think that the mode of being-in-the-world is an aspect of defining, where its activity primarily is based upon *understanding*, while being-in-the-ambiance is an aspect underlying being-in-the-world where the body *qua* functioning depends for its survival on the passive reception of various conditions of the external and internal ambiance. In Ichikawa's view then, being-in-the-ambiance precedes being-in-the-world, and this requires a dual form of the living body. Spatially designated, being-in-the-ambiance forms a lower stratum upon which being-in-the-world is erected. Being-in-the-ambiance refers, to use Heidegger's terminology, to a thrownness of personal existence, and hence indicates its passivity, while being-in-the-world refers to a "project" through the awareness of its thrownness, and hence indicates its activity. At any rate, these dual strata of personal existence qua body correspond roughly to the aspect of the structure of what Ichikawa calls subject-body; the being-in-the-ambiance is a somatic modality disclosed in the obscure, hazy horizon of consciousness while being-in-the-world is that which is revealed against a bright horizon of consciousness.

The mode of living body that is ambiguous in terms of its relationship to the ambiance entails the consequence that both the living body and ambiance are not rigidly fixed entities. On the contrary, the concretely functioning body changes its activities and its states in response to the change of meaning in the ambiance. Likewise, the ambiance changes its meaning in response to the living body's activities and states.[9] Consequently, the structure within which the living body directs itself to the ambiance and the meaning which it receives from the ambiance are both in constant generation, and it is through this fact that we can explain the novelty of our experience.

In this constant generation of structure and meaning, the living body directs itself to various meaningful objects in the ambiance, maintaining its individuality as a "disclosed, dynamic balance." In short, the living body has a holistic structure. Because the living body is constantly interacting with the ambiance, it is at times synthesized into a higher level of activity, and at other times is fragmented into a lower level of activity, where the respective terms "higher" and "lower" correspond roughly to the activities of "bright consciousness" and "obscure, hazy consciousness." Accordingly, the structure of the living body is said to assume a divisible whole. The living body is a "whole" insofar as it maintains its individuality in the ambiance, and it is divisible insofar as its directionality assumes a lower or higher level of activity.

Ichikawa perfunctorily distinguishes two aspects of the "divisible whole" of the living body, that is, the body's directionality to the ambiance in its constant interaction with the ambiance. He calls one of these aspects "orientational structure" (*kōseiteki kōzō*) in order to characterizes the state in which the living body is *not* consciousness of its directionality, or the state in which the process of the living body is not brought to consciousness.[10] As an example, we can cite habits, or skills which one has learned. Although Ichikawa seems to have in mind primarily the physiological function of the body, we could include impulsive actions within this category as well. Ichikawa calls the second aspect of the divisible whole of the living body the "intentional structure" (*shikōteki kōzō*) in which the directionality of the living body is said to accompany its consciousness or in which the process of directionality can easily be brought to the level of consciousness.[11] Both the "orientational" and the "intentional" structures are referred to collectively as the "directional structure" (*shikōteki kōzō*). In the discussion that follows, we shall articulate these two structures, beginning first with the orientational structure.

THE ORIENTATIONAL STRUCTURE

There are two points that Ichikawa wants to establish in his analysis of the orientational structure: (1) that the orientational structure serves as a preparatory ground for the function of the intentional structure, and thereby to substantiate his claim that cogito is dependent upon the living human body, and (2) that there is a certain degree of integration within the directional structure between its orientational and the intentional functions, and through this demonstration, to further investigate his claim that the body is the spirit. This investigation of the orientational structure and the intentional structure is discussed in light of the complimentarity Ichikawa finds between the orientational and the intentional structures.

Ichikawa distinguishes two kinds of directionality that belong to the orientational structures in which the living body does *not* have consciousness of its directionality: (1) one is a directionality that is self-functionally active in the living body, and (2) the other is a directionality that is cast externally to the ambiances.[12] As we have just noted, however, these two kinds of directionality do not involve *a consciousness of* the living body's orientation.

The first kind of directionality applies to the activities, physiologically speaking, that are dominated by the functions of the autonomic nervous system, the internal secretions, and to an extent, by the neuro-spinal nervous system. These activities are self-functional, and for this reason they rarely enter our consciousness under healthy conditions. They might even seem to function independent of the conscious, voluntary activities of a person. However, Ichikawa notes that the directionality of these self-functional orientational structures, though indirect, "prepares a general ambiance or condition so that the directionalities of intentional structure and externally cast orientational structure can function."[13] A failure, for example, of the homeostatic function endangers the life of the living body. Philosophically, then, the directionality of the orientational structure has the function of preparing "the ground for the living body's being active" in the ambiances "by assuming itself to be passive."[14] This reflects an articulation of the ambiguity mentioned earlier between the living body and the ambiances, or alternatively it specifies the meaning of the living body's being-in-the-ambiance.

Ichikawa recognizes that it is a negative characterization of orientational structure to say that the living body becomes active by assuming a passivity, since the self-functional activities do not seem to contribute positively to the activities of the intentional structure and externally cast directionality of the orientational structure. However, there is, says Ichikawa, a positive function in that the self-functional orientational structure "regulates a higher level of intentional structure, and at the same time is controlled by the latter."[15] The relationship that obtains between the orientational and the intentional structures, according to Ichikawa, is complementary. Generally speaking, the orientational structure has a positive meaning of preparing a "posture" which supports an intentional structure. For example, take Weber's discovery that the simple *thought* to move one's arm activates an expansion of the blood vessels in the arm prior to the execution of the movement.[16]

As mentioned previously, such a thought to move the arm does not involve a conscious intention to expand the blood vessels, and this is because the "principal role of our conscious states is generally to control or sketch the *externally directed* functions."[17] Yet, for the blood vessels to expand, then, one must presuppose a preparatory function in the orientational structure. With respect to the regulatory function of the orientational structure, take the example of pain. Generally speaking, the internal (or the intraceptor) sensations are vague and nondiscriminatory, except when there are abnormal conditions in the living body. Among these internal (or intraceptor) sensations, the most acutely felt pain is experienced in an internal organ. Ichikawa reasons that this is probably because pain functions as a danger sign to invoke a certain kind of regulation. Here, then, is an instance of the regulatory function that is carried out by the self-functional activities of the orientational structure.

In its preparatory function, the externally directed orientational structure either "promotes or curtails a volitional intentional action."[18] Take the example of a person who wishes to assume a certain bodily posture. The desire to assume a posture prior to the bodily execution establishes a conscious readiness. This readiness is not, strictly speaking, a working of consciousness, if we understand consciousness to be extensionless. One's posture has the function of regulating the level of consciousness by either lowering or elevating it. The degree to which our awareness is activated through the posture we assume is in proportion to the stability of the posture in question. For example, one's posture becomes increasingly less stable as one moves progressively through the positions of lying down, sitting, to standing, and finally reaches the point of bodily movement. In inverse proportion to the instability of the posture, one's level of awareness becomes increasingly activated. This suggests that the directionality of the orientational structure establishes a level of awareness and a degree of readiness in advance.

This notion that our posture prepares in advance for conscious activities, although most of the time we are not fully aware of this preparation, may be illustrated in the following manner. Ichikawa suggests that we carry out a simple experiment: he asks that we loosen up the tension in our faces, working gradually on the jaws, then around the mouth and the eyes, and finally moving behind the eyes.[19] The fact that we can relax these facial muscles indicates that even though we are not consciously attempting it, we usually "tense up our facial muscles in a certain pattern, making up a face."[20] It is on the basis of this underlying sketching, for example, that we are able to make "faces" that express approval or disapproval.

Ichikawa observes that the orientational structure has a more positive influence on the intentional structure than the preparatory function, and this influence is the regulatory function which the orientational structure exerts upon the intentional structure.[21] This is to say, the intentional structure incorporates within itself an orientational structure by which it is ultimately regulated. This is especially true of an orientational structure which has a regulated, yet flexible pattern such as walking. In attempting to walk, which is intentional, all of the muscles necessary to execute this activity comply with the attempt to walk, without this compliance being brought to the level of awareness. In such a case, Ichikawa argues, "I do not desire nor freely control each contraction and expansion of my muscles for every step of my walk."[22] The movement of the muscles deploys in a certain pattern (i.e., orientational structure) so that "the intentional structure (of walking) renders itself to the orientational structure,"[23] a regulated, yet flexible pattern of contraction and expansion of the muscles involved.

By showing the influences that the orientational structure has on the intentional structure in terms of the former's preparatory and regulatory functions, Ichikawa makes the point that these two structure are "closely linked,"[24] or closely integrated. He observes that, as a consequence of this integration, a "secondary ambiance" is formed, which is neither the internal nor the external ambiance. Ichikawa says:

> The orientational structure divides the ambiance, either positively or negatively, at a level prior to consciousness, forming around us a harmonious neutral zone with the various possibilities that are *dependable*.[25]

This generation of secondary ambiance is due to the preparatory and the regulatory functions of the orientational structure which enable the orientational structure to carry out its principle role of controlling or sketching the externally cast directionality. If the orientational structure and the intentional structure are not integrated, then the directionality of the intentional structure cannot be effected successfully, much less create a "harmonious neutral zone." The orientational structure prepares and regulates the intentional structure, and in so doing creates a harmonious neutral zone. To recognize the importance of this harmonious neutral zone, we need only consider the person whose movements of body and mind are not coordinated.

The preparation and the regulation by the orientational structure results in creating a harmonious neutral zone. It is so called because it saves us from facing a fatal situation. This creation of harmonious neutral zone implies that the distinction between the internal and the external ambiance, which was perhaps necessary in the beginning stage of our inquiry, is now unnecessary, for this harmonious neutral zone becomes a primary ambiance *for us*. For example, Merleau-Ponty's concept of bodily space presupposes Ichikawa's concept of the harmonious neutral zone, for without this harmonious neutral zone, the body's intentionality cannot create a bodily space. On the other hand, the dissolution of internal and external ambiance through the phenomenon of the harmonious neutral zone endorses, in turn, the validity of Merleau-Ponty's phenomenological discovery of bodily space. Ichikawa remarks that generally speaking, the orientational structure in its self-functional aspect builds up a zone of "survival possibility" (*seizon kanōsei*) and in its externally directed aspect a zone of "action possibility" (*kōdō kanōsei*).[26] Ichikawa uses the phrase survival possibility to stress that the life of the living body is dependent upon the passivity, though vital passivity, which the living body maintains in its relation to the ambiance. On the other hand, the phrase action possibility points up the preparatory and the regulatory functions of the orientational structure in its interaction with the ambiance.

THE INTENTIONAL STRUCTURE

Having thus outlined the regulation and control which the orientational structure exerts on the intentional structure, Ichikawa now seeks to demonstrate (1) that the intentional structure is dependent upon the orientational structure for its function and (2) that the intentional structure is grounded in the orientational structure. Ichikawa asserts that the "intentional structure...generates itself, being grounded in the orientational structure."[27] This statement claims that the intentional structure, the structure that is easily accessible to consciousness, is dependent upon the orientational structure, the structure that is not brought to consciousness in the course of its generation. Ichikawa's method of demonstrating this claim is first to point out the negative momentum involved in all of the activities of consciousness. That is, in order for an intentional object to be constituted by an intentional act, there must be a negative momentum intuited by the prereflective self, disclosing that the object in question is not identical with the act, or with the self performing the act. If they were the same, then there could be no constitution of an intentional object. Recognizing the negative momentum involved in all intentional acts, Ichikawa goes on to point out that the degree or the power of negation increases proportionally from mood, emotion, feeling, extending all of the way to perception. In other words, mood is the weakest in its power to negate an intentional object as not belonging to a self which has an emotion, while perception is at the other extreme end of the range, and has the strongest power of negation. This procedure is an application of Ichikawa's concept of the subject-body which is said to form a continuum extending from the transparent, bright cogito to the obscure, hazy horizon of cogito. In light of this understanding, mood belongs to the obscure, hazy horizon of cogito while perception belongs to the bright, transparent horizon of cogito.

Therefore, if Ichikawa can demonstrate that mood is *rooted* in the obscure hazy horizon of consciousness, or in the orientation structure, and if he can show that emotion, feeling and perception represents a progression in their dependence upon the orientational structure, his claim that the intentional structure is dependent upon, and grounded in the orientational structure would be substantiated.

The intentionality thesis as it was originally developed by Husserl maintains that consciousness is always consciousness of something, whether it pertains to emotion, feeling, perception or imagination, or for that matter, any mental activity. Put differently, consciousness has directionality (directionality here must be distinguished from directionality in Ichikawa) which enables us to connect a self with the world. This is indicated when it is said that consciousness is consciousness *of* something. In short, consciousness must have an intentional object, it must have a "something" of which we can be conscious. This something is said to be transcendent in Sartre because something qua something is outside of consciousness, while according to Husserl, it is said to be "transcendently immanent." It is said to be transcendent insofar as something qua something is beyond consciousness, but it is immanent insofar as it is constituted within consciousness. Both Husserl and Sartre recognize, however, that consciousness can be divided into two momenta: in Sartre between "for-itself" and "in-itself" and in Husserl between noesis and noema. These two momenta are connected by the act of consciousness, by the of in consciousness of.

At this juncture, Ichikawa questions if this positing of an intentional object can also apply to "mood" (*kibun*). He points out that mood does not have a clearly delineated intentional object, that is, a something of which we are conscious. He says, "it is difficult to easily determine whether a 'something' is a general appearance of the world or a general condition of self."[28] Naturally, one can argue that insofar as one is in a particular mood, this particular mood can be considered the something, the object of consciousness. But Ichikawa feels that such an argument is forced in order to make consciousness as transparent as possible, when in fact the argument is inconsistent with the experience of being in a mood. Being in a "mood is disclosed as an .

ambiguous relationship between the preobjective self and the world," and hence when one is in a particular mood, it seems to be an indeterminate state of "a general appearance of the world or a general condition of the self." This suggests to Ichikawa that unlike perception "mood, which establishes a 'distance' from an object, has the least negativity of positing it as not a self."[29] Ichikawa's contention is that when one is in a certain mood, the self is preobjective and hence is unable to establish a "distance" from the given state, understanding distance here as the inability to objectify oneself from a given state. Consequently, what appears is an indeterminate state of a general appearance of the world or a general appearance of a preobjective self. The important point Ichikawa establishes here is that, insofar as the mood can be considered a phenomenon of consciousness, its intentional power of positing its object, is the weakest, or alternatively it does not carry a negativity of positing an object as different from the self experiencing it. Ichikawa interprets this weakest power of negation in mood to mean that mood, among the various aspects of the intentional structure, is either the "closest to" or "deeply rooted in" the orientational structure. Mood, then, is the closest to the orientational structure because the orientational structure does not have the power to posit, for example, the external ambiance as distinct from the living body of one's own. As we can recall, the living body assumes a passivity with respect to its relationship with the external ambiance. Moreover, mood is deeply rooted in the orientation structure because mood, being fused with a somatic sensation, is swayed by the physiological condition of the living body. At any rate, it is important to take note of Ichikawa's point that mood, as an aspect of the intentional structure, is influenced by, and linked to the orientation structure. This, then, is a partial demonstration of Ichikawa's claim that intentional structure is dependent upon the orientational structure. In terms of the living body's being-in-the-ambiance, and by virtue of the dependency of mood upon the orientational structure, it discloses, to use Heidegger's terminology, a thrownness into the ambiance.

Ichikawa carries his observations on mood to a stronger position, asserting that "what has been said about mood is applicable to all intentional structures, but with a difference of degree."[30] We anticipated this position when we discussed the orientational structure in relation to the intentional structure, especially with reference to the preparatory and regulatory functions of the orientational structure. In their mutual complimentarity, the orientational structure, as a substructure of the intentional structure, prepares the ground for the intentional structure to function and, at the same time, regulates the latter in such a way that the intentional structure is given a direction for its function. Ichikawa now attempts to demonstrate such a relation, focusing his attention especially on the emotions and the feelings (those intentional structures with a self-functional tendency) and perception (an equally intentional structure with the externally cast directionality).

When we move from an analysis of mood to an analysis of emotion, we notice that the living body as a being-in-the-ambiance punctuates its intentional object more clearly than it does in the case of mood, although it does not do so as thoroughly as it does in the case of perception. In contrast to mood, emotion is marked by an intentional object, though such a marking may be nonpositional, or nonthetic at the time when an intentional structure of emotion is generated. Fear and anger, for example, always have their intentional objects which are linked with the perception of the state of affairs in the world. Marie, therefore, is fearful of the darkness, or a snake. A perception of the external world provides the emotion with an intentional object. But as Sartre points out in his *Esquisse d'une theorie des emotions*, these emotions carry within themselves a self-functional activity, a function that belongs, in Ichikawa's terminology, to the orientational structure. Sartre says, "En un mot dans l'emotion, c'est le corps qui, dirigé par la conscience, changes se rapports au mond pour que le mond change se qualitiés."[31] That is to say, the body, in transforming its relation to the world, changes the meaning (*la signification*) of the world, and this transformation is said to be performed magically (*magiquement*). In light of the consciousness of fear as an emotion, for example, it means that the mode of consciousness is magically transformed by means of the mode of the living body's being-in-the-ambiance. The magical transformation of the meaning of the world, then, blurs a clear perception of the state of affairs in the world. An emotion consequently achieves its goal, by "confer(ing) upon reason the qualities that I *desire*"[32] (emphasis added).

Interpreting Sartre's theory of the emotions in this manner, we can trace reasoning behind Ichikawa's claim that the intentional structure is dependent upon, and grounded in the orientational structure, at least insofar as an analysis of emotion is concerned. Since Sartre recognizes that emotion achieves its goal by magically transforming the meaning of the world through the body (*le corps*), Ichikawa translates Sartre's interpretation into what he calls an orientational structure. The term orientational structure is Ichikawa's designation for the generative process of which the individual is unaware. Without this orientation structure that magically transforms the body's relation to the world, emotion would not achieve its goal. Since this is the case, we have good reason to think that the intentional structure—in the present case, a generation of emotion—is dependent upon, and grounded in the orientational structure. The dependence and grounding of the intentional structure in the orientational structure is somatic in nature, for emotion achieves its goal by changing the *meaning* of the world *by means of* the body or the orientational structure, which in turn changes the mode of the living body's being-in-the-ambiance.

The degree to which perception, co-functional with the emotions, loses its discriminatory function is lessened in the feelings, and consequently the power of the feelings to magically transform the body's relation to the world is likewise weakened. In other words, the somatic dominance or the orientational structure does not have as strong a reign as was the case with the emotions. This does not mean, however, that feeling is characterized by other than the self-functional activity of the living body. In contrast to emotion, which shows a clear somatic dominance of the orientational structure, Ichikawa thinks that feeling has a quasi-intentional structure that stands between the orientational structure and the intentional structure. The use of the term "quasi intentional" indicates that feeling moves closer to the intentional structure in its larger sense in positing that its intentional object is not identical with the self experiencing it. Ichikawa says:

> Feeling has an intentional structure, an aspect of which is to make a specific object value-laden, while bestowing a magical power upon the externally functional activity. It has a quasi-

intentional structure as well which remains self-functional, dyeing not a specific object but the world with a certain value.[33]

Feeling, then, is said to be composed of dual affective modes; an intentional mode and a quasi-intentional mode. The intentional mode has a specific intentional object "dyeing it with a certain value," while the quasi-intentional mode bestows a general value upon the world. The latter is reminiscent of the characterization of emotion as having the power to magically transform the living body's relation to the world, and in this sense, the difference between emotion and feeling is a matter of degree. But, according to Ichikawa, this point alone is not a demarcating feature of feeling. In addition, feeling is said to "dye" a specific intentional object "with a certain value," perhaps with less intensity than in the case of emotion. The difference would seem to lie in the way perception accompanies both emotion and feeling in constituting a state of being-in-the-ambiance. With respect to emotion, the perception accompanying it loses its intentional object *in the midst of* a magical transformation, though it does not disappear as a factor constituting an emotion. This is what is meant by the statement that emotion's intentional object is nonthetically posited. In other words, positing an intentional object does not negate the self that is experiencing a certain emotion, but rather in its stead an intentional object nonthetically posited becomes a world, which incapacitates the discriminatory function of perception to establish its distance from an intentional object. On the other hand, the discriminatory function of perception with respect to feeling remains relatively undisturbed since it is not as intense an emotion. Ichikawa says:

> The *state* of feeling...does not seem, at first glance, to influence perception, but this is only superficial. Perception is influenced subtly at the level prior to consciousness by means of feeling's value bestowment.[34]

This point can be substantiated by Hadley Cantril's discovery of the "Honi Phenomenon," which manifests itself in the "distorted room." The distorted room, designed by Adelbert Ames Jr., is constructed in such a way that "it produces the same image on the retina as a regular square room if it is viewed from a certain point. Since the room is seen as square, persons or objects within the room looking through the windows become distorted."[35] The distortion of the room is said to occur when an observer does not have an affective attitude towards a person or a thing in the room. On one occasion, however, Cantril discovered that the room becomes distorted instead of the person in the room. He attributes this unexpected distortion to the observer's *affective* attitude towards the person in the room. According to Cantril, the distortion of the room instead of the person in the room is that the observer used the person rather than the context as a point of reference. Since the observer was the wife of the person in the room, and since she referred to him as "Honi" this phenomenon was named as Honi Phenomenon. Wittreich further experimented with Honi Phenomenon using married couples and he found that "if couples had been married less than a year there was a very definite tendency not to let the new marital partner distort as quickly or as much as was allowed by people who had been married for a considerable time."[36] The fact that the point of reference can be either the distorted room or the person in the room depending upon the observer's affective attitude toward one or the other leads Ichikawa to conclude that feeling's value bestowment is operative at a level beneath consciousness, and influences perception, particularly its intentional object.

When we consider mood, emotion, and feeling in light of our preceding discussion, the negativity in positing their intentional objects (i.e., the self in the generative process of these intentional structures is not identical with the intentional object) becomes stronger in the order mentioned. The strength of this negativity is inversely proportional to the influence that the orientational structure has on these intentional structures. But in the case of perception—an intentional structure with its directionality primarily cast externally—its correlation with the orientational structure is still further weakened. Conversely, the negativity of positing an intentional object as not self perceiving becomes stronger.

Perception is constituted within a field of consciousness where an intentional object as a focus of that field forms, to use the terminologies of Gestalt psychology, a figure with an oblique ground surrounding it. Although the demarcation between the figure and the ground in the field of consciousness is not experientially a clear-cut one, the division between the figure and the ground points to the *internal* structure of consciousness. Hence, this division does not itself surface to consciousness at the time when the generative process of an internal structure takes place, although it can be made conscious through reflection.

Ichikawa observes that this internal structure which makes a figure appear to consciousness *can* be linguistically incarnated in terms of the subject-predicate pattern in language, notably in Indo-European languages.[37] A figure which is thematized and rendered into a something comes to function as the subject of the sentence. However, this linguistically incarnated some*thing* is not a substance in the sense of *underlying* an appearance, or having an independent existence of its own: rather it is due to the thematizing function of the internal structure of consciousness that this something can be made the subject of a sentence. This "something" is an "empty figure" when it is conceived abstractly, and divorced from the actual working of consciousness. The truth of the matter, that is, the way in which consciousness functions, is more clearly expressed in sentences which begin with an impersonal pronoun such as "it is raining, it is hot." Or the way in which consciousness functions is more accurately represented in the subjectless sentences of Japanese. The subjectless sentences of Japanese capture the nonsubstantial and the empty characteristic of a figure within the field of consciousness as a function of thematization. The fact that something can be incarnated as the something in a sentence is analogous to the fact that a prereflective self can be made into an object upon reflection. However, at the time when perception takes place, the self is preobjective in that it escapes objectification while it enables the noematic content (i.e., a figure) to appear in the field of consciousness. Obviously, when Ichikawa speaks of the figure as empty, he is deeply influenced by Sartre, who thinks of consciousness as "nothingness" (*le néant*). Moreover, we can sense Merleau-Ponty's influence when Ichikawa speaks of the figure as a function of thematization, for a figure in Merleau-Ponty is said to be thematically given. These influences pervade Ichikawa's treatment of prereflective consciousness, which is necessarily involved in all instances of intentional structure.

How can the thematizing function of consciousness make a

figure appear in the field of consciousness? According to Ichikawa, it is a preconscious, nonthetic grasp of self. He argues that, since consciousness is always directed at something, it cannot be, at the same time, thetically aware of itself. But an awareness of this directing is possible through reflection. That it can be made conscious reveals that it is *nonthetically* aware of itself. In other words, there is a prereflective consciousness of self at work in constituting an intentional object. Even though the self does not surface to consciousness at the time when consciousness is directed toward something, it does not follow that:

> it is straightforwardly a nonpersonal consciousness nor is it in the undifferentiated subject-object state prior to its separation, for it is grasped as "my" consciousness upon reflection, never turning into the consciousness of Charlie Brown nor that of Margrid Dullas.[38]

Accordingly, consciousness conceals a prereflective consciousness of the self—the division that is distinct from, and yet more fundamental than, the division between the figure and the ground—and this is because consciousness is grounded in the orientational structure.

Ichikawa argues that the prereflective consciousness for the intentional structure is *constitutive of* consciousness, for this prereflective consciousness, consciousness itself, directed at a something, cannot function. This observation raises an interesting question about the status of prereflective consciousness. Ichikawa has just shown that prereflective consciousness cannot claim the ownership of a consciousness other than its own. But the fact that prereflective consciousness can be made conscious through reflection indicates that, in principle, it can change into an object in the same manner as any of the other objects of consciousness. Ichikawa argues that the ability of prereflective consciousness to become an object through reflection demonstrates that it does not have a privileged status, and is no different than any other object in the world.

Nevertheless, in its functioning, the prereflective consciousness of the intentional structure is neither an object within nor an inhabitant of the field of consciousness. This is the Sartrean position. But as constitutive of consciousness, the prereflective consciousness is a grasping of the self qua the functioning of the intentional structure. In short, it is not an ego-substance. However, we have argued that prereflective consciousness can be transformed into an object of consciousness through reflection. For example, when I can reflect upon the fact that "I see a beautiful woman," the reflected consciousness is not the same as the reflecting consciousness, since the latter involves another prereflective consciousness of myself in the act of reflecting. In other words, the act of reflection does not disclose an initial prereflective consciousness constitutive of "my seeing a beautiful woman." Therefore, we must be careful not to equate with reflected consciousness in which prereflective consciousness has originally been functioning with reflecting consciousness. We can repeat this process of reflecting-reflected *ad infinitum* and yet never be able to grasp prereflective consciousness in its total clarity as it is functioning in the first place. Hence, as prereflective consciousness is the grasp of my self constitutive of consciousness, it "cannot fall into a dubious object in the world, constantly fleeing from the total objectification by means of reflection."[39] At first, this statement *seems* to be inconsistent with Ichikawa's previous claim that prereflective consciousness can be transformed into an object through reflection. In short, Ichikawa seems to be asserting that prereflective consciousness can be transformed into an object and then arguing that it cannot. However, in the first instance, Ichikawa is asserting that objectified prereflective consciousness is no different than any of the other objects of consciousness in the world insofar as all of these objects can be made objects of consciousness. In the second case, he argues that prereflective consciousness cannot be objectified in toto and rendered entirely clear like all of the objects in the world. Ichikawa's points, then, are (1) that prereflective consciousness is not a *privileged* object of consciousness since it can be transformed into an object through reflection, in which case it becomes no different than any other object of consciousness, and (2) that prereflective consciousness cannot be transformed into an object that is totally clear, and cannot in Ichikawa's own words, "fall into a dubious object in the world, constantly fleeing from (total) objectification by means of reflection." In view of our previous discussion, this is because in all intentional structures the nonthetic comprehension of the self as "my self" is implicitly understood, and is based upon the *factual* division between consciousness and prereflective consciousness.[40]

Equally constitutive of consciousness is the intentional object, for without the intentional object, consciousness cannot exist. Incidentally, this recognition is one of the reasons why Sartre understood consciousness to be "nothingness." Husserl expressed the inseparability of consciousness from its intentional object when he argued that noesis (an act of consciousness) is "correlative with" noema (an intentional object), by which he meant that to each act of consciousness there corresponds its specific intentional object appropriate to the act. In other words, both the act of consciousness and its intentional object are constituted within the field of consciousness *at one stroke*. This means in terms of the figure-ground division, a figure as a focused something within the field of consciousness is thematically given, along with a horizonal "world" surrounding the figure which provides a preconscious ground.[41]

As we have seen, then, a prereflective self constitutive of consciousness can be brought into one's awareness to the degree that it becomes an object of consciousness once removed from the initial consciousness which constitutes it. Why, then, is it that a prereflective self cannot be revealed with *total* clarity within the field of consciousness? According to Ichikawa, this is because prereflective consciousness as a comprehension of the self within the intentional structure is grounded in the orientational structure. He says:

> The intentional structure in its living concrete totality is grounded in the orientational structure which is dimly seen in the so-called protopathic sensation and the somatic sensation. Controlling or suppressing the preconscious automatic functions, it synthesizes within itself all of the history of intentionality precipitated in the unconscious.[42]

When we consider the prereflective self, we discover that its translucency is a consequence of the fact that the intentional structure is founded upon an *opaque* orientational structure, and this opaqueness is concealed in terms of "all of the history of intentionality" within the orientational structure. Ichikawa argues this position because he conceives of the living body's directionality with respect to the ambiance as more primary than its intentionality. In other words, the living body's being-in-the-ambiance precedes its being-in-the-world which is disclosed through understanding. Consequently, when Ichikawa asserts that "all of the history of intentionality" is concealed in the orientational structure, one should not take "history" to mean a conscious dating of that which has taken place in and on the living human body. In this context, history seems to designate the *somatic* acquisition of a particular living body which is received through the generative process of various orientational structures such as the personal habits, idiosyncracies, tendencies that characterize this living body. According to Ichikawa, the opaque orientational structure is responsible for the translucency of the prereflective self, and this accounts for the fact that the reflected prereflective self appears "not as a colorless, pronoun-like 'I', but as an individual ego characterized by various tints."[43] Therefore, an "I" as a reflecting consciousness, because of the translucency of its prereflective self, remains also somewhat opaque, preventing "me" from understanding my self in toto. However, Ichikawa believes that there is a more fundamental reason than the translucency of the prereflective self which prevents a total disclosure of my self. He says:

> More fundamentally, it [i.e., the translucency of the prereflective self] is due to the reason that prior to reflection a prereflective self is already drenched in part in the structure beneath consciousness, and its intentionality is already controlled by meaning-generation at the level of the orientational structure which has the history of all directionalities.[44]

Ichikawa's statement that the function of the intentional structure is to synthesize within itself all of the history of intentionality implies that the prereflective consciousness or the self has to be seen as "drenched" in part in the orientational structure. If this were not the case, Ichikawa could not maintain that "all of the history of intentionality" is concealed in the orientational structure. Only when we concede that prereflective consciousness is constituted to a certain extent within the orientational structure, is it possible to understand that the prereflective consciousness in its intentional aspect "is already controlled by means of all directionalities." According to Ichikawa, then, the prereflective consciousness or the self can be regarded as a bridge that joins the orientation structure with the intentional structure, sharing a common, though partial, characteristic of each; its translucency is derived from the opaqueness of the orientational structure and its transparent constitutive function from the intentional structure. Consequently, "the objectified self remains translucent" because of "the intuition of opaqueness that exists prior to reflection."[45]

For Ichikawa, what does all of this imply with respect to the status of the Cartesian cogito as "pure" thinking? One might very well expect Ichikawa to argue that the Cartesian cogito is "colored" by an affective component in perception, or that it is "controlled," like prereflective self-consciousness, "by means of meaning-generation" at the level of the orientational structure. Perhaps realizing the difficulty of specifying the extent of "control" which is exercised by the orientational structure, or by the affective component of perception, Ichikawa points out the inadequacy of using the Cartesian cogito as a point of arrival for phenomenological reflection, though he deems it necessary as a point of departure.[46] The reason Ichikawa thinks that the Cartesian cogito is inadequate as the end of phenomenological reflection is that a Cartesian doubting cogito cannot be granted the apodicticity it claims to have in its absolute sense. For, although

> Descartes grasped apodictically the imperfection of *ego* as a doubting *cogito,* (since *ego* doubts because it is a being that lacks) after he had intuited *ego* apodictically as an indubitable *cogito.* The value of the apodictic intuition of *cogito* is dubious in its absolute sense, unless we conceive of God's guarantee as Descartes presupposed it.[47]

MINENESS OF THE BODY

We have implicitly dealt with the concept of mineness earlier when we examined Ichikawa's observation that a reflected prereflective consciousness or self is always revealed as my consciousness of self, that is, a self experiencing is always recognized as my self, which justifies a given experience as mine. To say that an experience is mine is to recognize a personalization of the lived experience of the body. In this respect, personalization includes the consciousness of the body as mine, along with its prereflective consciousness as my self, both of which have been presupposed so far by Ichikawa in his phenomenological attempt to render the lived body intelligible. The question which Ichikawa addresses in his phenomenological analysis may be formulated as: How does the body-consciousness as mine arise in grasping itself? Or alternatively, what is the phenomenological ground for personalizing the consciousness of the body as mine?

Ichikawa finds some affinity of thought in Tennesse Williams' *Cat On A Hot Tin Roof*, and he uses an appropriate passage as a convenient point of departure for his phenomenological investigation of the personalization of the body-consciousness. Williams writes:

> We're all of us sentenced to solitary confinement inside our own skins. Personal lyricism is the outcry of prisoner to prisoner from the cell in solitary where each is confined for the duration of life.[48]

Ichikawa thinks that Williams' statements raise two philosophically significant issues. The first issue may be formulated as: "How do we grasp our body if we are indeed 'sentenced to solitary confinement inside our own skins'?" Ichikawa believes that an adequate answer to this question will open up the phenomenological origin of the personalization of body-consciousness. The second issue may be formulated in the following way: if a self qua body (*shintai toshite no jiko*) is properly understood through the concept of the personalization of the body-consciousness, then our "solitary confinement inside our own skins" has to be mitigated as a primary way of characterizing the nature of our existence, because, according to Ichikawa, the self qua body is "essentially open to the outside and is a being connected with other people."[49] We will examine these two issues from the point of view of a failure of the personalization of body-consciousness.

Ichikawa's argument concerning the personalization of body-consciousness may be presented in the following manner.[50] As we have already seen, an intentional object of consciousness is constituted through the negation of the object to be constituted by means of the prereflective self, that is, in constituting an object, consciousness refuses prereflectively to identify itself with the object to be constituted. If the prereflective self and the object to be constituted within the field of consciousness were to be identical, there would be no intentional object to be constituted. For example, when I look at a beautiful woman, this woman as an object of my consciousness is not identical with myself. She is distanced from me and objectified within the field of my consciousness. In short, consciousness constitutes its intentional object through the negativity of its prereflective self not being identical with its intentional object. To put it differently, an intentional object is constituted through nonpersonalization. This is true of all of the so-called external perceptions. But what about the case of a pain in my back? Insofar as I can locate *where* it hurts, the pain has taken a distance from me, and insofar as I am aware of the pain, it is objectified and constituted in my consciousness. But this pain is not an intentional object, since I did not *intend* to have the pain. If, on the other hand, this back pain is so intense that there is no chance of taking a distance from it and objectifying it, it would be meaningless for me to talk about the back pain for the pain and myself would become indistinguishable, and could cause a loss of consciousness. Leaving this extreme case aside, internal perception can not be negated, unlike the case of the external perception, as being not mine.

Why is this the case? Ichikawa answers that it is because body-consciousness as it pertains to internal perception belongs to my self. In other words, it is personalized. This may be illustrated by the phenomenon of body-image, where we understand the body-image to mean here an intuitive apprehension of how we picture our body within ourselves. By way of clarification, Ichikawa suggests that we reflect phenomenologically upon the activity of searching with our hands in the dark.[51] In such an instance, needless to say, I can not look at my hand searching for an object, for darkness would conceal my object-body. But insofar as I attempt to feel with my hand for the object that I am looking for, my object-body is involved. For this reason, I am not attempting to locate the object from the perspective of the interiority of my subject-body. Both my subject-body and my object-body are synthesized as a body-image, which is attempting to locate the object in the dark. If they were not synthesized, I would be unable to pick out the right object when I felt its shape in the dark. This synthesis of my subject-body and my object-body is a synthesis that involves a discrepancy between the manner in which I live my subject-body and the manner in which I live my body qua object. According to Ichikawa, this "discrepancy" enables me to grasp my self qua body. Ichikawa writes:

> We can have a clear body-consciousness based upon the discrepancy between two modes of consciousness or dual structures because we are able to have internal and external perception at the same time with respect to [my] body which "I" live and personalize, while simultaneously making it an incarnate object and objectifying it.[52]

Needless to say, the synthesis that occurs is not conscious, rather it is a preconscious operation which enables me to perform the factual activity involved in groping with my hands in the dark. We can see here that Ichikawa's concept of my self qua body has its phenomenological origin in the lived experience of the body. The body that I live is personalized, giving rise to the concept of "mineness" with respect to the experiential correlate of the body. This experiential correlate in turn yields the idea of the "self" that goes through an experience by virtue of the constitutive function of consciousness. However, as we have seen, the self thus grasped is a thematizing function of consciousness, and is essentially devoid of an immutable figure when consciousness is not functioning. The self and the notion of mineness thus form the concept of my self, and come to be regarded as *open to* the outside world because their referential origin goes back to the lived body that is a momentum of establishing the objectivity of objects in the world.

The synthesis, however, does not produce an undifferentiated unity for my self qua body since it is based upon the discrepancy between the two modes of consciousness derived from the subject-body and the object-body. It is, Ichikawa thinks, an "ambiguous oneness" (*ryōgi teki ichigensei*). And, it is this ambiguous oneness, Ichikawa maintains, that philosophers and artists in the past have meditated upon as an ideal condition for human existence. For example, Merleau-Ponty cites an artist in *The Primacy of Perception* who says "In a forest, I have felt so many times over that I was not I who looked at the forest. Some days, I felt that the trees were looking at me, were speaking to me. I was there, listening."[53] According to Ichikawa, this kind of personal statement presupposes an instance of ambiguous oneness; a "oneness" between the subject and the object, between the interiority and the exteriority. Ichikawa explains that "artists grope for a way to express ambiguous oneness, and they dwell in the interiority of the world by transforming the world, *as it were*, into one's body"[54] (emphasis added).

Ichikawa's concept of ambiguous oneness perhaps requires further clarification. First, we must question why oneness is qualified by the adjective "ambiguous," why is it an ambiguous oneness? Throughout this chapter and chapter 1, we have observed Ichikawa's contention that the body is the spirit. This unity of the body and the spirit has been demonstrated through phenomenological descriptions of the living human body, and the unity which Ichikawa asserts has emerged vis-à-vis the synthesis which obtains between the subject-body and the object-body. In light of the phenomenological origin of this synthesis, the synthesis which Ichikawa has brought into the open has turned out to be a synthesis that brings forth an ambiguous oneness between the interiority and the exteriority, or the subject and the object. In other words, Ichikawa's unity is maintained in the synthesis that is present in ambiguous oneness.

CONCLUDING REMARKS

We must now critically examine Ichikawa's concept of "the synthesis that is present in ambiguous oneness." Ichikawa concerned himself with a phenomenological articulation of the lived body from the perspective of everyday mode of consciousness. This is what he meant by "the body qua phenomena," and his analysis of the structure of the body qua phenomena was presented only from the perspective of our everyday mode of consciousness, and therefore his analysis of subject-body and object-body was methodologically confined to this perspective. This is the reason why Ichikawa had to insert "as it were" to qualify his explanation of the concept of the ambiguous oneness which his penetrating phenomenological analysis brought to our attention. He says, and I repeat, that philosophers and artists have "groped for a way of expressing the ambiguous oneness and they dwell in the interiority of the world by transforming the world, *as it were*, into one's body" (emphasis added).

In my estimation, Ichikawa is correct in pointing out the possibility of "transforming the world into one's body," or better "transforming one's body into the world" so as to dwell both in the interior and exterior of the world. Although he thinks that this possibility is only metaphorical,[55] its actual transformation must be predicated on the assumption that there obtains a oneness in some sense between the subject-body and object-body, between the lived body and the world. It is theoretically impossible even to conceive of transforming one's own body into the world, unless there is a phenomenological basis of oneness between them for this transformation to occur. Although Ichikawa has demonstrated that the ambiguous oneness is a synthesis between subject-body and object-body, the ambiguity emerges in virtue of the fact that the phenomenological fact of the synthesis is a preconscious operation, and hence remains merely a possibility for everyday consciousness.

The status of the oneness as being both ambiguous and preconscious in Ichikawa's superb analysis which has brought out the phenomena qua body into the open, is traceable to his contention that cogito is dependent upon the body; he used insightfully the negative momentum of an I positing not identical with the object which is engaged by the I, that is, I am not identical with the object of my awareness. Ichikawa demonstrated skillfully that the power of negative *momentum* is the strongest in perceptual consciousness, and that it decreases as one moves from perception, to feeling, to emotion, and to mood: these various states are mapped, though implicit in Ichikawa's conceptual model, onto the continuum of cogito which ranges from the alleged transparency of our everyday consciousness to the obscure, hazy horizon of cogito.

If we can clearly demarcate, for the purpose of philosophical clarification, the continuum of cogito which ranges from the alleged transparency of our everyday consciousness to the obscure, hazy horizon of cogito, might it not be possible for us to conceive of a fuller sense of oneness than Ichikawa's analysis suggests? The question that we are raising here is whether or not the ambiguous, preconscious status of oneness is the final position that fundamentally characterizes the working of human consciousness. If it is not, it seems that a fuller sense of oneness must be unambiguous oneness, and it must also be conscious, not preconscious, operation that brings forth the oneness of the lived body. In order to obtain, then, the unambiguous, conscious sense of oneness, we must depart from the analysis focused solely on the everyday consciousness, but instead examine the lived experience which incorporates a *transformative* process of this everyday consciousness.

In order to see that there is in fact a fuller sense of oneness with the unambiguous and conscious status of oneness, we would like to examine in the next chapter another equally representative contemporary Japanese philosopher, Yuasa Yasuo.[56] Like Ichikawa, Yuasa explicates his own "body scheme" from a contemporary Western perspective with the view to articulating the Eastern mind-body theory. Because Yuasa incorporates the Eastern mind-body theory in the concept of his body-scheme, his analysis of the lived body departs from the confine of Ichikawa's phenomenological description, and incorporates a transformative dimension of everyday consciousness. He envisions the concept of body scheme to be comprised of the multilayered information circuits, correlating each circuit as much as possible with the neurophysiological structure of the living body. Yuasa's concept of the body scheme consists of four information circuits, and since it is conceived to be multilayered, it shows a decreasing transparency in terms of its availability to our consciousness, or it shows an increasing opacity as one moves from the surface to the deeper layer of the four circuits of information. This point somewhat parallels Ichikawa's concept of the continuum of cogito which ranges from the alleged transparency of our everyday consciousness to the obscure, hazy horizon of cogito. However, this continuum is further specified in Yuasa's body-scheme into the four informational circuits, (1) the external sensory-motor circuit, (2) the circuit of coenesthesis, for example, an awareness of our living body, (3) the emotion-instinct circuit, and (4) the unconscious quasi-body circuit. This specification will enable us, among other things, to understand clearly the sense of oneness which is achieved in the Eastern tradition of self-cultivation. Our philosophical investigation will now focus on the concept of Yuasa's body-scheme.

CHAPTER 3

Yuasa's Body-Scheme *

INTRODUCTION

In elucidating Yuasa's concept of "body-scheme," our primary focus is on his book, *Ki Shugyō Shintai*,[1] because Yuasa skillfully articulates theoretically the concept of the body from an Eastern perspective, while incorporating and utilizing a Western methodological procedure.[2] This stance which Yuasa assumes makes a marked difference from that of Ichikawa's treatment which was primarily confined to a Western (primarily phenomenological) perspective. Particularly interesting is Yuasa's careful analysis of the lived body, making it clear how Ichikawa's "ambiguous oneness" is transformed through the personal self-cultivation into "oneness of the body-mind." In my estimation, Yuasa offers a comprehensive and deeper analysis of the body than most philosophers, East or West, have thus far provided. His concept of body-scheme purports to explicate the inseparability and the oneness of the lived body-mind as it is *achieved* through the Eastern *prāxis* of personal self-cultivation. This achievement, then, is the theme of this chapter.

YUASA'S BODY-SCHEME

The concept of body-scheme[3] was introduced by Merleau-Ponty in *Phenomenology of Perception*. He incorporated and expanded Henry Head's idea of "body-image" as a way of giving a structure to the functions of lived-body.[4] Following this lead, Yuasa proposed his own body-scheme drawing on Eastern and depth-psychological insights. His concept of body-scheme is comprised

---

* An earlier version of this chapter appears in Maxine Sheets-Johnstone, *Giving the Body Its Due,* State University of New York Press, 1992.

of four circuits of interrelated information systems.[5] Yuasa analyzes the four circuits to determine how we live our bodies from
within, that is, our subject-body, at the same time correlating
these circuits, as far as possible, with neuro-physiological structures of the body—our object-body. Implicit in Yuasa's concept
of the body-scheme as the circuits of information is the idea that
the body-scheme is understandable and analyzable in terms of
energy phenomena, because if an information passes through a
circuit, there must be a carrier of this information, and this carrier must be understood as energy-phenomena.[6] Yuasa's over-all
strategy is to capture the dynamic and whole function of the
lived and living body (in relation to its living environment).

THE EXTERNAL SENSORY-MOTOR CIRCUIT

Yuasa calls the first circuit the "external sensory-motor circuit"
(*gaikai kankaku undō kairo*). This is a circuit connecting the
body to the external world through the sensory organs of the
body via stimuli received from the external world. The term
"sensory" refers to the function of the sensory organs which *passively* receive information about the external world via sensory
nerves attached to the sensory organs; the term "motor" in
external sensory-motor circuit designates an *active* motor
response on the received information, that is, an execution of
this response through the various limbs.[7] This is called a "circuit" because information received by the sensory organ goes to
the central nervous system (the brain) via sensory nerves to form
a centrifugal path; the brain in turn conveys the information to
the distal motor organs through the motor nerves to form a centripetal path. This circuit explicates in part the experiential
process, for example, of visually perceiving a tree.

THE CIRCUIT OF COENESTHESIS

The second circuit in Yuasa's body scheme is called the "circuit
of coenesthesis" (*zenshin naibu kankaku kairo*) and deals with
the information system that pertains to the *internal* sensations of
the body. Yuasa recognizes two subdivisions in this "circuit of

coenesthesis": the first one is called the "circuit of kinesthesis" (*undō kankaku kairo*), and the second the "circuit of somesthesis" (*taisei naibu kankaku kairo*).

The circuit of kinesthesis deals with kinetic movements of the body which function in close conjunction with the motor-nerves of the first circuit, the external sensory-motor circuit. This circuit is formed between the motor nerves and the sensory-motor nerves attached to the muscles and tendons of the limbs. In this circuit, each sensory-motor nerve functions as a centripetal path, conveying information about the condition of a distal motor organ (e.g., a hand or a leg) to the brain. The motor nerve, just as in the first circuit, functions as a centrifugal path, conveying the received information back to the limbs. Those who excel in the performing arts or in sports have a well developed circuit of kinesthesis; they can rapidly convey information about a condition of their limbs and coordinate this information skillfully with bodily movement. Yuasa notes that this circuit of kinesthesis supports "from below" the working of the first circuit. It is from below the first circuit because the experiential correlate to the circuit of kinesthesis is found in the *periphery* of the so-called ego-consciousness in functions such as thinking, willing, feeling and imagining.[8] Yuasa acknowledges that Husserl had already taken note of this kinesthesis in terms of "passive synthesis," a passive state prior to the active meaning-bestowing function of consciousness.[9] In general, this circuit is an information system ready to activate the body toward an action in the external world.[10] Together with the first circuit, this second circuits explains how in our everyday life we engage our immediate environments through perception and action. When Western philosophers deal with the dichotomy of mind and body, they focus on the problems arising from the division of these two circuits.

The second subdivision within the circuit of coenesthesis is called the "somesthesis" and is concerned with the condition of internal organs via the splanchnic nerves which are attached to the internal or visceral organs.[11] Splanchnic sensations convey the condition of a distal organ (e.g., a stomach) to the brain, forming a centripetal path. Under normal and healthy conditions, this sensation is vaguely perceived (i.e., protopathic sensation) unlike the clear localization of motor sensation. This is because the region in the cortex connected to the splanchnic nerves is small compared to the region regulating the sensory-motor nerves. However, when there is an abnormal condition in a visceral organ, a person may experience pain (i.e., epicritic sensation). This suggests that the circuit of somesthesis in a normal healthy condition recedes into the background, first behind the circuit of kinesthesis, and then behind the external sensory-motor circuit. Significantly, Yuasa points out that though no philosophers in the West have taken note of the importance of the issues arising from this circuit, some psychoanalysts in the Freudian and Jungian schools have paid attention to the circuit of somesthesis in light of their clinical experience, and in connection with Eastern methods of meditation.

Yuasa likens the circuit of coenesthesis to a biofeedback system. Changes that take place within this system are conveyed to the central nervous system and the latter in turn sends out responses to cope with changes in particular organ experiences. This self-contained system suggests that the body embodies a self-controlling mechanism, that is, biofeedback. Yuasa says that generally, the circuit of coenesthesis is translated experientially into an awareness of the self grasping the body, or simply an awareness of one's body. Insofar as it can be experienced, however vaguely, the circuit of coenesthesis belongs to consciousness.

Important in this connection is Yuasa's observation that the circuit of coenesthesis, particularly its somesthesis, maintains a close link between movements of the body and motile memory. When one learns to play the piano, for example, he/she acquires a knack for the placement of fingers through repeated practice. Once the technique is learned, however, the body *knows* in an instant how to respond to the next move that is required, that is, unconsciously or without forming an intellectual judgment. From this observation, Yuasa reasons that:

> [T]here is *an automatic memory system* at the base of consciousness for judgment, which stores past data, and checking a failed datum, it directs the datum in order for it to be a successful [execution] next time. The repetition of this process is a training. In other words, training is to *habituate* the body in a definite direction. For this purpose, the capacity of the memory system must be enhanced.[12]

A point to keep in mind regarding the "automatic memory system" is that it is situated below the external sensory-motor circuit and the circuit of kinesthesis, both of which belong to consciousness. What is more important in this connection is that the automatic memory system does not require a conscious effort of recall: *the body* learns and knows. This idea seems to be derived from a combination of Merleau-Ponty's concept of "habit-body" (*le corps habituel*) and Bergson's "learned memory" (*souvenir appris*), both of which designate an internalization of bodily movement for the utility of life. Yuasa admits, however, that the mechanism of bio-feedback for this automatic memory system is not clearly understood, because the relationship between the psychological function of (motile) memory and the corresponding physiological mechanism of the body is not yet known sufficiently.[13]

THE EMOTION-INSTINCT CIRCUIT

The third of the information systems in Yuasa's "body-scheme" is called "emotion-instinct circuit" (*jōdō honnō kairo*). This circuit has never been incorporated within concepts of body-scheme so far articulated. Yuasa's insight derives from his knowledge of depth-psychology and Eastern self-cultivation methods. He gives the following reason for the designation of this circuit:

> This circuit has a very close relationship with human instincts such as sexual desire and appetite. For this reason, I call it emotion-instinct circuit.[14]

First, he observes that this circuit is correlated with the autonomic nervous system, which controls and regulates the function of various visceral organs such as the respiratory organs (lungs), the circulatory organ (heart) and the digestive organs (stomach and colon). All of these functions are necessary to maintain the life of the body. If the function of any of these organs fails, an individual body cannot sustain its life. For this reason, "this circuit is fundamental for maintaining not (the motor-function of) the body but its life."[15] A healthy condition of the body is maintained when an appropriate balance of tension and laxity obtains between the sympathetic and parasympathetic nerves which cofunction in the autonomic nervous system. If an excessively tense condition is prolonged, it will offset the balance between the sympathetic and parasympathetic functions. The experiential correlate of the imbalance is stress. However, only cumulative stressful conditions make us aware of the condition of our body.

How, specifically, does Yuasa account for an occurrence of stress using the emotion-instinct circuit? He explains that the autonomic nerve which controls and regulates the emotion-instinct circuit carries within its fibre both the centrifugal and centripetal information paths, unlike the previous two circuits which have independent centrifugal and centripetal paths. The centripetal information system of this emotion-instinct circuit conveys the information concerning the condition of a visceral organ to the brain, the central nervous system. However, Yuasa points out that this centripetal circuit does *not* reach the cortex (neoencephalon). This means that the activities of the visceral organs are performed usually below the conscious level.[16] In other words, we do not have a conscious awareness of their functions under normal and healthy conditions. They function independent of our will. In contrast, the centrifugal path of this circuit sends out to the distal visceral organs those stimuli which the brain receives from the external world vis-à-vis the sensory organs, converting them into an *emotional response* (i.e., pleasure or pain), which turns into stress or a stressful response.

Yuasa notes that emotion generated out of this emotion-instinct circuit has a special significance compared to perception and thinking. Although both perception and thinking can be mapped approximately onto corresponding sensory organs or onto physiological counterparts,[17] emotion when experienced is not localized in any particular organ. Yuasa interprets this to mean that emotions such as anger and sorrow take over the whole of the body, that is, they are holistic in nature.[18] They affect the whole body.

THE SUMMARY OF THE THREE CIRCUITS

Yuasa explains how the preceding three circuits are interrelated. He says:

FIGURE 1
YUASA'S THREE INFORMATION CIRCUITS

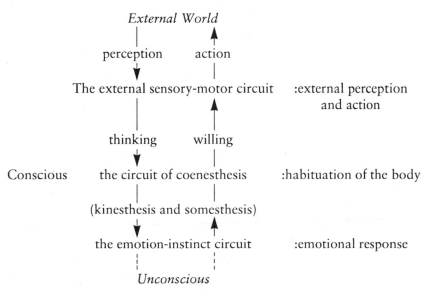

The relationship among (them)...may be summarized as follows. The sensory stimulus (received) from the external world
enters the first "external sensory-motor circuit" that is in the
uppermost surface layer (of the body-scheme), and passing
through the second circuit of coenesthesis, reaches the third
emotion-instinct circuit that is the lowest layer (in the scheme)
where the emotional response of pleasure or pain is generated.
This response returns to the second circuit, and eliciting its
movement, it further activates the first circuit, which is
expressed as a bodily movement in the external world.[19]

As may be evident, one of the characteristic features in Yuasa's
three-circuited body-scheme is that he conceives the scheme as
forming a multilayered information system: starting with the
external sensory-motor circuit, he recognizes underneath it the circuit of coenesthesis and at the lowest layer the emotion-instinct
circuit. This schematization suggests that the control which one
can exercise on these circuits decreases as one recedes from the
first external sensory-motor circuit and progresses to the third
emotion-instinct circuit. The difference in control correlates with
an awareness of the body which decreases in transparency, or in

increases of opacity as one moves from the first to the third circuit. For a visual presentation of this point, Figure 1 may be helpful.

According to Yuasa, there is no direct and immediate relationship between the first external sensory-motor circuit and the third emotion-instinct circuit. For example, the fact that one cries does not immediately impair the capacity for visual perception. However, the capacity of the first circuit is dependent on the second circuit of coenesthesis. As noted earlier, this is because the second circuit is closely connected with the motile memory which assists the habitualization of the body. Therefore, an athlete who has mastered a set of certain techniques for moving his/her body through training, for example, embodies an enhanced capacity of the second circuit which in turn heightens the level of activity in the first circuit.

In fact, this is the goal of Western sports, perhaps symbolically represented by the phrase muscle man.[20] It suggests to Yuasa that the goal of Western sports is not conceived in connection with, and in consideration of, the organs governed by the autonomic nervous systems. Psychologically this means that the training method of Western sports does not take into account the idea of controlling the emotion-instinct circuit.[21]

Since the goal and training method of Western sports are mentioned, it is appropriate here to contrast them with those of Eastern self-cultivation methods which have influenced various Japanese cultural activities such as martial arts, tea ceremony, *ikebana*, and the like, and which seem not to require the same discipline as sports. The methods Yuasa has in mind in this regard are represented by "*sāmadhi* through constant motion" or "*sāmadhi* through continual sitting,"[22] both of which are an ideal to be achieved in self-cultivation methods. In contrast to the goal of Western sports, Yuasa sees one of the goals in personal self-cultivation to be that of "control(ling) the patterns of emotional response," or more broadly, the function of the emotion-instinct circuit. He states:

> The goal of personal cultivation is to change the patterns of emotional response (i.e., complexes in personality) by controlling emotions and integrating the power of the unconscious within consciousness.[23]

There are two points to be clarified and elaborated in this quote: (1) to "control emotions" and (2) to "integrate the power of the unconscious within consciousness." Since the second point concerns the last and fourth circuit of Yuasa's body-scheme, I shall reserve it for later. For now, our concern is the point of controlling emotions. What does "controlling emotions" mean within the Japanese cultural tradition of personal self-cultivation and how does Yuasa interpret it? He does not mean an exercise of conscious will to suppress emotions, as is suggested, for example, in Kant's ethical theory.[24] Concurring with Aristotle's concept of virtue as a habit-formation, Yuasa interprets controlling emotion to be a process of habit-formation that works on the third emotion-instinct circuit.[25] He explains the process of habit-formation within his theory of body-scheme as follows:

> The information entering the first external sensory-motor circuit reaches the third emotion-instinct circuit, and an emotional response to this information ricochets back to the second circuit which *habitualizes* the body, forming a definite passage among the three layers of these circuits.[26] (emphasis added)

This process is an instance of conditioned reflex which otherwise is not functional in our "natural attitude." Initially, the passage among the three circuits is a temporary conjunction, but through repeated practice, it will become a *definite* conjunction.[27] Since Yuasa conceives of controlling emotions as a process of habit-formation, that is, repeated training, the control in question is developed naturally. The process depends largely on the body, not on the mind, that is, not on the exercise of conscious will to suppress the emotion. An assumption in Yuasa's understanding of controlling emotions is that it is possible to correct the modality of mind by correcting the modality of the body—emotion being the modification of the body as Spinoza has it.[28]

In the process of habituating the second circuit of coenesthesis as a way of controlling emotions, Yuasa takes note of the importance of breathing exercises which are emphasized in all forms of Japanese training and self-cultivation methods. Physiologically, the respiratory organ is regulated and controlled by the autonomic nerves and motor-nerves; the respiratory organ has an ambiguous character of being linked both to the voluntary and involuntary muscles. This means that one can consciously control the rhythm and pattern of breathing, and in turn affect the physiological functions governed by the autonomic nervous system. More importantly still, one could affect the emotion-instinct circuit since, as Yuasa observes, the autonomic nervous system is closely connected to emotion:

> The function of autonomic nerves is deeply linked to emotions (both positive and negative emotions such as anger, sorrow, hatred, joy, love and peace, that is, pleasure and pain). If the negative emotion is always stressed, a pathological state will result, but on the other hand, if the positive emotion is always strengthened, it will nurture more mature psychological traits (that is, the pattern of emotion as a habit of the mind/heart).[29]

The goal of the Eastern method of training and self-cultivation is then designed to habituate naturally the third emotion-instinct circuit through breathing exercises that conscious will can control. What is implicit here is the Eastern discernment of the correlativity between state of mind and state of body in the rhythms and patterns of breathing. For example, when one is angry, the pattern of breathing is irregular and its rhythm rough. When this insight is generalized, it means that controlling emotions in personal self-cultivation:

> enhance[s] *the degree of correlativity* between the movements of mind and those of the body, thus producing a closer relation of unity between the mind and body. Ultimately, it pursues a spiritual goal of developing an all-round personality.[30] (emphasis added)

We witness in this quote an important thesis of the Eastern mind-body theory, namely, that the relationship between mind and body is originally one of unity or oneness which a practitioner restores through prāxis.

Having touched on the subject of controlling emotions, I would now like to investigate the point that was left unattended, namely Yuasa's point that the goal of Eastern methods of training and personal self-cultivation is to "integrate the power of the unconscious within consciousness." An examination of this point will in turn enable us to understand more concretely the meaning of unity or oneness that is said to obtain through prāxis between mind and body in the Eastern, particularly Japanese, tradition.

THE CIRCUIT OF UNCONSCIOUS QUASI-BODY

The "circuit of unconscious quasi-body" (*muishikiteki jun shintai*) articulates the fourth and the last circuit in Yuasa's body-scheme. The term "unconscious" used in this designation indicates that this circuit is not accessible to our everyday consciousness. The term "quasi" qualifying "body," on the other hand, indicates that the body at this level does not conform to the idea either of the subject-body or of the object-body which phenomenologists have thus far investigated and elucidated. It defies our ordinary understanding, and yet is in some fundamental sense connected to the body.[31] Yuasa characterizes this fourth circuit of unconscious quasi-body as follows:

> This fourth circuit is an *invisible circuit,* insofar as we examine it anatomically, and so it cannot be perceived by means of external perception. And when it is viewed psychologically, it is *a potential circuit below consciousness,* which consciousness in an ordinary circumstance cannot detect.[32] (italics in the original)

According to Yuasa, this "quasi-body" does not have an anatomical counterpart because our sensory perception cannot detect it; hence it is "invisible" for external perception. Yet Yuasa claims that it is psychologically "a potential circuit below consciousness." This suggests that although the "quasi-body" is potentially invisible to us, and hence unknown to the everyday consciousness, the practice of various self-cultivation methods can render the invisible circuit "visible," that is, bring its function into awareness. If it can become actual, we should understand the unconscious quasi-body as only *relatively* invisible—in other words, as potentially visible.

Yuasa incorporates the circuit of unconscious quasi-body within his concept of body-scheme in consideration of the *ki*-meridian system which acupuncture medicine has recognized for thousands of years in the Far East. The connection of unconscious quasi-body with ki-meridian is explicit in Yuasa's statement: "I shall call the system of ki-meridian 'unconscious quasi-body'."[33] According to acupuncture medicine, the ki-meridians form an invisible network beneath the surface of the skin which covers the entire body, and which serves as a grid through which the ki-energy flows.[34] Ki-energy can be detected only in a living body, not in a corpse. Yuasa describes the nature of ki-energy as it is presently understood:

> [T]he substance of the unknown energy *ki* is not within our [present] understanding. It is a flow of a certain kind of energy unique to the living organism which circulates in the body, although it is uncertain yet what generates such a function. To be more specific, when the flow of *ki* is examined psychologically, it can be perceived as an extraordinary sensation, as a lived body's self-grasping sensation in a unique situation on the surface of the circuit of coenesthesis. (e.g., a case of a ki-sensitive person.) Furthermore, when it is seen physiologically, it can be detected on the surface of the skin which is a boundary wall between the body and the external world. [35]

When Yuasa refers to the experiential detection of ki-energy as it flows through the body, he has in mind the medical application of the acu-points that are distributed on the twelve major ki-meridians. He mentions, for example, that stimulation applied by an acu-needle on the acu-point called *san-li*, located roughly on the outer side of the shin within the stomach-meridian, produces a change in the stomach which can be verified by x-ray. Of course, there is no anatomical connection between the point on the shin and the stomach in terms of the nervous system. Yet with respect to the medical use of the acu-points, the existence of the ki-meridians is uncontestable. They have proved a source of successful medical treatment of the living human body for many hundreds of years.

For our present concern, Yuasa's reference to the psychological detection of the ki-meridians as a "lived body's self-grasping sensation" in a ki-sensitive person is significant in that this psychological experience is based upon experimental research performed by Nagahama Yoshio. Nagahama discovered that a ki-sensitive person could detect "vibrations" when an acu-needle is inserted at a point on the body.[36] The tracks along which the vibrations are felt correspond, according to Nagahama, to the ki-meridian system that charts the distribution of the acu-points as they are recorded in the old Chinese treatises.[37] It is important to emphasize here that in Yuasa's body-scheme the unconscious quasi-body circuit lies deeper than the circuit of coenesthesis (especially the circuit of somesthesis), for ki-vibrations in the ki-sensitive person are generated "on the surface of the circuit of coenesthesis," suggesting that the effect of the unconscious quasi-body circuit surfaces from below the circuit of coenesthesis. Furthermore, when Yuasa mentions the physiological detection of the "ki-vibrations," he has in mind the difference in conductivity of ki-vibrations as compared to the conductivity of nerve-impulses. The movement of ki-vibrations is said to be much slower than the movement of nerves-impulses.[38]

In the case of a ki-sensitive person, ki-energy is said to be felt or intuited as a sensation of power from below the circuit of coenesthesis. In light of the previous three circuits then, this unconscious quasi-body mediates between the first two circuits and the third emotion-instinct circuit. The first two circuits at least in part belong to "consciousness" and the third as Yuasa has noted has a close connection with the unconscious. Thus the unconscious quasi-body mediates between consciousness and the unconscious through the flow of ki-energy.[39] The philosophical consequence which Yuasa draws from this observation is enormously important. Yuasa states:

> The ki-meridian system is related closely to both mind and body, both spirit and matter, and is a middle system that influences them. For this reason, it is a third term which cannot be explained by Descartes' mind-body dichotomy, but it forms a mediating system that links the mind and the body. Herein lies, it seems, a *break-through* point that reforms the paradigm of empirical science [established] since Descartes.[40] (emphasis added)

Given this observation that the ki-meridian system, and hence Yuasa's circuit of unconscious quasi-body, is a mediating third term between mind and body, the question naturally arises if this claim is empirically verifiable. For an answer, Yuasa refers us to the practice of meditation and its conceptual analysis within the framework of his concept of body-scheme.

Yuasa notes that meditation "bring[s] the activity of the third emotion-instinct into awareness."[41] In order to see why this is the case, we must first understand what meditation is. Here, Yuasa draws our attention to the status of the external sensory-motor circuit in seated meditation. He says:

> To meditate in a sitting position means to stop the muscular movements of the limbs while cutting off the sensory stimuli of the external world. By means of this, the external sensory-motor circuit is brought to a state of standstill.[42]

The circuit of kinesthesis is by implication rendered inoperative, because this circuit functions in close conjunction with the first external-sensory motor circuit. In seated meditation, then, both the external sensory-motor circuit and the circuit of kinesthesis are rendered inoperative. Yet the circuit of somesthesis, which has a close connection with automatic memory system, and whose experiential correlate is a self-grasping awareness of one's body, is still functional. Yuasa continues:

> When we meditate, we assume a posture of looking into our body (e.g., the interior of the abdominal cavity inside the skin). However, nothing is seen in the interior of the body since it is dark. The condition of the activity of various internal organs is in most parts buried in the unconscious, except that we are aware of it in a limited degree as a vague sensation of the visceral organs as a whole. What is felt in this case is only the condition of the activity of the circuit of coenesthesis as a *self-grasping sensation of one's body*, that is, as an *awareness* of the whole of one's body.[43] (italics in the original)

This is a description of meditation in its initial stage, but as meditation deepens, Yuasa notes that:

> [O]ut of this self-grasping sensation of one's body, emotional complexes gradually start appearing in the form of wandering thoughts and delusions. To use the terminology of Gestalt's psychology, meditation can be regarded as a training where emotional complexes surface as images (figures) whose canvas is the self-grasping sensation of one's body as its background (ground). According to the view of the body (espoused) by Eastern medicine, emotion in this case is understood as a flow of ki-energy.[44]

Important in this regard is Yuasa's observation that emotion is identified with the flow of ki-energy.[45] What Yuasa means then by "bringing the emotion-instinct circuit into awareness" is that the ki-energy qua emotion appears during meditation as "wandering thoughts and delusions" against the background of self-grasping awareness of one's body. The meditator incorporates and assesses the meaning of these images. Since wandering thoughts and delusions are referred to as "patterns of emotional response" or "emotional complexes," we may ask why patterns of emotional response or emotional complexes are experienced as wandering thoughts and delusions. Yuasa seems to be echoing C. G. Jung's idea that the unconscious has an autonomous function with creative power. When the level of activities of the first external sensory-motor circuit and the circuit of somesthesis is lowered in meditation, the autonomous function of the unconscious surfaces into awareness as wandering thoughts and delusions, that is, ki-energy appears as images. Once the wandering thoughts and delusions are all cleared, that is, once they no longer appear in the course of the meditation practice, creative energy begins filling the meditator. It is in recognition of this experiential fact, Yuasa says that meditation is a way of "integrat(ing) the power of the unconscious within consciousness." Interpreted philosophically, this means an achievement of a higher degree of correlativity between movement of mind and movement of body.

We have just observed how ki-energy qua emotion can be brought into awareness in seated meditation. A question naturally arises if the same result obtains in moving forms of meditation such as Japanese archery[46] or recitation of *nembutsu*[47] while constantly walking. The principle involved in these practices, Yuasa claims, is the same as that of seated meditation. Both seated and moving forms of meditation are the "practice of entering into a quiet and immovable state by relaxing the mind and the body."[48] In martial arts, in particular, this principle is expressed as "letting the mind and ki-energy accord with each other" (*shinki icchi*). Yuasa interprets this to mean that:

the mind appropriates the flow of ki-energy through its feeling-awareness. That is, ki-energy is not the function which the ordinary, everyday consciousness can perceive, but is a new function which the consciousness (mind) becomes gradually capable of perceiving.[49]

It is here that we can appreciate the fact that the circuit of unconscious quasi-body, initially characterized as the invisible, "potential" system below consciousness, proves visible and becomes actualized in awareness.[50] When this occurs, oneness of body and mind is experienced. Traditionally, this state is expressed as "Oneness of the body and mind" (*shinshin ichinyo*) by Eisai (1141–1215), as "Casting off the body and mind"[51] (*shinshin datsuraku*) by Dōgen (1200–1253) and as "Crystallization of the mind and body" (*shinjin gyōnen*) by Myōe (1173–1232).

CONCLUDING REMARKS

We would like to conclude this brief exposition of Yuasa's concept of body-scheme with a few philosophical observations, while providing a brief transition to part 2 of our investigation. Yuasa's concept of body-scheme is epistemologically dualistic and ontologically nondualistic. The dual aspect is present in Yuasa's concept of body-scheme because he recognizes an existential transformation in the practice of personal self-cultivation. The concept of lived body that emerges from Yuasa's body-scheme is one of *achievement*.

The dualism with which Yuasa starts his investigation must be distinguished from Cartesian dualism.[52] Descartes' dualism is an ontologically *disjunctive* dualism, admitting no interaction between two separate realities, the mind and the body (or spirit and matter). Yuasa's body-scheme, on the other hand, suggests an epistemologically *provisional* or *correlative* dualism. It is provisional because the third and the fourth circuit of Yuasa's body-scheme are separated epistemologically in our natural attitude[53] but, as Yuasa has demonstrated, dualism can change into nondualism through the *transformative* practice of self-cultivation. He accepts this transformation to be an empirical fact, tested through long historical and cultural traditions in Japan. Theoretically, it suggests that there is a functional correlativity between mind and body, that is, the functions of both mind and body can be enhanced through prāxis. Yuasa has elucidated the correlativity in his analysis of the third emotion-instinct circuit and the fourth unconscious quasi-body circuit. In his final analysis, cor-

relativity is demonstrated in the experience of body-mind oneness. Ontologically, then, the original relationship of mind and
body is nondualistic in nature. In fact, Yuasa's provisional dualism and nondualistic position presuppose one another: unless
mind and body were provisionally dualistic in our natural attitude, it would be impossible even theoretically to conceive of
their oneness. Were this not the case, the practice of self-cultivation, with its transformative dimension, would be meaningless.
Generally, this conception of mind and body is in accord with
the implication of traditional Eastern concepts such as nirvana,
satori, and tao, that is, the implication that there is a higher epistemological perspective achievable through the process of personal self-cultivation and this higher epistemological perspective
is correlative with the ontological status of reality. Unless one
achieves a higher epistemological perspective, true reality does
not appear.

Now, we would like to provide a brief transition to part 2 in
order to indicate a direction of our investigation. In articulating
Yuasa's concept of body-scheme there has emerged, among other
things, an important point which calls for further investigation.
It is concerned with a transformative process which, Yuasa
believes, can change the provisional or correlative dualistic attitude, characteristic of our everyday mode of existence, into a
nondualistic mode of existence. In this connection, Yuasa mentions such Japanese religious figures as Eisai, Myōe, and Dōgen.
Among these figures we want to focus on Dōgen (1200–1253)
and delve into his philosophy of body, because he is one of the
most profound, outstanding Zen masters in Japanese intellectual
history with a keen philosophical sensitivity, unparalleled perhaps even in the entire Buddhist tradition.

For this purpose we shall focus our analysis in part 2 on the
experiential meaning of the practice of seated meditation, or
what Dōgen calls "just sitting" (*shikan taza*). A primary reason
that we focus on Dōgen and his philosophy of the body is
because we believe that by investigating his philosophy of the
body, we can better understand in more concrete detail the transformative process leading to the nondualistic sense of oneness
between the body and mind together with its philosophical
implications. Moreover, since Dōgen's experience of satori, an

enlightenment, linguistically expressed as casting off the body and the mind, was achieved vis-à-vis the seated meditation, which is a somatic modality of person, we believe that a careful analysis of this seated meditation will provide us with a clear experiential meaning of the mind-body oneness.[54] In order to articulate this experiential meaning, we will attempt to respond, throughout part 2, to two major questions: (1) how does the body go through transformations in the process of just sitting, (2) what kind of epistemological perspective does this process of transformation bring forth?

PART 2

A Medieval
Japanese Concept
of the Body:
Dōgen Kigen

CHAPTER 4

Buddhism and
Dōgen's Concept of the Body

INTRODUCTION

Dōgen Kigen (1200–1253) is a founder of the Sōtō school of Zen Buddhism in Japan,[1] and is generally considered one of the most original religious thinkers in Japanese intellectual history. Even among Zen masters in East Asia, past and present, Dōgen's writings are unparalleled in depth and insight. Since he is a master of Zen tradition, which emphasizes the practice of seated meditation almost to the exclusion of any dogmatics or theoretical doctrines, an examination of his philosophy on the body will provide us with a deeper understanding of the role that the body plays in our life than the ones offered from the natural, everyday standpoint. In part 2, therefore, we shall examine Dōgen's philosophy by focusing on his concept of the body, particularly in connection with the practice of seated meditation that Dōgen called "just sitting" (*shikan taza*).

When we take Dōgen's concept of the body as central to an understanding of his philosophy, the following preliminary considerations should first be observed. A concept of body is implicitly assumed throughout Dōgen's *magnus opus*, *Shōbōgenzō* (The Treasure of Right Dharma Eye), as well as his other writings, in the practice of just sitting. As a Zen master, Dōgen practiced and exhorted his students to practice just sitting, which is, needless to say, a *somatic* modality of a person. Just sitting forms the experiential core of Dōgen's philosophy and is therefore presupposed as a matter of course in his writings.

The importance of this practice in Dōgen's philosophy can be inferred from the fact that he placed the utmost importance on this practice, to the exclusion of all other practices (at least in the early period of his writing career) as a single peaceful entrance to understanding the Buddha way.[2] What this suggests is that Dōgen's religious philosophy culminates in this simple practice of just sitting. Therefore, it is an essential element in his teachings and may properly be understood in contemporary Western terminology as an existential project, insofar as its orientation and commitment is concerned. Moreover, Dōgen's own enlightening experience is said to have been achieved under the tutelage of Nyojō during the practice of just sitting. Dōgen's confirmatory experience is linguistically expressed as "body and mind casting off, cast off are the body and mind!" (*shinjin totsuraku totsuraku shinjin*). In this confirmatory expression, we have a clear glimpse of the important role that body plays in Dōgen's philosophy. The importance of body is apparent because Dōgen asserts "*body* and mind casting off," instead of "*mind* and body casting off."[3] This confirmatory expression can for now be interpreted generally as a practical consequence of letting the body or somatic modality take a precedence over mind.

Accordingly, in order to interpret Dōgen's concept of the body in light of an existential project and a confirmatory expression, it is important to bear in mind that a person must allow the practical to take precedence over an intellectual or theoretical understanding of the Buddha way.[4] That is, the practice of just sitting is a precondition for understanding the Buddha way. In fact, to ignore or to dismiss this process would necessarily result in a failure to grasp the essence of Buddhism, especially that of Dōgen. It is therefore essential to recognize that, although an intellectual grasp of Dōgen's concept of body is possible through its philosophical articulation, this understanding is limited to the theoretical and can in no way be regarded as a substitute for the existential project itself. Hermeneutically, this attitude must be kept in mind in order to understand his *Shōbōgenzō* (The Treasure of Right Dharma Eye) where Dōgen explicitly deals with the concept of body. To disregard the practical aspect of just sitting is to invite a superficial reading of the text which must confine itself to the literal meaning of the "words," an academic exercise that will leave the subtle, experiential depths of Dōgen's philosophy unexplored.

In dealing with Dōgen's concept of the body in the next four chapters, we shall keep in mind the following two major questions: (1) How does the body go through transformations in the process of just sitting? (2) what kind of epistemological perspectives does this process of transformation bring forth?

TRADITIONAL BUDDHIST CONCEPT OF THE BODY

As a preparatory to responding to the above questions, it might be helpful to provide a brief explication of the traditional Buddhist concept of the body, a concept of the body which Dōgen accepted. For this purpose, the following passage from Dōgen's *Shōbōgenzō* is illuminating:

> Bear in mind that the human body in this life is tentatively made up of the four elements and five aggregates [*skandhas*], which are produced in a harmonious combination of direct and indirect causes, always accompanying eight kinds of sufferings [*dukkha*]. How does the body remain [the self-same] in the [constant] transformation of generation-extinction? Since you are in the dark, you do not know it yet. Pity yourself for not realizing it even though you go through [constant] generation-extinction.[5]

There are three points in the above quotation to which we would like to call our attention for further clarification, especially for those who are unfamiliar with Buddhism. (1) The concept of the body consisting of the four elements and five aggregates, (2) the human body undergoing generation-extinction based on the harmonious combination of direct and indirect causes, and (3) the transformation that occurs through "generation-extinction" even though a person is unaware of it.

Buddhism traditionally understands the human body to consist of four elements and five aggregates (*skandhas*), which Dōgen accepted as an initial position without providing his own analysis of these terms. What, then, are the four elements and five aggregates?[6] The four elements are the Earth, Water, Fire, and Wind. The inclusion of these four elements in the concept of the human body suggests that the human body as it is conceived in the Buddhist tradition shares the "same" elements that constitute the natural world or physical nature. The human body in its constitution is inseparable, at least in part, from nature, for those elements are "natural" elements pervasively present in nature.[7] What is philosophically presupposed here is a correlation between macrocosm qua the physical nature and microcosm qua the human body.

In terms of the lived experience of the human body, we may understand that Earth, Water, Fire, and Wind correspond respectively to firmness, fluidity, body-heat, and mobility. When these elements are not "harmoniously" maintained in the human body, it experiences a sick state, for example, in terms of a temperature or of dehydration.[8] These elements are also the life source whose nature does not differ from the invigorating activities of the natural world. Since we in the contemporary age are accustomed to viewing the human body in terms of the observations that make up Western medical science which analyzes the object-body, a Buddhist's approach to the body may seem archaic, and even perhaps groundless. However, we may remind ourselves of the fact that Western medical science has made its gains, albeit extraordinary ones, originally through the examinations of *corpses*. However, under normal circumstances, it is practically impossible to resurrect a corpse. Medical science holds, then, an unwarranted methodological assumption that the living human body is understandable vis-à-vis the analysis of a corpse. Moreover, as long as it deals with, if not the corpse, the object-body, a whole and holistic function of lived body cannot be understood; the focus on the object-body presupposes that the living human body assumes a status no different from a material object that is lifeless. A concern for life is completely obliterated in this presupposition. These methodological attitudes eventually led the West to maintain that humans are superior to nature, as was developed in the "Age of Enlightenment." In contrast, a Buddhist's view, which includes these four natural elements, is based upon an observation of the *living* human body. A Buddhist view is much closer in spirit to the view of the micro-macro cosmos cherished earlier before and during the Renaissance.

In addition to these four elements, the human body in Buddhist thought is also maintained as consisting of the five other aggregates (skandhas) namely, (1) the physical form (*rūpa*), with its six sense organs, (2) their corresponding faculties of receiving external stimuli (*vedanā*), (3) the faculty of synthetically representing what is received (*samjñā*), (4) the dispositional tendency as a potential formative energy (*saṃskāra*), and finally (5) discriminatory consciousness (*vijñāna*). One must observe in understanding these five aggregates that there is no one aggregate singled out as having a "privileged" status in the constitution of the human body, as for example, Descartes gave a privileged status to *ego cogito*, claiming that the mind is easier to know than the body.

Although each aggregate can be elaborated in more detail, let us observe for the purpose of our interpretation two striking features of this concept of the human body. Obviously, what is most striking about the Buddhist's categorization of the human body is that it includes consciousness. From Descartes on, the concept of the body in dominant Western philosophy has been understood as that which stands in opposition to the mind in its ontological status.[9] Kant, for example, assuming a similar philosophical stance, maintained that the body is unknowable, a thing-in-itself, although accessible to understanding through empirical intuition (spontaneity and receptivity), through which the "concept" of the body is synthetically constituted by means of transcendental categories.

In this century, however, phenomenologists have attempted to overcome this kind of dualistic view of the person. In particular, Merleau-Ponty in his *Phenomenology of Perception* analyzed the lived body and concluded that perceptual consciousness is incarnate, and is rooted in the human body. Although Merleau-Ponty recognized the incarnate character of consciousness, we must point out that his concept of the body is the one described and analyzed in light of the standpoint of everyday consciousness.[10] The basic assumption, however, underlying both Merleau-Ponty's and the Buddhist's concept of the human body is that in order to understand what humans are, the concept of the human body must be approached holistically as an individual living *whole*. This approach to the body could be contrasted with the assumption that the cogito of Descartes and the transcendental subjectivity of Kant, both of which are divorced from the human body, must be taken as an absolute beginning as well as a terminating point in philosophy. At this juncture, however, it is important that we bear in mind that consciousness included in the concept of the human body is a somatic or incarnate consciousness in the sense that it is rooted in the human *soma*, or body.

If perceptual [ego-]consciousness is used as a basic stand-point from which to analyze the human body, the Buddhist's inclusion of saṃskāra, a dispositional tendency with the poten-tial formative energy, as a constituent of the concept would be concealed, and therefore, left unexamined. Indeed, the inclusion of this aggregate in the concept of the human body is perhaps more striking than the inclusion of incarnate, discriminatory consciousness. As a dispositional tendency, saṃskāra captures a psychological aspect of the body, which may be understood with regards to one's likes and dislikes, insofar as they surface in our everyday consciousness. Since the reason for one's likes and dis-likes can be given only in a tautological manner, that is, "I like x because I like it," Buddhism considers them inherently in the human body. In other words, saṃskāra as a dispositional ten-dency is a potential formative energy and is a contingent given in the formation of the human body; human body is "that which has been formed" independent of our everyday consciousness.

This is, for example, a further specification of Heidegger's concept of "thrownness" as we interpreted it in the previous chapters. In our everyday experience, we experience the working of our dispositional tendency as it moves from the depths to the surface of consciousness, most conspicuously in terms of desires and passions. Consequently, this aggregate reveals a contingent aspect of the human body in its most profound sense. The importance, then, of including the aggregate, saṃskāra, in the concept of the human body is the Buddhist contention that the human existence must be analyzed from a perspective which is concealed from our everyday ego-consciousness. The assumption here is that an empirical "ego" has a much deeper root than Cartesian ego cogito.

This point echoes Ichikawa's contention which we examined in part 1, namely that the intentional structure (e.g., perceptual consciousness) is regulated by, and dependent upon the orienta-tional structure, that is, the hazy, obscure horizon of conscious-ness in the subject-body. The same idea is also expressed by Yuasa's "emotion-instinct" circuit, whose transparency in terms of its experiential correlate is rendered opaque increasingly as one moves from "external sensory-motor circuit" to the circuit of "coenesthesis."

From now on, when we use the term "empirical ego" it will designate the function of somatic, incarnate consciousness influenced through the working of saṃskāra, our dispositional tendency with the potential formative energy. The term, "perceptual consciousness," should be understood to refer to an aspect of the function of the empirical ego, whose noetic act is directed mostly towards things in the physical world, or towards the residue resulting from this act vis-à-vis our reflection. We shall also use "everyday consciousness" to designate, in general, both the functions of empirical ego and perceptual consciousness.

This cursory discussion of the four elements and five aggregates, which has placed special emphasis on incarnate consciousness and dispositional tendency as a formative energy of the human body, allows us a rough, though necessarily partial at this stage, understanding of Dōgen's concept of human body. In thus understanding the human body, however, we must be careful not to think of the four elements and five aggregates as self-subsistent entities, for, as Dōgen asserts, these *tentatively* constitute the human body in this life. As will become clear, these aggregates of the human body, according to Dōgen, are subject to a constant generation-extinction, which in turn, provides a rationale for Dōgen to maintain the tentative or provisional character of the constitution of the human body.

At this point, then, we can turn to the discussion of the second issue, namely that the human body goes through a constant generation-extinction based upon the "harmonious combination of direct and indirect causes," and through this analysis we shall establish the point that the human body is the basis for all that appears.

HUMAN BODY: THE BASIS FOR ALL THAT APPEARS

For the purposes of interpretation, we shall focus on the thesis that the human body goes through a constant generation-extinction, an instance of Dōgen's treatment of causality, that is, the "harmonious combination of direct and indirect causes." In order to elucidate this point, we can turn our attention to a passage from *Vimalakīrti Nirdeśa Sutra*, which Dōgen elaborates in the fascicle "Kai-in Zanmai" ("*Samādhi* of Oceanic Reflection"). "Samādhi of Oceanic Reflection" is an ultimate state of meditational experience cherished in the Hua-yen school of Buddhism. Generally speaking, samādhi is a state of oneness in which the observer and the observed merge into a subtle feeling of inseparability through an exhaustively transparent state of mind, which we might designated by the phrase "samadhic awareness." To indicate a vast scope of this experience, the Hua-yen school of Buddhism uses the phrase, samādhi of oceanic reflection, comparing it to an ocean. Referring to this state of experience, which reflects, like a bright and clear mirror, everything that is,[11] Dōgen quotes a passage from *Vimalakīrti Nirdeśa Sutra* maintaining that:

> [t]his body is synthesized merely in terms of numerous dharmas. At the time of generation, only dharmas get generated and at the time of extinction, only dharmas become extinct. [Therefore,] when dharmas are generated, one does not say that an "I" is generated and [likewise] when dharmas become extinct, one does not say that an "I" becomes extinct. Between earlier and later thoughts [*nen*], they do not depend upon each other. Between earlier and later dharmas, they are not opposed to each other. This is called the *samādhi* of oceanic reflection.[12]

We shall examine later what "dharmas" mean in this context, but our present concern is to identify the content of the above passage as pertaining to the samādhi of oceanic reflection. From the last statement in this quotation, we learn that the description given above pertains to the samādhi of oceanic reflection. The concept of the human body, we may be assured, is given through the perspective of this samadhic experience. We may for now define samadhic awareness, when applied to the concept of the body, a state of being where there is no opposition between subject-body and object-body, or more positively where there is a lived oneness, accompanying an exhaustively transparent state, between the subject and the object, a consequence of which is a creation of a field such that the *raison d'être* of each thing is revealed in toto within its causal matrix. The exhaustive transparency attained in the samadhic experience is a practical, existential consequence of clarifying, to use Ichikawa's terminology, "the obscure, hazy horizon of cogito"; or within Yuasa's conceptual framework of "body-scheme" it is a clarification of "emotion-instinct circuit," particularly its dispositional, habitual pattern of mind/heart. As such, we should realize that this perspective is different from our everyday perspective of empirical ego-consciousness; different, then, also from the one that is accessible to us through the philosophical reflection upon the lived experience of both our subject-body and object-body.

Referring to the meaning of dharmas in this context, Tamaki substantiates the interpretation that the concept of the human body is given through the perspective of samadhic awareness when he asserts:

> Dharmas are not mere *things*, nor are they *minds*. They *exist* in the *samādhi* of oceanic reflection, that is, in the world of Buddha that is the universe itself, and they are *things* seen from this world.[13]

Using phenomenologist's terminology, Tamaki's explanation can be reinterpreted as follows: things as noematic content of experience as they are given in our everyday perspective go though an epistemological reorientation, a shift from the everyday to the samadhic, and thereby the dharmas acquire a meaning of "things seen from" the perspective of samadhic awareness. For now we may assume that this epistemological reorientation is effected by means of a somatic transformation, particularly by means of just sitting.

We will see this assumption developed as we progress in this part, but for now, let us consider the question: "How is the human body conceived of from such a perspective?" In responding to this question, we must make certain to clearly distinguish the samadhic awareness as such from its conceptual recapitulation. Needless to say, the preceding quotation from *Vimalakīrti Nirdeśa Sutra*, pertains to the latter, and what we are interested in is Dōgen's existential and experiential understanding of this passage.

"This body" referred to in the foregoing quotation from *Vimalakīrti Nirdeśa Sutra* cited in the fascicle "Kai-in Zanmai," indicates, to use Ichikawa's terminology again, a synthesis of "subject-body" and "object-body." According to the contention made in this passage, the human body is said to consist of nothing but "numerous dharmas." According to Nishiari,[14] dharmas in this context mean specifically the four elements and five aggregates. However, this interpretation is not very informative for us since we have already seen that "the four elements and five aggregates" represent the preliminary way in which Dōgen understands the concept of the human body. On the other hand, again according to Tamaki,[15] dharmas mean things seen from the perspective of samadhic awareness. Elsewhere, Tamaki interprets numerous dharmas to mean "myriad phenomena" (banshō).[16] According to Tamaki's interpretation, then, the concept of the human body as synthesized by numerous dharmas is seen as a synthesis of myriad phenomena, when it is seen as a noematic content of samadhic awareness. This approach will shift the understanding of the human body from the seemingly categorical four elements and five aggregates, or dharmas as mere things, to an experiential one, though highly elevated one. That is, with this interpretation, what seems to be a categorical, conceptual framework of the four elements and five aggregates acquires a "phenomenal" character. In stating this, however, care must be taken to understand what myriad phenomena means. A phenomenon in this connection cannot mean, for example, that which appears to consciousness if we understand consciousness to mean *only* our everyday perceptual, ego-consciousness, since the contention is that the "phenomena" in question are the ones revealed within the perspective of samadhic awareness. This suggests that the consciousness meant here is other than everyday perceptual ego-consciousness. In contrast to the latter, let us for now understood the consciousness in question to mean "samadhic" awareness, that is, an awareness unique to samādhi as defined above as a oneness between the subject and object. Consequently, Tamaki's myriad phenomena can be interpreted as that which appears to samadhic awareness.

If myriad phenomena are that which constitutes the human body, and furthermore, if this human body qua myriad phenomena appears to samadhic awareness, the concept of the body is the basis for all that appears. This position is, of course, in contrast with the consciousness oriented philosophy in which everything that appears, appears only to everyday consciousness.

DŌGEN'S CONCEPT OF GENERATION-EXTINCTION

In the previous section, we have interpreted dharmas as phenomena appearing to samadhic awareness, and thereby conceived of the body as the basis for all that appears. This will bring us to an analysis of how Dōgen understands the "appearing," which he discusses vis-à-vis "generation-extinction of dharmas." Since the term generation-extinction suggests a temporal process, Dōgen's task here is to analyze it in light of temporality constitutive of "synthesis of this body."

In referring to "this body" as seen from the perspective of samadhic awareness, Dōgen states: "A temporal situation (*jisetsu*) of the so-called samādhi of oceanic reflection...is a temporal situation in terms of numerous dharmas."[17] Dōgen's contention is that the idea of "This body is synthesized" must be seen in terms of an understanding of the temporal situation. Without the temporal aspect, the very concept of "synthesis" can not obtain, let alone this body, for synthesis is of a temporal character. The concept of synthesis presupposes temporality. In other words, for Dōgen, the inclusion of temporality in the concept of the human body is a necessary condition for asserting that "This body is synthesized."

Thus, being synthesized, this body is said to form one whole aspect (*ichigōsō*) consisting of numerous phenomena. That is to say, this body is sustained cohesively as a whole.[18] Each person has an individual body unique to him/herself. But this body as a synthesized cohesive whole, on the other hand, cannot, so Dōgen argues, be identified with the whole of numerous phenomena. He maintains that "'this body' is not in turn the whole (of numerous dharmas)."[19]

Paradoxically, Dōgen asserts that this body is a whole of numerous dharmas, but rejects the converse that numerous dharmas are the whole of this body. However, we can understand this paradoxical assertion to mean that in each temporal situation, this body is synthesized *coherently* in terms of numerous dharmas, but *all* of the numerous dharmas do not in turn appear in synthesizing this body. In light of our earlier distinction between everyday consciousness and samadhic awareness, all of the numerous dharmas do not appear to everyday consciousness, but they do appear to samadhic awareness. This interpretation avoids placing this body at the center of all other phenomena, for a given configuration of this body is not exhausted at a given time by a constitution of all of the numerous dharmas; it can change into another configuration. This understanding of the body is consistent with the Buddhist concept of the body as sharing the same elements as the elements in nature, in that the human body does not assume a privileged status in the matrix of beings. Simultaneously, this interpretation allows us to recognize the changing process of this body. What is referred above as this body is no other than an individual, living body that we are.

In order to understand the idea of change in the configuration of this body, we must return to Dōgen's passage in "*Samādhi* of Oceanic Reflection," and examine his ingenious way of discussing the generation of dharmas. He says: "At the time of generation, only dharmas get generated." The concept of generation is paired with the concept of extinction, that is, generation-extinction. That is, the concept of the human body can be brought to a full understanding only if it is seen in light of both generation and extinction. This again introduces a temporality into the concept of this body, for this body is conceived as undergoing a temporal change of generation-extinction.

At the time of generation, only dharmas get generated. The contention is that this is what and how the human body *is*, taking "is" to mean the temporal process of existence. Let us then observe that dharmas and generation are conceived as correlative; generation is of dharmas, and dharmas without being generated are nothing. They obtain their respective meanings only when they are paired, otherwise, these concepts become vacuous. Moreover, in light of the concept of synthesis, "dharmas" indicates a "what" of synthesis while "generation" functions as a "how" of synthesis. Consequently, in order to complete the *momentum* of synthesis, time brings together a what and a how of synthesis. Therefore, dharmas, generation, and "time" are regarded as essential components of synthesis—synthesis that brings forth a whole human body. The concept of the body thus presented suggests that it is an ever renewing "configuration," independent of the consciousness of the empirical ego.

At this point, we may pause to question why Dōgen chooses to understand the human body in terms of generation-extinction. Although there are a number of reasons why he takes this position, in view of Dōgen's overall existential and religious project, the most fundamental one is his recognition of the contingent *fact* of human existence concerning life and death. Dōgen says:

> Human body thus goes through generation-extinction. Even though we long for it otherwise, it never remains the same. There has never been anyone throughout the past who has survived his physical death by longing otherwise.[20]

This recognition of contingency is related to Dōgen's soteriological motive, namely, that the process of generation-extinction allows one to achieve the unexcelled, perfect enlightenment (satori).[21]

Theoretically, if there is no generation-extinction, and hence no change, then there would be no possibility of attaining the unexcelled, perfect knowledge. If this were the case, the meaning of practice would be nullified; it would become infeasible to aspire for the unexcelled, perfect knowledge, let alone hope to attain it. Dōgen could not accept this consequence, for he firmly believed in the "right dharmas" of Buddhism. Dōgen exalts that "the thus-come [tathāgatha, i.e., the Buddha] alone has clarified this dimension of momentary [generation-extinction]."[22] For our present concern, what seems to be Dōgen's guiding reason is that by characterizing the human body in terms of the generation-extinction of dharmas, he avoids the error of understanding the human existence from the narrow perspective of everyday consciousness as well as mistakenly conceiving of it as something substantial. Furthermore, the most important consequence for us to take note of is an epistemological concern regarding the meaning of generation-extinction. Dōgen says:

> This generation of dharmas does not leave a trace of generation behind. For this reason, generation cannot be perceived [chikaku], nor can it be known [chiken]. This is called "not saying that an 'I' is generated."[23]

The reasoning that is employed in the original passage from *Vimalakīrti Nirdeśa Sutra* is that the generation of an "I" cannot be maintained simply because generation is always the generation of dharmas, but not of the generation of an I. The assumption here is that dharmas are ontologically objective. Dōgen, however, reinterprets this position and gives an epistemological explanation for it, arguing that "generation cannot be perceived nor can it be known," for "generation does not leave a trance of generation behind." Dōgen's reinterpretation does not mitigate the assumption that dharmas are ontologically objective. In fact, if generation cannot be known and cannot be perceived, it would naturally follow that an I as a substantial entity cannot be generated, since what is generated are dharmas as "objective" entities. Dōgen says that, "the other person neither learns, nor comes to a realization, nor makes a discriminatory thinking that these dharmas are generated."[24] In this context, "the other person" refers to an empirical ego, seen from a samadhic awareness.

The reference to the other person is made in view of the fact that samadhic awareness is dissociated, under normal circumstances, from the empirical ego which claims the mineness of its experience. From another perspective, in order for Dōgen to assert that generation-extinction cannot be known nor can it be perceived, he must stand outside of the experiential domain in which generation takes place, otherwise, his claim about the unknowability of generation-extinction is unintelligible. The domain upon which Dōgen stands in asserting the unknowability of generation-extinction, as I maintain, is the domain of samadhic awareness. From this position, we can in turn surmise that the domain where generation is operative is other than the domain of samadhic awareness. The domain where generation-extinction is operative must be a domain with which we are most intimate and familiar. That is, it must be a domain of everyday consciousness oriented mostly toward the natural world, or toward a "residue" resulting from natural world in terms of memory and reflective thinking. Accordingly, when generation is said to be unknowable and unperceivable, these epistemic functions are of this domain.

One may contest Dōgen's claim of the unknowability of generation-extinction by arguing that one can know it through reflection. However, if we understand dharmas to be phenomena appearing to samadhic awareness, this objection does not arise, since "reflection" is a recapturing of the past content of *everyday* consciousness.[25] Moreover, this recapturing cannot be performed completely, since the reflecting consciousness cannot bring forth a consciousness reflected upon in toto. When Dōgen claims the pervasive working of generation-extinction, his claim encompasses the whole of the human body, which is the concept represented by the four elements and five aggregates. Yet, one might continue to argue that whatever is gained through reflection upon the working of generation-extinction constitutes a knowledge of a process, and from this knowledge we can *infer* that the whole human body goes through generation-extinction. Obviously, however, an inference is not the same as knowing and perceiving generation-extinction. This is where reflection differs from a samadhic knowledge.

We must ask why Dōgen claims the unknowability of generation. He says.

> A generation is always an arrival of a temporal situation, for time is a generation. It must be; "what is this generation? A generation!" ...[G]eneration is a generation of synthesis. It is "in terms of all dharmas" which is the generation of this body and which is the generation of an "I." ...It is the generation of an "I" which is unsaid. A time of generation is these dharmas, but it is not the twelve hours [of the clock time], nor is it three worlds arising in competition.[26]

What is this generation? This question is responded, at first glance in an unintelligible manner: "Generation!" The point to be taken here, however, is that the act of questioning is itself an instance of generation. If we generalize from this observation, any activity can be viewed as an instance of generation, whether the activity is mental, physical or whatever. This point becomes clearer when it is understood that the phrase, "temporal situation," can be altered to read "temporal fruition." (Both phrases would be acceptable translations of the Japanese term *jisetsu*.) The alternate "temporal fruition" captures the sense of Dōgen's meaning when he asserts that "time is a generation," since time in light of the alternate rendition is a fruition of dharmas by means of generation. Any activity is bound by time, and for it to be actualized, there must be "an arrival of temporal situation," or a temporal fruition. The very nature of actualizing activity requires that there is a time or temporal fruition appropriate to it. This kind of temporality, as Dōgen maintains, is obviously not clock time with its equally punctuated intervals of time. But, on the other hand, each clicking of the clock time is a temporal fruition, for these sounds to be heard there must be an act of listening. Clearly Dōgen conceives of generation qua temporal fruition as more fundamental than the clock time. A philosophical point that Dōgen makes by introducing a temporal aspect into the concept of generation is that this body is generated through temporal fruition, in which each generation renews a configuration of this body.

Considered in light of the mind-body issue, Dōgen's claim that the generation-extinction of dharmas cannot be known, implies that there is a dualistic tendency of mind and body in our everyday existence. Since Dōgen's claim is that we cannot have a complete knowledge of generation-extinction by means of our everyday consciousness, the knowledge we have of it through reflection does not fully cover the scope of the generation-extinction of dharmas. For example, our physical object-body, and our dispositional tendency with a potential formative energy, both equally constitutive of the concept of the human body in Dōgen's scheme, can not be brought to a clear understanding of their working, and hence also the understanding of their generation-extinction. They remain, to a great extent, opaque. This means that the phenomenologist's subject-body, or the body lived from within, cannot be experienced in toto through our everyday consciousness. This is the reason, for example, that Ichikawa could not but give a definition of subject-body as ranging from a bright, transparent consciousness to a hazy, obscure horizon of consciousness. Referring to this kind of dualism, Yuasa uses the terms, "commonsensical dualism" (joshiki teki nigenron), or "provisional dualism" (zanteiteki nigenron).[27]

On the other hand, we must also consider another implication, contrary to the dualistic tendency between the mind and the body discussed above, namely that the mind and the body, thus distinct in our everyday existence, can be brought to a oneness in samadhic awareness. For, if the generation-extinction of the human body can be known to samadhic awareness, then there will be a total coincidence between the distinct mind and body. Accordingly, the human body when it is viewed as comprising the four elements and five aggregates would become a total transparency. Needless to say, we must hasten to add that there must be an infinite degree of integration between the dualistic tendency of the mind and body operative in our everyday existence and its oneness in samadhic awareness. We shall return to this theme later.

GENERATION-EXTINCTION OF AN "I"

We have just seen that one of the implications of the *unknowability* of the generation-extinction of dharmas, or phenomena as appearing to samadhic awareness, is that Dōgen's scheme admits of two opposing strands when it is applied to the mind-body issue: (1) a dualistic tendency between mind and body, and (2) their oneness or nonduality. The locus of these implications lies in the understanding of a knowing subject, or an empirical ego, an I. If we are to understand Dōgen's claim of the unknowability of generation-extinction, we must first examine the nature of a knowing subject, I, or the empirical ego, in relation to the thesis of the generation-extinction of dharmas. For Dōgen to discuss I in this context is natural, since the concept of the human body includes within it a somatic, incarnate consciousness, which is a function of the empirical ego, or an I as a knowing subject.

In discussing the generation of this body, Dōgen makes a seemingly paradoxical inversion of the original passage from *Vimalakīrti Nirdeśa Sutra* quoted in *Kai-in Zanmai*, by claiming that an I (*ga*) is also generated, for he explicitly states, "it is 'in terms of numerous dharmas' which is the generation of this body and which is the generation of an 'I'." This is in direct contradiction with the original claim in which it is maintained that an I is not generated in the synthesis of this body. On the surface, it seems that Dōgen's contention of the generation of an I is a rejection of the no-self theory (*anātman*), a cardinal tenant which all forms of Buddhism cherish. However, when he makes this claim, Dōgen qualifies himself by saying that "It is a generation of 'I' that is *unsaid* (*fugen naru gaki nari*)" (emphasis added). His reason for observing the generation of an I is that "(The) unsaid does not mean un-expressed (*fu-dō*), since expressing (*dōtoku*) [the generation of an "I"] does not lie in verbal expression."[28] Although it is difficult to fully comprehend Dōgen's elliptic explanation, he seems to be saying that only because the generation of an I is not linguistically realized, this does not mean that it is the case experientially, as well. For example, when I engage myself in any act, whether it is a physical or mental act, an I is not brought to the level of awareness in the midst of the act. An I is a prereflective cogito. But, upon reflection, I realize that this prereflective I is necessarily involved in my act. This means that even though the presence of an I is not directly experienced in any act I undertake, it nevertheless is always reflexively present.[29]

If this is a correct understanding, what would be the domain of experience in which an I is generated? Our earlier interpretation suggests that it must be the domain of our everyday consciousness, which contrasts with the domain in which samadhic awareness is experienced. Accordingly, the I which Dōgen says is generated in the synthesis of this body, must be an empirical, everyday ego, which directs its glance mostly to the natural world, or the residue resulting from the glance. Dōgen's analysis seems to be phenomenologically closer to the lived everyday experience.

Extrapolating from the correctness of this position, some Western philosophers make the mistake, Dōgen likely would argue, of turning this generation of an I into a transcendent entity, which subsists through time. However, the appearance that there is such a thing as a transcendent I is given by the fact that, whenever I reflect upon myself, there is always found an aspect of I as the bearer of experience. On the other hand, Dōgen's position is that the generated I undergoes an extinction, and the extinction is an extinction of dharmas. If as Dōgen maintains, an I goes through a constant generation-extinction, it logically follows that whenever a reflecting glance is cast over an experience, there must be the appearance of I. However, Dōgen argues that it is generated, and destined to disappear when reflection ceases.

As we can see, this position still allows Dōgen to hold the no-self theory (anātman), because, if a generated I undergoes an extinction, this I cannot be maintained as an entity persisting through the process of generation-extinction. Rather, this I is in the constant flux of generation-extinction. This position that Dōgen maintains is advanced in view of an occurrence of dharmas.[30] He writes:

> The very time of not saying that an "I" becomes extinct is a time of these dharmas becoming extinct. Extinction is an extinction of these dharmas.[31]

Applied to the preceding example of the reflecting act and the act reflected upon, an I which has become accessible through reflection exists in virtue of the act of an I which is freshly generated, which turns the initial I that has engaged itself in the act into an object. The initial I is thus turned into an object of a new I, and consequently as it is turned into an object, it "becomes extinct," that is, loses the status of an I by virtue of the generation of a new I. This transition from generation to extinction is analogously spoken of as "Suddenly a fire arises," for out of nowhere, a new I is generated. In more conceptual terms, Dōgen characterizes the transition from generation to extinction as follows:

> A temporal situation of the extinct I is unsaid and temporal situation of the generated I is unsaid; even though both are the birth of the unsaid, they are not the same death of the unsaid. It is already an extinction of earlier dharmas and that of later dharmas. It is the dharmas' earlier and later thoughts [*nen*].[32]

The "unsaid" in respect to the extinction of an I should be understood in the same way as the unsaid in respect to the generation of an I. That is, although the extinction of an I is not verbally expressed, it is experientially undergone without this process being brought to everyday consciousness. If we accept a constant appearance and disappearance of an I in terms of the generation-extinction of dharmas, the status of an I as a temporally subsisting entity has to be rejected. Thus, Dōgen says, "The nonstopping time of generation-extinction is 'who' undergoes generation-extinction?"[33] The interrogative "who," in Dōgen's view, expresses, among other things, ultimately the nonsubstantial character of an I as well as the negation of "mineness." More importantly, who in Dōgen expresses a practical, existential transcendence of the individuality associated with the human body, both subject-body and object-body, along with the memory embedded in them. This was, for example, part of the meaning of "*Samādhi* of Oceanic Reflection."

CONDITIONS FOR TRANSITION FROM "I" TO "WHO"

What are the epistemological conditions that make possible a transition from an I to a who? These conditions, I believe, can be specified by analyzing the meaning of "dharmas' thoughts" (*hō no nen*) as in the passage: "It [i.e., generation-extinction] is the dharmas' earlier and later thoughts (*nen*)." (For the sake of simplicity, we shall disregard here the temporal aspect mentioned in respect to dharmas.)

What then are dharmas' thought? Dōgen's own understanding of the term, "dharma," in the context of the synthesis of this body, is "that which is undefiled." He says, "Being dharmas, it [i.e., an extinction] is not accidental dust (*kakujin*). Since they are not accidental dusts, dharmas are undefiled."[34] In light of this explanation, dharmas' thought would mean "undefiled thoughts." Indeed, this understanding of dharmas' thought has a religious significance for Dōgen, for he further identifies undefiled thoughts with "buddhas and patriarchs."[35] However, in order to specify the conditions for a transition from an I to who, we might go one step further and ask what is the philosophical meaning of dharmas' thoughts, and in particular, what is its epistemological implication?

A clue to unpack the meaning of dharmas' thoughts seems to lie in interpreting the term "accidental dusts" (*kakujin*) correctly. "Dusts" here refers to that which covers, and specifically in this context, to desire, or to use Yuasa's terminology, all that arises from the emotion-instinct circuit. Desire is an aspect of potential formative energy realized as a dispositional tendency (samskāra) which is rooted in the body. Accordingly, we come to a better understanding of the meaning of the generation-extinction of an I, which we discussed in the preceding section: the generation-extinction of an I carries with it the accidental dust, or the desires of the body. When Dōgen points out the generation of an I, his emphasis seems to fall more upon this aspect, laden with accidental dust, than upon the alleged "transparency" of everyday consciousness. In this respect, then, an I is not characterizable merely by its alleged transparency but rather is deeply rooted in the somaticity, namely, the desires. Everyday consciousness, according to Dōgen, is far from "transparent" but a "murky" consciousness.

Accordingly, we are led to recognize that desire is that which covers, and this "covering" is due to desire. To put it positively, dharmas are that which is uncovered. This point reiterates Tamaki's earlier interpretation of dharmas as appearing within a samadhic awareness. Moreover, that which covers is said to be "accidental." An antonym for the adjective accidental is "intrinsic," or even perhaps "essential." Therefore, dharmas' thoughts comes to mean that which is uncovered and intrinsic or essential. But what does this mean epistemologically? In light of the above interpretation, the contrast between accidental dusts and dharmas' thought corresponds to a contrast between the covered and the uncovered. Epistemologically, this polarity suggests that there must be a transition from the covered to the uncovered—a process of epistemological reorientation, and dharmas' thoughts are that which is uncovered.

To summarize the above observation, we may say that since desire accidentally prevents that which is uncovered from its uncovering, and since desire as that which covers is rooted in the body, the transition from the covered to the uncovered involves a somatic modification or transformation.[36] We shall examine this transformation in more concrete terms when we deal with Dōgen's own confirmatory experience of "casting off the body and mind," and with the practical process leading to this experience.

With this specification of the epistemological conditions that makes a transition from an I to who possible, let us venture into a further speculation concerning the deeper meaning of dharmas' thoughts. In so doing, I would like to suggest that Dōgen intends in his phrase dharmas' thoughts to express a certain kind of objectivity. If this kind of objectivity is demonstrated, it would constitute a further specification of the epistemological conditions we have just laid bare. In order to demonstrate a sense of objectivity implied in the phrase dharmas' thought, we shall focus on an analysis of the Japanese term, *nen*, which is rendered here as "thoughts." The use of this term implies that dharmas' thoughts are experiential, because the term, nen, provides this added sense. The Japanese term, nen, is made up of the characters symbolizing "the present" and a "mind," and can hence be rendered as "the present mind." If we interpret nen in the broadest possible way, it would mean "whatever is in the present mind." This interpretation captures a temporal as well as a noematic aspect of experience.

What would be the meaning of dharmas' thought in light of this interpretation of nen? "Dharmas' thought," it would seem, is contrasted with "my" thought, taking my here to mean an empirical ego's sense of belonging or possession. In other words, dharmas' thought, is understood to be a negation of mineness—a minimum condition for the transition from an I to who. This also follows from the previous observation that Dōgen does not accept a transcendent I which sustains itself qua itself, although he grants the appearance of an empirical I, albeit in the form of generation-extinction.

By using the phrase, dharmas' thought, Dōgen is striving for what may be termed "trans-subjectivity." For now we may understand this term, trans-subjectivity, to mean a domain which exists behind or beneath the individual subjectivity of everyday consciousness. The term, "beneath," or "behind," although suggestive of spatial dimension, should be taken epistemologically as concealed from our everyday perceptual consciousness. In relation to the concept of samadhic awareness, the concept of trans-subjectivity can be understood as a domain in which samadhic awareness is operative. Accordingly, dharmas' thoughts is the noematic content of samadhic awareness in the domain of trans-subjectivity. We might also recognize the domain of trans-subjectivity to be, at least in part, the place in which samskāra as a formative energy in its raw form is operative on the way to the surface of everyday consciousness. From the standpoint of Cartesian ego cogito, this domain of trans-subjectivity is concealed, and therefore would be regarded as designating the body, an extended thing which is denied for its knowability as to its intrinsic qualities.

The above observation is consistent with our interpretation that dharmas' thoughts are that which is uncovered intrinsically or essentially, by means of a somatic modification or transformation. We may recall that the process of generation-extinction is claimed to be unknowable from the standpoint of everyday perceptual experience. This position suggests that the process of generation-extinction is not *subjective*—an epistemological attitude characteristic of our everyday perceptual experience, since subjectivity is a salient mark of everyday consciousness. From this position, however, it does not immediately follow that the process is objective if this "objectivity" is a polar concept of subjectivity, but this objectivity may be regarded as trans-subjectivity. Judging from the use of the term dharmas' thoughts, with its implied negation of mineness, Dōgen seems to be claiming that this domain of trans-subjectivity is also objective in character. The sense of objectivity proposed here is not merely the concept derived from the observation of external physical things vis-à-vis everyday consciousness, but rather objectivity in the sense of a common quality that every human being qua body shares once the somatic transformation or modification is effected by means of the practice of just sitting. This sense of objectivity is a reality observable by means of a samadhic awareness: a reality which remains for most of us concealed beneath the surface layer of everyday consciousness.

Dōgen claims that having thoughts (nen) is characteristic of every human being, for he asserts:

> Who is not 'you'? For those having earlier and later thoughts are all 'you'. 'I' am the same. Who is not an 'I'? For [having] earlier and later thoughts are an 'I'?[37]

The I and the "you," affirmed here as forming a community are held together by the common bond of having "earlier and later thoughts." This was, for example, a true meaning of "consciousness" (con + scire) in the history of Western philosophy.

As is evident from the above quotation, Dōgen's world is not solipsistic but rather may be characterized as "intercorporeal" in contrast to the intersubjective. While the term, "intersubjective,"

connotes the common ground of subjectivity, and is thus limited
to the confine of interiority, particularly of ego cogito, the intercorporeal suggests the common involvement with others in terms
of the whole of a person qua body "out in the open" in space.
This intercorporeal world is not directly affirmed by virtue of the
fact that we all have thoughts as a universal characteristic of
being human qua body. Rather, it only suggests an intersubjective character of the community of people. An implication of this
realization, however, confirms the interpretation that Dōgen's
world is intercorporeal. We may recall that Dōgen includes a
somatic, incarnate consciousness within the concept of human
body in the sense that this consciousness is rooted in the body.
Since thoughts occur in consciousness qua human body, it is the
place in which thoughts occur. The body is a supporting framework within which thoughts take place,[38] and the somatic, incarnate consciousness that is rooted in the body serves as a basis for
an objectivity, an objectivity which Dōgen implies through his
use of the term dharmas' thought.

However, it alone is not adequate to claim an objectivity of
dharmas' thoughts because the intercorporeal world affirmed by
means of having earlier and later thoughts in a human qua body
pertains only to the everyday consciousness which is naturally
given. Therefore, Dōgen sets a condition for attaining the objectivity of dharmas' thought. This condition is a practical, existential condition, which in turn entails an epistemological consequence. He says, "If you let [dharmas] be nondependent and
nonopposed, it would be a near perfect expression [*dōtoku*]."[39]
The term, *dōtoku* (expression) is used as a confirmation of having attained an unexcelled enlightenment (satori), which presupposes a self-cultivation in accordance with Zen sitting rules. As
such, we should take it to be a linguistic recapitulation of samadhic experience. The assumption here is that a person without the
experience of satori cannot "let dharmas (be) nondependent and
nonopposed."

But what does this mean? The opposite of "nondependent"
and "nonopposed" is "dependent" and "opposed." If we follow
Dōgen's argument, he implies that the mode of our everyday
existence is characterizable in terms of that which is dependent
and opposed. In light of the contrast we made earlier between

the covered and the uncovered, the dependent and the opposed may be considered to be an experiential description of the covered, while being nondependent and nonopposed may characterize the uncovered. However, the immediate difficulty in understanding what Dōgen means arises because he provides no specification of "what" is dependent and opposed in our everyday experience. But for the present, if we take this "what" to be noematic contents of our everyday consciousness, it follows that that which is dependent and opposed is a relation between noemas, or to use Dōgen's terminology, between earlier and later thoughts.[40] Consequently, we may understand that our earlier and later thoughts are dependent and opposed to each other. The opposition between earlier and later thoughts suggests that they are not experienced with freedom and spontaneity, and this in turn suggests that each earlier and each later thought is not experienced to its fullest. That is, they are dependent upon each other. Experientially, we know its implication only indirectly, for example, through an accumulation of stress. If it is not incorrect to interpret the mode of our everyday experience in this manner, it is now possible to have a glimpse of the meaning of dharmas' being nondependent and nonopposed.[41]

When we expand this interpretation of "dependence and opposition" and apply it to the mind-body issue, the following consequence is entailed. The reason that a series of noema are experienced in our everyday existence as "opposed to" and "dependent upon" each other is that there is a provisional dualism between the mind and the body operative in the field of our everyday existence. That is, there is *something* which makes a series of noema to appear opposed and dependent. This something must be rooted in the body, for there is nothing which is capable of opposing, and making a series of noema dependent upon each other in the alleged transparency of our everyday consciousness. This was, in fact, a partial meaning of saṃskāra as a contingent formative energy in the human body.

We have specified the theoretical conditions which permit the transition from an I to a who in terms of a transformation from the covered to the uncovered, and correspondingly in terms of the transformation from the dependent and opposed to the nondependent and nonopposed. The very possibility of this transformation rests theoretically upon Dōgen's acceptance of the thesis of the ceaseless and pervasive working of generation-extinction qua dharmas which exclusively claims its function upon this body. We must now examine, in more concrete terms, the *practical* procedures that give rise to the above mentioned transformation. This leads us directly to an analysis of just sitting.

CHAPTER 5

Dōgen and the Body in Meditation

INTRODUCTION

In the preceding chapter, we have singled out the epistemological conditions that make possible a transition from an I to a "who" in terms of the distinction between "the covered" and "the uncovered." "The covered" by virtue of "accidental dust," may be regarded as a mode of everyday existence, while the uncovered may be regarded as a mode of samadhic existence. Seen in this manner, a transition from the covered to the uncovered would roughly correspond to an existential movement from everyday existence to samadhic existence. As our analysis has revealed, the former is further specified through an experiential description of "dependence" and "opposition," while the latter through "nondependence" and "nonopposition." This movement is existential in nature, involving somatic transformations which constitute an epistemological reorientation. However, the descriptions of nondependence and nonopposition are too vague and too general, to be a full fledged account of what I term epistemological reorientation. In order to specify this "epistemological reorientation" in more concrete terms, we must now examine the detailed, practical procedures involved in somatic transformations. According to Dōgen, this is effected through the practice of just sitting, and consequently we turn to an analysis of "just sitting" in this chapter. By directing our investigation in this manner, we shall lay down preparatory steps to respond systematically to the two major questions which we initially set out for this part, namely: (1) "how does the human body go through transformation(s) in the process of 'just sitting'?" By providing a successful response to the first question, we will establish a basis from which to approach the second question, (2) "what kind of epistemological perspective(s) does this process bring forth?"

PREPARATION

In *Gakudō Yōjin Shū* (The Essentials in Studying the Way), Dōgen discusses several essential points that must be observed as preparatory to undertaking a study of the Buddha way, or to be more specific, what Dōgen would have termed the practice of just sitting. While on the surface these points do not seem to have a direct bearing on our philosophical inquiry, since they were given for those who seek a religious undertaking of understanding and living the Buddha way, Dōgen's thought is inseparable from a religious significance which adds its own richness to the study of Dōgen's philosophical insight. These points provide practical advice for those who are preparing to undertake the practice of just sitting.

Before undertaking the practice of just sitting, Dōgen deems it necessary to aspire to *bodhi* (*bodaishin*), an unexcelled, perfect knowledge. This aspiration, Dōgen claims, is entailed by the observation of the impermanence (*mujō*) of life, for when one realizes a pervasive presence of impermanence, "one does not arouse [the pettiness of] one's ego [*koga*], and does not entertain the idea of fame and personal gain."[1] Yet, if everything experienced is impermanent, the obvious danger is the conclusion that all experiences are meaningless, and this in turn invites nihilism. This position, Dōgen refused to accept. According to Karaki Junzō,[2] impermanence for Dōgen was "the fundamental fact" of life. However, from the viewpoint of his existential project, what Dōgen offers here is an insight cherished in the Buddhist tradition; the tradition that entertaining the pettiness of the ego is a hindrance to attaining the unexcelled, perfect knowledge. Therefore, the pettiness of ego must be abandoned, for it functions as a limiting condition in a person's attempts to attain the unexcelled, perfect knowledge. Dōgen seeks a dimension of experience the scope of which is wider than that of ego cogito.

However, bodhi must not be pursued, Dōgen warns, with the intention of becoming a buddha, nor with a casual attitude. He writes:

> Buddha-dharma must not be attained with a mind [*u-shin*] nor with no-mind [*u-shin*]. If a practicing mind and the [Buddha-] way do not coincide with each other, one's body and

mind is not in peace. If it is not in peace, it cannot rest in enjoyment.[3]

The correspondence between a practicing mind and the Buddha way is said to be achieved when one does not take an attitude of like and dislike in the pursuit of the Buddha way.[4] In light of our previous discussion, this is a purification of one's dispositional tendency arising from one's potential formative energy (saṃskāra). This point of pursuing Buddha way neither "with a mind [*u-shin*] nor with a no-mind [*mu-shin*]" may seem paradoxical, if not contradictory, for if one were to aspire to the unexcelled, perfect knowledge, it would seem logical that one must have the intention of attaining it, or becoming a buddha. But Dōgen asserts that this is not a proper way. His reason for rejecting this approach to the Buddha way is that the very attitude of having the intention of becoming a Buddha is an attachment and begins to function as a hindrance, for the unexcelled, perfect knowledge, is said in its negative characterization to be a "freedom from" attachments of any kind. The intention of attaining the perfect, unexcelled knowledge becomes a focus of one's pursuit.

The next important point which an aspirant must acknowledge, Dōgen observes, is to have faith in the Buddha way. "Those who believe in Buddha way must have faith that one's self is originally in the way; they must not vacillate in doubt, nor entertain delusions or crooked ideas; it neither increases nor decreases, nor does it err."[5] This faith safeguards an aspirant in his pursuit of the Buddha way, for disbelief would prevent him from making progress in just sitting. In general, vacillating mind is inconducive to attaining to anything, especially the unexcelled, perfect knowledge. But at the same time, Dōgen recognizes that, "Generally speaking, it is most difficult to encounter persons who believe that they are in the Buddha way."[6] The above three points: (1) having an aspiration for bodhi, (2) having no intention of becoming a buddha and (3) having faith in Buddha way, together represent the preparatory attitude which an aspirant must observe. Dōgen describes this attitude as "neither dwelling on, nor becoming stagnant both in mind and body."[7]

Together with the above points, Dōgen emphasizes that the aspirant must pursue the Buddha way under the "right" teacher. He says:

> The way of practice, I would say, is dependent upon the
> authenticity or inauthenticity of a guiding master. The caliber
> [of an aspirant] can be likened to good material and the master
> to a carpenter. Even good material can not be made to mani-
> fest its excellent beauty without a good carpenter. Even a
> crooked piece, when handled by a good hand, immediately
> manifests its subtle finish. It is obvious from this that truth or
> falsity of satori is dependent upon the authenticity or inauthen-
> ticity of a guiding master.[8]

One of the reasons why Dōgen insists upon studying the Buddha
way under the right teacher is to guarantee the transmission of
"right dharmas" (shōbō). In practical terms, this right teacher is
essential in guiding the aspirant in meditation, for the aspirant
may mistakenly understand various hallucinatory and/or pathological states, frequently engendered during the practice of just
sitting, as auspicious signs for satori. In other words, the importance of the right teacher lies in "checking" a confirmatory experience, which would guarantee the continuous succession of right
dharmas. Dōgen speaks of a qualification for an "authentic"
teacher as:

> One who has clarified the right dharmas regardless of his age or
> of the length of his career, and received a seal of authentication.
> An authentic teacher does not place a priority on words, nor on
> intellectual understanding. With an extraordinary caliber and
> an abundance of vigor, he is not trapped in his own opinion,
> adhering to his personal sentiments. He is a person whose prac-
> tice and whose understanding corresponds with each other.[9]

This observation is born from Dōgen's own experience in China
where he wandered for two years seeking a right teacher before
he met Nyojō. Wandering in search of the right teacher is a tradition established in Zen Buddhism. Aside from the qualification
which Dōgen states in the above quotation, what he means by a
right or authentic teacher must include, as I surmise, an agreeable personal propensity with the aspirant. Otherwise, the aspirant cannot sustain the rigorous task of undertaking the practice
of just sitting successfully enough to reach the final goal. A radical difference between the personal propensity of a guiding master and his disciple would end up in confrontations, and
inevitably in disappointment on the part of the aspirant.

ATTITUDE

When encountering the right teacher, Dōgen defines the attitude which an aspirant should take in undertaking the Buddha way. He says:

> When one first enters the gate in studying the Buddha way, one cultivates himself in accordance with the instruction while listening to his teacher. At this time, there are things to be kept in mind. That is, dharmas moving the self and the self moving dharmas. When the self [*ware*] moves dharmas well, the self is strong and the dharmas are weak. On the other hand, when dharmas move the self, dharmas are strong and the self is weak. Ever since the transmission of dharmas, there have been these two temporal occasions.[10]

In an age where self-assertion is extolled and where aggression masquerades under the cover of "individualism," it seems that an aspirant should assume the attitude of "the self moving dharmas," instead of "dharmas moving the self." Moreover, where "activity" rather than "passivity" is promoted, there seems to be all the more reason to take this attitude of the self moving the dharmas. But when an aspirant "cultivates himself (or herself) in accordance with the instruction" given by the teacher in the sense indicated by Dōgen, this attitude of the self moving dharmas must be rejected as an aberrant way of undertaking the practice of just sitting. This is, according to Dōgen, because it would result in making the "dharmas weak." Rather, Dōgen insists that an aspirant must take the attitude of the "dharmas moving the self." Insofar as an aspirant *takes* this attitude, we must recognize that he makes a sustained active effort. From this point of view, what is seemingly "passive" in assuming the attitude of the dharmas moving the self turns out to be active. In other words, activity associated with the self moving dharmas, is a superficial, "animal" reaction.

But why, we may ask, does Dōgen regard dharmas moving the self as more correct than the self moving dharmas in the aspirant's pursuit of the Buddha way? Consistent with Dōgen's position, the attitude of dharma moving the self is implied in the condition set for having an aspiration for *bodhi*, namely, the condition that an aspirant must leave or abandon the ego-self. Here I am using the Japanese terms *koga* and *ware* synonymously when I interpret that "an aspirant must leave or abandon the ego-self," although there is a subtle linguistic and philosophical difference between these words. For our present concern, we can ignore the difference between koga and ware, because the distinction is immaterial for our discussion. However, what is philosophically significant in this context, is that Dōgen suggests that there is a dimension of experience higher and greater than that of the ego-self. According to Yuasa, the reason that Dōgen rejects the attitude of the self moving dharmas as an improper way of pursuing Buddha way, is that this attitude posits an empirical ego as an incorrigible ground for understanding man.[11] This interpretation follows from an understanding of "dharmas" as objective in character. If the term, "the ego-self," suggests a dimension of subjectivity, the term dharmas may be conceived of as designating a dimension of "objectivity." We have had a glimpse of what this objectivity may be like, when we discussed earlier the meaning of "dharmas' thought." At any rate, what Dōgen is asserting when he says that an aspirant must let dharmas move the self, is his philosophical contention that there is a dimension of experience greater than that of the ego-self. This dimension of experience is obviously related to the unexcelled, perfect knowledge. Our task here is to elucidate this dimension of experience through an analysis of the somaticity of a person, especially, through the practice of just sitting.

According to Dōgen, this dimension of experience, which is higher and greater than that of the ego-self, can not be opened up or revealed existentially through an intellectual understanding of the Buddha way. Rather its disclosure or revelation has to be relegated to the practice of just sitting. Dōgen says:

> The rule [of Zen cultivation] is to avert the path of intellectual understanding by eradicating the root of all mental functions [*ikon*] by means of [just] sitting. This, I maintain, is an expedient means of guiding a beginner's mind. Afterwards, [an aspirant] casts off his body and mind and discards delusions and satori. This is the second step. If one were to eradicate the root of all mental functions by means of sitting, eight or nine out of ten people would be able to see the way instantly.[12]

In this quotation, Dōgen talks about letting dharmas move the self in practical terms as "eradicating the root of all mental functions." Or to be more precise, he argues that by eradicating the root of all mental functions one learns to let dharmas move the self. But what does eradicating the root of all mental functions mean? The method of accomplishing this eradication is clearly stated: it is accomplished "by means of [just] sitting," which is a somatic modality of a person.

THE GOAL OF "JUST SITTING"

But what is the *root* of these functions? Insofar as what is to be eradicated is the root of these functions, the eradication does not directly pertain to these functions, but rather to a source or ground out of which these functions are activated. If this eradication is successfully accomplished, we can surmise that a modification of these mental functions would obtain. Among the five aggregates (*skandhas*) which constitute the human body, what are considered to be "mental functions" are (1) the faculty of receiving external stimuli (*vedanā*), (2) the faculty of synthetically representing what is received (*samjñā*), (3) the incarnate consciousness, and (4) the dispositional tendency with its potential formative energy (samskāra). Among these mental functions, then, the dispositional tendency with its potential formative energy seems to be a prime candidate for the meaning of the root of these mental functions. In identifying the root of these mental functions, however, we must be aware that the dispositional tendency as such is an explicit aspect of samskāra, while its potential formative energy is an implicit aspect. When interpreted in this manner, we cannot straightforwardly identify "the root of all mental functions" with the dispositional tendency per se, because it touches only tangentially on these mental functions. It appears, as it were, as the tip of the iceberg. Underneath it exists a vast reservoir of potential formative energy.

Nakamura interprets,[13] "the eradication of the root of all mental functions by means of sitting" (*ikon zadan*) to mean the eradication of "the consciousness which is the ground of desire (*kleśa*)." This reading suggests that there remains a consciousness which is not infested with "desire" after eradication. But more importantly, the incarnate consciousness is observed to be rooted in desires. Tamaki, on the other hand, interprets the same phrase to mean that "the operation of the human mind and its functions passes into disappearance."[14] The key term to an understanding of Tamaki's interpretation is "human" (*ningentekina*). Since he does not specify what emerges after the eradication of the "human mind," we must say that his characterization is negative. In light of Nakamura's interpretation, Tamaki's assumption is that consciousness with desire is human, and therefore it implies that consciousness without desire is other than human. Although both Nakamura and Tamaki differ in phraseology, they seem to be saying the same thing. Nakamura, I believe, is correct in pointing out the eradication of consciousness infested with desire, while Tamaki is also insightful in insisting that "the operations of the human mind and its functions" disappear in the rigorous training of cultivation. Speaking generally about the Eastern meditation, Yuasa Yasuo in his *Tōyōbunka no Shinsō* (The Depth of Eastern Cultures), observes that "the cultivator through his own efforts brings his body and mind, as much as possible, to a near death state wherein his life energy is balanced to zero."[15] Similarly, a Japanese Zen monk Hakuin, though he belonged to a different Zen tradition than Dōgen, refers to it as a great death (*daishi*). In view of these observations, the eradication of the root of all mental functions demands the aspirant to go through a radical transformation of his being.

If it is correct to understand what activates the human mind is desire (*kleśa*), it would seem to follow naturally that the elimination of desire would result in something other than the operation of the human mind. In light of this observation, saṃskāra, as a source or ground with its potential formative energy that activates "all mental functions," is eradicated insofar as it is the source or ground of desire (kleśa). If this observation is not in error, then it would seem that consciousness with desire, or in our earlier terminology, everyday perceptual ego-consciousness, undergoes a modification, which I maintain, constitutes an epistemological reorientation, although we have yet to see in more precise terms what this epistemological reorientation is. At any rate, Dōgen's contention is that the epistemological reorientation cannot be achieved through one's intellectual understanding.

An aspirant, says Dōgen, "enters the Buddha way by adjusting [one's] body and mind."[16] "Adjusting (one's) body and mind" refers specifically to the procedure involved in the practice of just sitting. Our discussion now brings us to an analysis of just sitting.

AN ANALYSIS OF "JUST SITTING"

Once these preparatory points have been firmly established, the aspirant is ready to undertake the practice of just sitting (*shikan taza*). Dōgen inherits the idea and the practice of just sitting from his Chinese master, Nyojō. The modifier "just" in just sitting is used to single out the method of sitting, and to distinguish this method from other practices, but it is also used to signify single-mindedly devotion to, and concentration on sitting. Dōgen held the belief that just sitting is a "dharma gate of repose and bliss,"[17] and he understood, specifically, that it entails somatically assuming the lotus position, or a variation thereof. Further, he believed that a general aim of just sitting is to "learn a retrogressive step through which to turn back [the externally cast] light to inner illumination."[18] This retrogressive step indicates a turning away from the activities of our everyday existence. Epistemologically, it means to halt the working of external perception and everyday consciousness. By so doing, this retrogressive step is a movement into the interiority of the empirical self. Dōgen's contention is that external perception, as a naturally endowed function which directs the empirical ego to the things of the natural world, will not enable a person to discover his authentic self. Hence, Dōgen contends, when this process of retrogressive step is learned, "the body and the mind will naturally drop off and the original face will presence itself."[19] This retrogressive step may be likened to phenomenological reductions of the natural world, but the difference between these processes is that the former prescribes a specific, practical procedure of "adjusting the body and the mind" to assume the lotus position, while the latter is a mere intellectual exercise through the use of free imagination. This retrogressive step, therefore, is a practical procedure that not only permits an "inward looking" attitude allowing the discovery of "the original face," but it is also a corrective for the externally cast "light" to be more illuminating than it is naturally given. Herein lies one of the existential significances of just sitting.

To achieve the optimum condition necessary to learn a retrogressive step, the ambiance in which just sitting is practiced must be conducive to halting the workings of external perception. Thus, Dōgen outlines the detailed procedures:

> For *sanzen*, a quiet room is suitable. Eat and drink moderately. Cast aside all involvements and cease all affairs. Do not think good or bad. Do not administer pros and cons. Cease all of the movements of conscious mind. *Sanzen* has nothing whatever to do with sitting and lying.[20]

In making the last statement, Dōgen marks off the practice of just sitting from everyday activities, for in learning a retrogressive step through the practice of just sitting, one must learn to *disengage* himself from the world. Ideally, the everyday activities must eventually assume the form of just sitting, but in the incipient stages of the practice of just sitting, one must first learn the retrogressive step. For this reason, the ambiance in which just sitting is initially practiced requires that there is a least amount of disturbance which might activate the external sensory organs. Thus, by blocking off, as much as possible, incoming stimulation from the external ambiance, one must free oneself from the engagements of the world. The essential point to be learned is to "cease the movement of the conscious mind," insofar as it is engaged in the everyday world. What is implied in this observation is that there is a mode of awareness distinct and different from that of everyday consciousness. Also implicit in Dōgen's instruction to cease the movement of the conscious mind is a "practical everyday" dualistic tendency existing between the mind and the body.

In order to lessen the gap between the mind and the body operative in the everyday existence, Zen instructs the aspirant to adjust the body and the mind. The adjustment of the body refers specifically to the various correctives prescribed for the aspirant assuming the lotus position.[21] Once the bodily posture has been adjusted to correspond properly to the lotus position or its variation, Dōgen instructs the aspirant to adjust his breathing and his mind.

[T]ake a deep breath, inhale and exhale, rock your body right
and left and settle into a steady, immobile sitting position.
Think of not-thinking. How do you think of not-thinking?
Non-thinking. This in itself is an essential art of *zazen*.[22]

The instruction to adjust one's body and one's mind, when starting a session of just sitting, begins first with the body, and then
with the breathing and finally with the mind. (In concluding the
session, this order is reversed.) These directions specify the procedure in taking a retrogressive step, and they describe a conscious movement from the external world into the internal
world. The mediation between the external world and the internal world is performed by regulating one's breathing. Breathing
here is not simply an inhalation and exhalation of air, as analyzed in chemistry. Rather the philosophical significance of regulating one's breathing is to adjust or readjust oneself to the harmonious rhythm of nature, to the four elements which in part
comprised the concept of the body. Here, breathing functions as
a bridging mediator between the grossness of the material world
and the subtlety of the interior world. According to Tamaki, the
method of breathing which Dōgen prescribed is "neither short
nor long."[23] That is, he recommends that the aspirant avoids, for
example, strenuous breathing methods employed in some of
yogic *prāṇāyānas*. Once the breathing has been properly adjusted, one "settle[s] into a steady, immobile sitting."

In the course of just sitting, one must be careful not to fall
into a torpid state of dullness, nor into a wandering state of dis-
traction. Both are inconducive to the right form of just sitting—
"rightness" here is understood as conducive to "cease all the
movements of the mind." In the midst of just sitting, one is supposed to "think of not-thinking." What does it mean, then, to
think of not-thinking?

SAMADHIC AWARENESS

What is philosophically interesting and significant is the paradoxical statements regarding the practical procedure leading to
the state of awareness in seated meditation, namely the statements: "Think (*shiryō*) of not-thinking. How do you think of

not-thinking (*fu-shiryō*)? Non-thinking (*hi-shiryō*)!" Since these statements are a Zen dialogue, originally uttered by Yakuzan Kudō (751–834), they will escape our understanding, if we attempt to apply to them the laws of "logic" used in our ordinary discourse. For example, to say that the goal of meditation is to think of not-thinking is a contradiction, and therefore, our everyday logic demands that we immediately dismiss it as non-sensical.[24] If we are to avoid this kind of hasty judgement, we must first understand that these seemingly paradoxical statements are a *practical* guide given by a master to his disciple as a way of entering into a state of samadhic awareness. At the same time, these statements point to a linguistic recapitulation of the experience involved.

With this preliminary remark in mind, when we read the preceding Zen dialogue as it is stated, the goal of seated meditation is to think of not-thinking, a state distinguished both from "thinking" and from "not-thinking." The mode of thinking necessary in order to attain this state is by means of nonthinking, as Dōgen states: "In order to think of not-thinking, one invariably employs nonthinking."[25] What interests us here, then, is a philosophical analysis of the experiential meaning of think of not-thinking.

Thinking, according to Akiyama Hanji, is "all the conscious functions, including perceptions, discriminatory thought, desires and delusions. In other words, it is a general term for all of the states of knowing, feeling and willing."[26] In light of our preceding discussions, this mode of thinking characterizes the domain of everyday consciousness. Not-thinking, on the other hand, insofar as it is a negation, is the denial or the rejection of thinking. But as such, Akiyama continues, it must be "an elimination (of thinking) by eradication, or an empty-nothingness [*kūmu*]."[27] The negative, "not," which precedes the term, thinking, is not primarily the logical negation, but is entailed in a somatic negation of thinking. The term, "somatic negation," is used foremost to indicate that not-thinking is induced by the form of seated meditation, and that its logical negation is entailed by it. This is because the seated meditation is somatic in character, that is, assuming the lotus position, or the half lotus position. Although the logical negation does not alter the being of a person, for it is

merely the matter as it can be set down "on paper," or entertained "in the mind," the somatic negation, on the other hand,
transforms the being of a person. Especially relevant for our purposes here, is the transformation of the manner through which
the things of experience are transformed, and this change we earlier characterized as an epistemological reorientation. In this
respect, "negation," as it is used in somatic negation, may be
taken to be a practical procedure for epistemological transformation, or reorientation. However, if this negation results in unconsciousness in the sense that the process of somatic negation falls
outside of consciousness, there cannot be consciousness, let alone
thinking in its somatically negative form. In this case, the mediator involved in this practical procedure becomes indistinguishable from a rock qua rock, for example. Obviously, this is not
what is meant by the somatic negation. Consequently, we are led
to assume that not-thinking is a certain mode of consciousness
induced by the somatic negation, and this mode of consciousness
is different from that of thinking. It may be more appropriate to
understand it as a certain kind of somatically induced "awareness," for this term is not associated with the various "features"
of consciousness made salient within the phenomenological tradition. Moreover, the term awareness will effectively allow us to
avoid an association with the intentionality thesis. The above
interpretation is consistent with the attitude which the aspirant is
advised to assume, namely to disengage himself or herself from
the world in order to "cease all of the movements of the conscious function." Furthermore, it is in line with our interpretation of "eradicating the root of all mental functions."

Now that we are in possession of respective meanings for
thinking and not-thinking, it would seem to follow that we
should turn our attention to an analysis of the logical meaning
and the status of think of not-thinking. However, as we concluded earlier, this approach is a dead end, since it will lead us to the
intellectual and logical plane: and on this plane, the statement,
think of not-thinking, is a contradiction. Dōgen's strategy is
rather to dissolve the contradiction through the practice of seated meditation, that is, by changing the somatic modality. Therefore, it would seem that a more profitable approach to an analysis of think of not-thinking is to focus our attention on the

means by which the aspirant is led to this experiential state. When we take this approach, however, we must be careful not to confound think of not-thinking with nonthinking, for the latter is merely the means to the former. At any rate, Dōgen maintains that the means by which the aspirant can attain the experiential state embodied in think of not-thinking is by nonthinking (*hi-shiryō*). Necessarily, then, in order to understand what think of not-thinking means, we must unpack what nonthinking is.

Using the language of phenomenology, T. P. Kasulis charac-terizes the state of nonthinking (*shiryō*), as being "nonpositional (neither affirming nor negating)" in its noetic aspect, and "pure presence of things as they are" in its noematic content.[28] To say the noetic act is "neither affirming nor negating" means that the consciousness of an experiencer assumes no specific "attitude" or "stance." It entertains neither being or nonbeing. Hence, the noetic aspect is said to be "nonpositional." With this mode of consciousness, its noematic content is said to be the "pure pres-ence of things as they are." The reason why the noematic content is said to be "pure" is that it is not tinted with or colored by one's subjectivity, a correlativity which is entailed by the non-positional noetic act. Or, more positively, we can use Husserl's terminology from *Ideas*, and describe the noetic act as "neutral-ized."[29] But this is somewhat misleading, for in Husserl's case, this neutralization is effected *without* involving the transforma-tion of the somatic modality of a person, that is, it is only accomplished through the intellectual endeavor of "transcenden-tal reductions." On the other hand, as we have been observing, nonthinking is a mode of awareness that is induced in a specific form of somaticity, called just sitting. The point is that the noetic analysis must include within it a reference to, or a consideration of, the somatic transformation. To say that a noetic act is non-positional informs us only of the mode of consciousness as it is divorced from the somaticity of a person, and not of the influ-ence or the effect that a somatic transformation has on the mode of consciousness.

In order to supplement the above interpretation, we will now turn to a noted contemporary practitioner of Dōgen Zen, Sawaki Kōdō. Describing the content of Zen meditation through non-thinking, Sawaki writes:

In such a Zen meditation, the residue does not remain even in the occurrence of thought or in the hearing of sounds. Sounds are *simply* heard, and thoughts *simply* occur and then they naturally disappear, just like the incoming and the outgoing of breath.[30] (emphases added)

This account recalls our earlier treatment of "generation-extinction of dharmas" as the description of samadhic awareness with respect to its noemata. In light of our analysis, what is insightful about the above quotation is Sawaki's observation that while the practitioner of Zen meditation is sitting in the mode of nonthinking, there is no "residue" left in generation-extinction of dharmas; or specifically in his example, thoughts or "sounds" leave no residue. Nothing, in other words, becomes a "seed" for later fruition, and this implies that the reflective capacity is not operative in the same way as it is in our everyday waking moments. But why is this the case? It would seem that the crucial term in the above quotation is the adverb, "simply," and therefore, the key to an understanding of the state of nonthinking lies in unpacking simply in its context "Sounds are *simply* heard, and thoughts *simply* occur." This leads us to an analysis of how samadhic awareness functions.

What does "simply" mean in the context sounds are simply heard and thoughts simply occur? In our everyday experience, sounds are not simply heard, for if we accept Merleau-Ponty's hypothesis and use his terminology,[31] there is a network of "bodily intentionalities" (*l'intentionalit du corps*) which is cast *in potentia* or in advance towards the things in the world, and which forms an invisible intentional arc between the perceiver and the perceived. Based upon this mechanism, Merleau-Ponty contends, a perception becomes an actual perception. We catch the sound through the auditory organ via the network of bodily intentionalities. In contrast, as we have observed, the seated meditation prepares a person to disengage himself from the world. This means that the degree to which the bodily intentionalities are activated is lessened in the seated meditation. (The degree to which this activation is lessened, I would surmise, is in proportion to the depth of nonthinking.) This disengagement from things in the world is confirmed by Sawaki when he says that there is no striving of mind whatsoever in this mode of seated meditation.[32] To go back to our example, sounds are heard but there is no *selective* bodily intentionality at work. In other words, the sensory organ responds to external stimuli in such a way that it is not invested with, or charged with the activation of its function. More generally, the body is not prepared to activate itself as well as be activated. To use Merleau-Ponty's terminology again, the body ceases to cast even *in potentia* the intentional arc, and thereby avoids to establish a connection between the mediator and the external world through the invisible intentional arc. Sawaki mentions Dōgen as uttering, "I did not hear the thundering sound such as this, although, I was aware of it."[33] Dōgen's observation suggests that there still exists a more refined relation between the mediator and the external world than Merleau-Ponty's concept of the intentional arc. For our present purpose at this point, suffice it to note that the "nucleus" of everyday consciousness has taken the "retrogressive" step deep into the domain which is concealed from our everyday consciousness, where the nucleus is to be understood as the center and the source of "intentionality." In this respect, the intentionality we are discussing is somatic in character, if it indeed can still be called intentionality. At any rate, retrogression into this domain "eradicates the root of all the mental functions," and as a result, the everyday consciousness enters into a new domain, is completely transformed, and becomes samadhic awareness.

We must be clear, however, that Dōgen does not offer an explicit clarification of the term, nonthinking. At least, he does not offer it in terms readily understandable to a nonpractitioner of just sitting, or to a novice in seated meditation. Yet, what he says is sufficiently indicative enough in order to have a glimpse of what nonthinking may be like. Dōgen writes:

> Non-thinking resides in "who," and the "who" supports me. The immobile sitting, though it may be myself, is not merely a measure of thinking, but makes the immobile sitting emerge. Even though the immobile sitting is [no other than] the immobile sitting, how does the immobile sitting think of the immobile sitting? This being the case, it is neither the measure of Buddha, nor the measure of dharmas, nor the measure of satori, nor the measure of comprehension.[34]

"The immobile sitting" derives its name, from the "immobility" of a mountain which rises high in the sky but has its base secured firmly in the earth. Therefore, it means figuratively to sit like a mountain. Moreover, this immobile sitting is said by Dōgen to "reside in 'who'." In the context of the above passage, who is a reiteration of who as it is used in "Who undergoes generation-extinction," and it indicates, among other things, the absence of mineness, or the personalization of the experience in immobile sitting. Or more positively, who indicates a field where a union between the subject and object takes place, while disclosing the *raison d'être* of things in the matrix of causality. As such, immobile sitting goes beyond the boundary of our everyday experience. If the presence of "mineness" or "personalization" of experience is characteristic of everyday, human consciousness, since it can always be revealed through reflection, then, as Tamaki noted earlier in reference to the eradication of the root of all mental functions, the experience of immobile sitting is unquestionably characterizable as nonhuman, extraordinary experience.

Dōgen tells us in the preceding quotation that nonthinking is not restricted merely to the "measure of thinking," but is also transformed into "immobile sitting." The consequence of this transformation, perhaps, can be identified with the think of not-thinking, although Dōgen does not specifically make this connection. However, if this is correct, it turns out that to think of not-thinking as a goal of meditation is no other than the immobile sitting, which is a somatic modality of a special kind. As we look closely at the preceding quotation, we can notice that the immobile sitting embraces in its scope the measure of thinking, but at the same time goes beyond it. This means that the immobile sitting is more than the measure of thinking, both in terms of not-thinking and in terms of non-thinking, although we are left with some uncertainty of what the measure of thinking is. An indication of the scope of immobile sitting is carried in Dōgen's rhetorical question, "How does the immobile sitting think of the immobile sitting?" The expected response to this rhetorical question is negative, and by anticipating a negative response, Dōgen rejects the identification of the measure of thinking with the immobile sitting. Because of Dōgen's rejection of this identification, he asserts in his attempt to capture the meaning of the immobile sitting that "the immobile sitting is neither the measure of Buddha, nor the measure of dharmas, nor the measure of satori, nor the measure of comprehension." Tamaki argues that this line of thought means "the immobile sitting continually discloses itself."[35] To say the least, Dōgen's explanation of the immobile sitting is extremely difficult to comprehend for those of us who stand outside of the immobile sitting, since to think of not-thinking, in our interpretation, is itself identified with the immobile sitting.

However, we might venture here into speculation. When the term "immobile" is applied to the somatic form of sitting, it suggests that there must be absolutely no movements whatsoever insofar as the noetic act of immobile sitting is concerned. That is, there is an awareness that nothing moves. Otherwise, the immobile sitting cannot be so named, and would be without meaning. When we assume that this is correct, it is somewhat more understandable that Dōgen requires a string of negatives to characterize the immobile sitting such as "*neither* the measure of Buddha, *nor* the measure of dharmas, *nor* the measure of satori, *nor* the measure of comprehension" (emphases added). As far as the noematic content of this awareness is concerned, there is literally nothing. Therefore, the only way in which Dōgen can express the state of immobile sitting by means of language is through the negative characterization, because only in this way can he discourage those ordinary people who do not have the experience of immobile sitting from employing misunderstood characterizations to describe the state such as satori, or dharma, etc. But, it is perhaps misleading to use such terms as "noetic" and "noematic content" in this connection, for these terms suggest that the immobile sitting is reducible to the terms of the function of consciousness. Dōgen asserts that "the immobile sitting is (no other than) the immobile sitting." Obviously in light of this statement, immobile sitting is not merely an aspect of consciousness. Although the statement is cast in a tautological manner, and hence is uninformative, we will be more successful in our attempts to understand what immobile sitting is, if we choose terminology truly reflective of the meaning of this tautological statement. What is certain, however, is that to think of not-thinking is consummated in the specific somatic form which is itself immobile sitting. It is important to realize that the consummation of think of not-thinking by means of the immobile sitting, is not the reduction of think of not-thinking to the function of the body in the sense of the extended thing devoid of thinking. As we recall, Dōgen's concept of the body includes an incarnate consciousness, among other things. Consequently, a fruitful investigation in search of new terminologies that would allow us to understand the meaning of the immobile sitting seems to lie in examining Dōgen's position on the mind-body issue, for immobile sitting is said at once to embrace the measure of thinking, which, broadly speaking, pertains to the dimension of the mind, while going beyond it by means of the specific somatic modality, a dimension of the body. This, then, is the topic to which we now turn our attention.

ONENESS OF THE BODY-MIND

The term, "body-mind" (*shinjin*) is suspected of being a Japanese neologism, and is rarely found as a phrase in Chinese.[36] We have observed earlier that the traditional Buddhist concept of the human body is comprised of the four elements and five aggregates, and that this concept of the body includes a somatic or an incarnate consciousness. In light of this, the term, body-mind, seems ambiguous, since the concept of the human body already includes "mind." To avoid this ambiguity, the meaning of the body paired with the mind as in the phrase, body-mind, must be specified: it designates a material form (*rūpa*). Therefore, the contrast between the body and the mind corresponds to the distinction between the body qua the material form and the mind comprising the rest of the aggregates, although it is moot to include saṃskāra in the constitution of the mind alone.[37] Broadly speaking, however, the term, body-mind, which Dōgen uses throughout his writings, parallels the Cartesian distinction, although with the crucial difference that Dōgen views the mind as incarnate in the body. It is to this sense of body-mind, then, that Dōgen refers as capable of being brought to oneness. We will follow this specified sense of the term, body-mind.

The places where Dōgen explicitly deals with the mind-body issue are found in *Bendōwa* (Negotiating the Way), as well as in

Shokushin Zebutsu (This Mind is the Buddha). We will focus on examining the treatment of this issue as it appears in *Bendōwa*, for Dōgen's treatment of the mind-body issue in *Shokushin Zebutsu* is essentially the same. Dōgen's argument is developed in response to the position which he attributes to the Senika heresy. This position holds that there is an immutable mind-nature, or spiritual intelligence with which man is endowed, and which does not perish even after bodily death. Furthermore, among other things, this is advanced as a way of overcoming the fear of death. Dōgen summarizes this position as follows:

> Even though once this body is born, it is carried away to perish, the mind-nature does not perish. When one recognizes well that there is a mind-nature impervious to generation-extinction, the body assumes a tentative appearance, since the mind-nature is an original nature [of man]. The mind is ever abiding through time and does not depend upon [the passage of] the past and present time.[38]

This is a dualism somewhat similar to that of Descartes who, in part, advocated a mind-body dualism in order to affirm the immortality of the soul. Dōgen ridicules the Senika heresy, saying that "it is even more foolish than holding the pebbles and broken pieces of roof-tile as if they were the treasure of gold."[39] This ridicule is based upon Dōgen's thesis that everything is subject to generation-extinction. He says:

> Buddha-dharma maintains that the mind and the body are one [*shinshin ichinyo*] without separating the appearance from its nature. If one were to hold that the position of [the mind] abides in time, then all of the dharmas abides, and the mind is not separate from the body.[40]

Here, Dōgen's criticism is clear; it is directed against the inconsistency of holding that when both are regarded as forming an integrated whole, the one part (i.e., the mind) is considered immutable, while the other (i.e., the body) is not, or that while the former is mutable, the latter is not. The assumption in rejecting this position is that the mind and the body are not separate, but rather form an integrated whole, or oneness. We can sense in Dōgen's rejection that his concern is with "this" side of life, rather than the "other" side, for he does not want to accept that immaterial substance subsists through time after bodily death. Dōgen, further, criticizes the Senika heresy, contending that:

> Even though it is delusory thinking in light of Buddha wisdom which has left behind [the matter of] life-death, this discriminatory mind which understands the mind to be abiding through time independent of the body, goes through generation-extinction, and is not abiding in time at all.[41]

Dōgen's application of the thesis of generation-extinction is thorough, for he points out that the mind which entertains the idea of mind-nature abiding through time, nevertheless, itself goes through generation-extinction, temporally vanishing into oblivion in the next moment. He advances the above criticism from the position that:

> In the position which maintains an extinction [of firing desires, i.e., nirvana], all dharmas goes through extinction, without separating the appearance from its nature.[42]

Nirvana as an ultimate goal in Buddhism is used here as a way of refuting the existence of the mind-nature, for Nirvana is understood, albeit negatively, to be an extinction of "all dharmas" synthesizing the human body. Apart from Nirvana, Dōgen harbors a few suppressed motivations for advancing the thesis of oneness of body-mind. Foremost is Dōgen's strong conviction that, if one accepts the existence of a spiritual intelligence, or mind-nature, emphasis upon just sitting becomes superfluous, and this he could not accept. Moreover, the spiritual intelligence was believed to have the power of shaping one's likes and dislikes, the sense of good and evil, and pain and pleasure in encountering the appropriate occasions which give rise to them.[43] In Dōgen's mind, all of these must be shaped through a personal cultivation. But far more important than this is Dōgen's philosophical dissatisfaction with the position that holds the dualism of various kinds which are implied in the Senika heresy. Rather, his position is the oneness of body-mind (*shinshin ichinyo*).

Although Dōgen's argument is directed at refuting the existence of the mind-nature that persists through time, and that results in separation of the body from the mind, or appearance from its nature, his "oneness of the body-mind" is problematic.

What does this phrase oneness of the body and the mind mean? The meaning of "oneness" is not immediately clear, except that, as I have indicated earlier, it can be interpreted as an integrated whole of a person. "Oneness of the body-mind" is supposed to be a reflective restatement of the heightened state of just sitting. That is to say, when a meditator enters into a deepened state of immovable sitting, an integration between the mind and the body is brought to such a degree that it does not admit of the bifurcation between the mind and the body, or between the subject and the object. And, as such, it is foreign to our everyday experience.

In order to properly understand the significance of oneness of body and mind, it is helpful to know a larger methodological procedure accepted in Dōgen's scheme of thought, and more generally in Buddhism. This brings us to the discussion of Zen's theory and practice. How are they related to each other?

ZEN'S THEORY AND PRACTICE

At this point in our discussion, we have to turn our attention to the relative relationship obtaining between Zen practice and its theory. As we have already observed, Dōgen rejects idle intellectual speculation, and this can be interpreted to mean that practice precedes theory in Zen. A theoretical formulation of any Zen contention, therefore, is advanced first by verifying a lived experience through practice. In other words, any theoretical formulation is a reflective restatement of one's lived experience in meditation, although the rigor of such a formulation depends upon the capacity of the individual Zen master. At any rate, the ambiguity or the conflict in the interpretation of *shin shin ichi nyo* may be dissolved if we apply a distinction between practice and theory. In the course of Zen cultivation, the aspirant may understand *shin shin ichi nyo* to mean "making the body and mind one" or "reaching the oneness of the body-mind," which is for the aspirant an ideal to be achieved. On the other hand, through deepening his Zen cultivation, the aspirant comes to understand the oneness of the body-mind, that is, he or she comes to understand when *shin shin ichi nyo*, as the oneness of body-mind, is practically as well as theoretically verified. At such a time, there is no distinction between achieving an ideal and the ideal achieved, between practice and theory. The aspirant, to use Dōgen's phrase, becomes a person whose "practice and understanding coincide with each other." In the course of this verification the understanding of *shin shin ichi nyo* undergoes, we may surmise, an epistemological reorientation through the transformation of the somaticity.

From the preceding analysis, it is evident that Dōgen's attitude towards the body-mind issue embraces two somewhat incompatible positions, although one is supportive of the other, while conceivably admitting of almost an infinite degree of integration between them. When it is observed that the body and the mind become one via the process of just sitting, the body and the mind, although integrated, are considered to be distinct in our everyday experience, yet they are but one in the samadhic experience. According to this account, the dualism operative in our everyday experience is not a fixed, absolute dualism which does not admit, both practically and theoretically, of its transformation into nondualism. For this reason, Tamura calls Dōgen's position "relative dualism,"[44] much the same way that Yuasa characterizes the Eastern meditative tradition in general as assuming "commonsensical" or "provisional dualism." Therefore, when this transformation is effected, the apparent dualistic tendency loses its significance and turns into nondualism. This transformation is in fact, the efficacy of "learning a retrogressive step." In light of this, a nondualistic position is achieved through integration in just sitting, the apparent dualism in everyday experience can be rejected as an inauthentic, erroneous way of understanding the mind-body issue. But if this is held to be the case, the meaning of just sitting, and Dōgen's emphasis upon it will be nullified, and consequently lost. Therefore, from Dōgen's perspective, the apparent duality of body and mind must be sustained irrespective of nondualism. In terms of Dōgen's scheme then, both the relative, commonsensical dualism, and the nondualism that is achieved through just sitting support and sustain each other. Tamura characterizes this as "the relative qua absolute,"[45] while reinterpreting "the relative" and "the absolute" respectively to mean dualism and nondualism. In Dōgen's own words:

> In Buddha-dharma, practice and authentication are equally the same. Because the practice [of just sitting] is within authentication, the beginning mind in negotiating the way is therefore the whole of original authentication.... Because practice is already an authentication, there is no limit to authentication. Because authentication is the practice, there is no beginning in practice.[46]

Here, one can sense Dōgen's strong sentiment towards the practice of just sitting. He expresses this sentiment also when he asserts that "Although this dharma is amply present in each and every person, it never becomes present without practice, and it cannot be attained without authentication."[47] It is clear, then, that, apart from the practice of just sitting, Dōgen does not recognize an authentication (shō), an equivalent of satori. It is for this reason, for example, that Takahashi criticizes Dōgen's religiosity as not aiming for universal salvation.[48] In the foregoing analysis, the important point for us to keep in mind is that Dōgen's position on the body-mind issue admits of two strands; one the relative, or provisional dualism of everyday experience and the other nondualism achieved through just sitting, and that one is supportive of the other, together they allow an almost infinite degree of integration.

When we take the meaning of oneness of the body-mind to be a state of samadhic awareness, disregarding, for now, the relative, commonsensical dualism also implied by shinjin ichi nyo, we must ask how it fares with the description of immobile sitting. Does oneness of the body-mind designate experientially the same depth of samadhic awareness as the immobile sitting, or is the latter a still deeper state of samadhic awareness? As we recall, the immobile sitting is said to be "(no other than) the immobile sitting," and moreover is claimed to embrace the measure of thinking, while at once going beyond it vis-à-vis think(ing) of not-thinking. In light of this, we must conclude that the oneness of the body-mind cannot be identified straightforwardly with immobile sitting; it must be a stage within, or on the way to, immobile sitting.

If we accept the above interpretation that we can single out two strands in Dōgen's attitude towards the body-mind issue, namely the relative, provisional dualism which is operative in our everyday existence, and the nondualism operative in samadhic experience, it follows that the "oneness of the body-mind" cannot be understood from the perspective of our everyday existence. Epistemologically, this means that the function of external perception as it is directed toward the natural world, is incapable of experiencing, much less understanding, the oneness of the body-mind, and hence is useless in articulating the meaning of the oneness of the body-mind. This shortfall is also entailed in the interpretation we gave to learning a retrogressive step in which we argued that it is to disengage oneself from one's involvement in the natural world. This implies that, if the oneness of the body-mind is indeed experienced in samadhic awareness, there must necessarily be an epistemological apparatus that operates in samadhic awareness quite distinct and different from the order that is operative in the everyday perceptual consciousness. Logically, in order for oneness to be experienced, this oneness must be grounded in something common to both the body and the mind, that is, common and equally shared by both as they function in samadhic awareness. And in order to reach this ground, one must practically trans-descend into the source out of which both the mind and body appear. Otherwise, it is pointless to assert the oneness of the body and the mind.

This leads us to the next step in our analysis of Dōgen. Considering his nondual position on the body-mind issue, how does the description which he gives to the experience of a deepened state of meditation bear out the the sense of oneness. This topic will be examined vis-à-vis an analysis of casting off the body and the mind (*shinjin totsuraku*), an event that marked Dōgen's authentication.

CHAPTER 6

Dōgen and the Body in Transformation

INTRODUCTION

Our topical concern of this chapter is an analysis of Dōgen's confirmatory experience of casting off the body and the mind (*shinjin totsuraku*).[1] This experience expressive of this phrase was an extraordinary event that was marked off from the events of Dōgen's everyday existence, and therefore from the domain in which, as we have observed in the preceding chapter, the common sensical, relative dualism between the mind and the body is operative. According to the rendition of *shinjin totsuraku* as casting off the body and the mind, that which is cast off is the dualistic tendency obtaining in everyday existence, and therefore the experience implied by this phrase is other than the everyday experience. In our subsequent philosophical analysis of casting off the body and the mind, then, we shall see in more concrete terms the meaning of "oneness of the body-mind," and the meaning of "eradicating the root of all mental functions," which is, we have observed, the goal of meditation.

Dōgen's confirmatory experience of casting off the body and the mind is said to have taken place when Nyojō admonished a monk who was dozing off during the practice of sitting. Nyojō apparently shouted at the monk, uttering "*Sanzen* ought to be casting off the body and mind! How do you expect to achieve this when you just doze off?" Upon hearing this admonition, Dōgen allegedly experienced something deep, something which transformed the whole of his being. The expression of which Dōgen gave to this experience is: "(I have) cast off the body and the mind; the body and the mind are cast off." But, what was the nature of this experience?

Takazaki advances the hypothesis that Nyojō did not utter "you ought to cast off the body and the mind," but must have

131

said "you ought to cast off the mind-dust (*shinjin*)," contending that Dōgen perhaps misunderstood the Chinese phrase, "mind-dust" [*shinjin*] for "body and mind" (*shinjin*).[2] In order to substantiate this hypothesis, Takazaki offers several pieces of evidence, two of which seem to be most conclusive: (1) Throughout Nyojō's writings, there is no reference to *shinjin totsuraku*, casting off the body and the mind, although *shinjin totsuraku*, casting off the mind-dust, occurs once. The absence of this phrase would suggest that *shinjin totsuraku* as casting off the body and the mind was not part of Nyojō's vocabulary. (2) In Dōgen's diary, *Hokkyoki*, which he kept during his sojourn in China, there is an entry in which Dōgen asked Nyojō the meaning of *shinjin totsuraku*, to which Nyojō is said to have replied: "*Shinjin totsuraku* is a seated meditation. When one just sits, he discards five kinds of desire (related to the five sensory organs),[3] and eliminates five kinds of barriers (*gogai*)."[4] This mention of five kinds of desires and barriers may be seen as a partial specification of "the root of all mental functions," although its fuller understanding must be seen in light of Dōgen's own confirmatory experience of casting off the body and the mind.

In view of Takazaki's observation, it would indeed seem that Dōgen broadened, and perhaps deepened, his teacher's understanding of confirmatory experience, for casting off the body and the mind implies a wider scope of experience than casting off the mind-dust, that is, discarding or eliminating these desires. No doubt, both would require a movement away from the relative, common sensical dualism, in a bid to attain nondualism, but the degree, and the intensity of the experience described by the phrase casting off the body and the mind would certainly go deeper than the experience involving an elimination of desires. While the mind-dust which blankets and clouds the mind is certainly inseparable from the body, casting off the body and the mind suggests the removal of the bottom of a bucket, as it were, out of which these desires surface to our everyday consciousness. This is indeed in conformity with the meaning of eradicating all the mental functions, discussed in the previous chapter. Furthermore, Takazaki points out that according to Nyojō's understanding, the criterion for "encountering buddhas and patriarchs" which may be taken as an equivalent of enlightenment (satori), is satisfied by "eliminating even one kind of desire and/or one kind of covering desires [*kleśa*]."[5] If, on the one hand, Dōgen broadened the scope of experience, at least, insofar as the linguistic expression implies, but on the other hand, Nyojō's confirmation in "checking" Dōgen's experience rested upon this minimum criterion,[6] we must ask ourselves how deep Dōgen's experience of satori was at the time when Nyojō granted the seal of transmission. Since there is no way of directly responding to this issue with certain verifiable evidence, we should instead address ourselves to the question: what was Dōgen's experience which culminated in the linguistic expression casting off the body and the mind? In carrying out this attempt, we must make a methodological decision. Since Dōgen does not speak of the event of his casting off the body and the mind explicitly, we must avail ourselves of the descriptions which he gives of the experience of satori in *Shōbōgenzō*. In fact, this is the approach which we have consistently applied in the foregoing analyses. Consequently, our concern shifts from attempting to understand the particular event of Dōgen's casting off the body and the mind to its general and formal description.

TRANSFORMATION OF SYNTHETIC FUNCTION

Although, generally speaking, there are a number of individual variations of what triggers an occasion for satori, there is agreement that it must be experienced as relaxed, perhaps even ecstatic, periods "after the extreme tension."[7] In Dōgen's case, we are told that the release came upon hearing the words spoken by Nyojō. This kind of altered response to stimulus in reaching satori is not unusual. We know from the Zen tradition, for example, that Kyōgen Shikan had a great satori upon hearing a stone hitting bamboo. Under normal circumstances, however, without a prolonged period of sitting via a process of sedimentation, this kind of event cannot be an occasion which triggers a satori, a Zen enlightenment.[8] Among other things, this suggests that the meditator's readiness to activate auditory perception is unusually heightened at a time immediately prior to satori experience. Of the five sensory organs, the ears are more open to the external world in a deepened sitting than the remaining senses, and hence are most susceptible to stimulation. However, as we have seen in our discussion of "nonthinking," the manner of responding to sounds coming from the external world is set off from a direct reaction to the sounds. In the meditator's initial phase of nonthinking, she or he receives the sounds via auditory perception, but she or he *is not moved* to respond to them, because she or he is in the state of "immovable sitting." As she or he advances deeper into the mode of nonthinking, however, the sounds she or he hears could occasion the breaking of the barrier between hearing sounds and sounds that are heard. Alternatively, this might be expressed as follows: the auditory affectivity in its readiness for operation is initially brought to zero in an advanced stage of nonthinking, but the suppressed affectivity bursts into full operation upon being triggered. At such time, the meditator *feels* that there is no difference between hearing the sounds and the sounds that are heard. That is, he achieves a oneness with them. We may consider this an instance of what Dōgen calls "transforming the body upon turning the brain" (*yakushin kainō*). Here, we have a glimpse into a meaning of what oneness of the body-mind means.

This does not mean, however, that among the five sensory perceptions, only the auditory perception is accentuated, although it would seem that it functioned to occasion satori in Dōgen's case.[9] For example, Reiun is said to have had a satori upon *seeing* the blossoming of a peach tree,[10] which suggests a heightened visual perception. Generally speaking, however, it would be reasonable to assume that the synthetic center for all five sensory perceptions is brought to a heightened affective mode—the "synthetic center" which Aristotle speaks of as the organ of "common sense" (*sensus communis*) and which he regarded as common to all sensory perceptions.[11] This heightened synthetic center, we may regard as "supersensory" in the sense that it goes beyond an ordinary, everyday function of the sensory organs. In order to substantiate the contention that the synthetic function for all of the five sensory perceptions is heightened in samadhic awareness via its affective mode, that is, an emergence of supersensory function, we shall now examine Dōgen's analysis of the confirmatory experience of Dōzan, the first patriarch of the Sōtō Zen Buddhism.

Referring to Dōzan's confirmatory experience, an experience in which he is said to have attained an authenticating satori by "hearing the voice with the eyes," Dōgen writes:

> In studying the first patriarch's expression of "hearing the voices with the eyes," the eye is the organ [through which] the voices of insentient beings preaching dharmas is heard. The eye is the presencing voices of the insentient beings preaching dharmas. You ought to study your eyes extensively. Because *hearing* the voice with the eyes is the same as hearing the voice with the ears, they are yet different. You should not understand that there is the organ of the ears in the eyes, nor should you understand the eyes and the ears stand in the relation of interchangeability, nor should you understand the voice presences in the midst of the eyes.[12] (emphasis added)

Ordinarily, our ear is the auditory organ, but what Dōgen claims in this quotation is that one can also hear with the eyes! Many are tempted to dismiss the latter as Zen nonsense, for most of us have not heard of, let alone witnessed, such a seemingly confused experience, and therefore would regard it as an improper use of the language, a semantic confusion, or at best an attempt to be metaphorical. However, I interpret it to be an instance of synesthesia, in which there is indeed a "confusion," and an exchange of sensory faculties.[13] Needless to say, it is a confusion insofar as we take the five sensory organs to have their own fixed, and determinately assigned functions without a possibility of going beyond them so as to let the supersensory function emerge. According to Dōgen, this notion of exclusive function arises because ordinary people "have not clarified on their own the extreme limit of (their) body and mind."[14] What the above quotation implies is that there is a sensory function beyond the ordinary, fixed and determined functions; these functions can be transcended, allowing the supersensory function to emerge, which occurs when the body and the mind are brought to "the extreme limit" in the practice of just sitting. If this does indeed take place, confusion is an inappropriate word to describe the synesthesia which is said to have occurred, for example, in Dōzan's experience of satori.

This special use of synesthesia to describe an experience of satori will become clear when we recognize that the perception of the eye can be different from, and yet the same as, the ear. Dōgen demonstrates that he is not unaware of the difference in function between the eyes and the ears as they operate in our everyday existence, when he states: "Since hearing the voice with the eyes is the same as hearing the voice with the ears, they are yet *different*" (emphasis added). What is affirmed as the "same" must be the somatic act of hearing in samadhic awareness, where "somatic act," in sharp contrast with *cogito* as act, indicates the whole involvement of a person, while the "difference" must mean the individual function of each sensory organ. When this experience is actually lived, the meditator feels that his or her everyday sensory, *somatic* self is indeed "cast off." The term which Dōgen uses to describe this lived experience is no-body [*mushin*], meaning that there is no lived feeling of one's own (object-)body which is opposed to the mind.

The preceding analysis of Dōzan's confirmatory experience via synesthesia should *not* suggest that every case of confirmatory experience of satori is obtained vis-à-vis synesthesia. The value of this type of analysis, however, lies in leading us to a general analysis of the act aspect of the supersensory synthetic function. Consequently, we must take the position that the act aspect of supersensory synthetic function is more significant than an analysis of the alteration of sensory circuits. We can, for example, imagine that an emergence of supersensory function, would affect the manner in which synthesis functions, when, for example, it is a synthesis of understanding the sounds as sounds. Insofar as the sounds are identified as sounds, the power of recognizing the external stimuli, in general, must not be impaired, while at the same time, the mode or manner employed in recognizing these external stimuli must be transformed.

What then is the mode of synthesis operative at the moment when casting off the body and the mind occurs? It is worth while to point out that the *manner* of recognizing an external stimulus must be radically different from the one operative in a normal, natural situation. Most importantly, what distinguishes this type of perception from everyday, normal perception is the degree of affectivity. In the extraordinary experience of casting off the body and mind, the supersensory synthetic function is charged with a power much stronger than the normal, everyday power, since the power which would otherwise be used in the activation of the sensory organs is reserved via a process of sedimentation. This infusion of power occurs partly because the activation of perceptual consciousness is lowered in a deepened state of samadhic awareness, and hence the power of ordinary synthetic function is also weakened prior to the experience in question. If the power of synthesis is unfortunately lost, pathological phenomena (e.g., Zen sickness) would be experienced. Because of this contingency, the practice of "just sitting" has its threatening side.

The power of supersensory synthetic function which we have been discussing is a form of judgement. Consider the following simple, everyday example. Upon seeing a flower, we immediately recognize that it is a flower, "immediately" in the sense that the judgement takes place without the intervention of intellectual reflection. To recognize a flower in this manner requires a form of judgement, a prereflective judgement which can, though, be realized reflectively by taking a subject-predicate form. To use Husserl terminology, it is pre-predicative judgement; a pre-predicative or pre-reflective judgement, since the judgement takes place spontaneously, and without thinking. If the judgement is pre-predicative or pre-reflective, it is moot, however, whether the act of judgement is solely rooted in cogito as Sartre, for example, has conceived it to be. Merleau-Ponty, avoiding the use of the term, "pre-reflective," has employed the term "bodily intentionality," contending that this type of intentionality prepares in advance an intentionality associated with perceptual consciousness, and hence it is more primary than (pre) reflective cogito. Considering a "perspectival" givenness of every perception, which presupposes a bodily presence relative to the thing perceived, it would seem that some aspect of the body is involved in forming a pre-reflective or "pre-predicative" judgement. I shall argue in later sections that a form of judgement is somatic in character and that it is achieved via an attunement.

What we have so far referred to as "epistemological reorientation" by means of somatic transformation has now been brought into a sharper focus, namely, to the clearly delineated feature of a mode of judgement. In light of this, when the practice of just sitting, is viewed epistemologically, we can see that it is aimed precisely at transforming the mode of judgement given naturally to our everyday existence into the mode of judgement in samadhic awareness. It is from this prospect that we can view more clearly the rationale in Dōgen's rejection of the "dharmas moving the self" as inconducive to attaining an understanding of buddha dharmas, that is, as inconducive to attaining this mode of judgement possible in samadhic awareness.

By unknowingly positing itself as a "valid" ground from which to make judgement, the empirical self carries its own supposedly valid ground for making judgement. As we have seen in dealing with the samādhi of oceanic reflection, samadhic awareness is devoid of the sense of mineness, especially the ego infested with a host of its desires. Dōgen's contention would be that this empirical self must shatter its own ground, and leave itself open to whatever is judged in order for a mode of judgement operative in samadhic awareness to be activated, since the self carries within itself a host of unexamined presuppositions, presuppositions which are unknowingly retained for the sake of its own survival. We can now understand the true meaning of eradicating the root of all mental functions to the degree that it involves, as Yuasa points out, lowering life-energy to its zero balance, or as Hakuin insists, undergoing a great death prior to satori experience. This understanding of eradicating the root of all mental functions also suggests the rationale for Dōgen's rejection of the intellectual pursuit of the buddha dharmas, as well as for a partial meaning of casting off the body and mind.

So, when we ask the manner or the mode of the supersensory synthetic function which is operative in casting off the body and the mind, we are concerned with articulating the mode of "judgement." In passing, I would like to advance the thesis that it is a somatic act that performs a judgement in the experience of casting off the body and the mind, in contrast with cogito as act, and since it is a somatic act, there is no involvement of an intentional glance, which is, after all, the function of the empirical self, and which is cast off in samadhic awareness. In this sense, it is misleading to say that the somatic act "performs" a judgement, for "performance" may imply an intentional act. The somatic act must be taken as a performance without intending; as a performance "without thinking," in the sense in which T. P. Kasulis uses hi-shiryō as nonthinking. We use the term somatic in recognition of the point of its origin as well as of its intrinsic features. It is induced by means of the practice of just sitting, which is a modality of one's somaticity. To be more specific, the judgement in question is charged with affectivity which is rooted in the somaticity of a person. However, I contend that the somatic act in performing a judgement may better be characterized as an instance of "attunement" in which the somatic act and what is judged form a *harmony* between them. We shall see shortly how this interpretation bears out Dōgen's experience of casting off the body and the mind when we deal with "the felt inter-resonance" (*kannō dōkō*). The important point to bear in mind at this juncture is that the act aspect of the supersensory synthesis in samadhic awareness is somatic in character, and the judgement that is formed is an attunement.

We shall now examine how the concept of the somatic act emerges from Dōgen's further elaboration of hearing the voice with the eye. Dōgen writes:

> Simply make it your express business to learn "hearing the insentient beings preaching dharmas" with your eyes. The gist of the first patriarch's expression is that "the ear has difficulty encountering the insentient beings preaching dharmas." The eyes hear the voices, and furthermore one's pervasive body [*tsūshin*] hears voices and the entire body [*henshin*] hears the voices. Even if you cannot somatically investigate hearing voices with the eyes, you ought to somatically appropriate [*taitatsu*] and cast off "the insentient beings are capable of hearing the insentient beings preaching dharmas."[15]

There are three significant points in the latter half of the above passage to which we would like to turn our attention, and upon which we would like to elaborate. By enlarging upon these three points we can demonstrate that the use of the term, somatic act, is appropriate in referring to a mode of judgement (via an attunement) which, we claim, is operative in samadhic awareness as it has been sedimented within a person qua meditator. The first of these points is Dōgen's assertion that "the entire/pervasive body hearing the voices" is more important than "the eyes hearing the voices." The second point is Dōgen's conviction that this expansion of sense perception is necessary in practice in order to experience that "the insentient beings are capable of hearing the insentient beings preaching dharmas." And the third point is that, in order to experience that the insentient beings are capable of hearing the insentient beings preaching dharmas, Dōgen urges the aspirant to achieve what he calls "somatic appropriation" (taitatsu). We shall examine the first and third points now, since they are interrelated, and reserve our analysis of the second point for later when we will deal with the felt inter-resonance, since the third point is a logical consequence of the first and second points.

The first question we will explore is the experiential meaning of Dōgen's contention that "the entire/pervasive body hears the voices" as it is related to the eye hearing the voices. We have taken the eye hearing the voices as an instance of synesthesia, and have concluded that it means the emergence of supersensory synthetic function beyond the multiple sensory organs. In our everyday experience there is a boundary of sensibility set forth by means of the sensory organs. That is, the lived feeling of one's body extends as far as the sensory organs are functionally capable. Alternatively, this may be understood as a natural delimitation of one's body-image, where the body-image is an awareness of one's relative spatial location lived from within so that it is more or less marked off by the delineation of the boundary of one's skin. In contrast, I would like to interpret the entire/pervasive body hearing the voices, to be among other things, a lived feeling of *spatially expanding* the limits of the body-image of one's everyday lived body, since these limits are imposed by the function of the everyday mind, and which is transcended in the experience of casting off the body and mind. I advance this interpretation of a spatial expansion of one's body-image in consideration of the following: the term, "*henshin*," translated as "the entire body," indicates the spatial spread of a lived body, and the term, "*tsushin*" implies a permeation within this spatial spread. In Dōgen's own words, "The total body [*zenshin*] is a total mind. There is no obstruction when one becomes a total body."[16] When these terms are translated into experience, they suggest that the lived body is transformed into an affective sensorium in its paramount sense of the term; its scope becomes broader than the one embraced by the experience of sensory perception, and its power of synthetic function becomes more keen and more intense. When the body in this sense is achieved, it seems reasonable to refer to its enactment as a somatic act.

Dōgen claims that this somatic act is effected by means of somatic appropriation. Somatic appropriation is an achievement term, specifically designating the existential project of just sitting in its consummate form. Now, that which is somatically appropriated in the present context, is the lived feeling of spatially expanding the limits of our everyday lived body, the limits that are imposed upon the body by means of the functions of the five sensory organs. The somatic act, then, is that which issues from the somatically appropriated body and mind. Accordingly, we can for now think of the somatic act as an enactment of what is somatically appropriated, which, as we shall see shortly, forms the basis for making a judgement via an attunement.

TRANSFORMATION OF AFFECTIVITY

Our analysis now centers on the concept of affectivity as it is related to the experience of casting off the body and mind. Affectivity in this context designates a way in which a meditator is influenced by both his or her emotive state and the object that is engaged through samadhic awareness.

In the preceding analysis of casting off the body and the mind, we have concerned ourselves with an elucidation of the epistemological aspect, namely the sensory perception and its transformation. The purpose of this discussion has been to prepare the ground for a better understanding of a mode of judgement (via an attunement) which, we contend, is operative in samadhic awareness. This was, in fact, an analysis of what Nyojō meant in part by the phrase *shinjin totsuraku*, namely, to "discard the five kinds of desires (related to the five sensory organs)." We must now turn our attention to an affective aspect of the experience of casting off the body and the mind, for it is a major contributing factor in the formation of judgement vis-à-vis attunement.

Logically, the concept of affectivity requires that affectivity is grounded in the bilateral interplay between what does the affecting and what is being affected. In fact, to eliminate one of the terms in this formula renders the concept of affectivity vacuous. "Bilateral interplay" may be understood to be a dynamic exchange in the role of "affecting" and "being affected" due to a mutual permeation, that is, that which does the affecting can be turned into that which is being affected. This is to say that in order for X to be an affective agent, it must be both active and passive, both affecting and being affected. Generally speaking, when a person is situated in space, a person qua body and his surrounding ambiance reveal an instance of this bilateral interrelationship.[17]

As traditional Western epistemology conceives it, our sensory perception is a salient example of this affectivity, "salient" insofar as the capacity of the sensory organs permits us consciously to "take note of" or to "recognize" the feature(s) of the surrounding ambiance. As we have already observed, we carry out this function in our everyday existence pre-reflectively, or to use Husserl's terminology we perform a pre-predicative judgement. When we base our epistemology on sensory perception, a function of the body that is naturally given, and when we view it as functioning solely within the range of its natural endowment, whatever is outside of the range of its capacity to perceive is disregarded as admitting of no knowability. This is, for example, what Kant proposed in his First Critique when he recognized "sense intuition," directly connected with the sensory perception, as the sole window to the external world. In making this move, he disregarded the subtle aspects of the phenomenon of affectivity obtaining between a person qua body and his or her ambiance; for example, he left no room for the features which are revealed in samadhic awareness, that is, in Kant's case, a rejection of intellectual intuition. Moreover, he thought only of a *lateral* relationship between the sensory organs and the ambiance, by absorbing everything experiencable within the obvious and salient function of the sensory perception. Needless to say, for Kant the human body was a thing-in-itself which was denied its own knowability.

When we turn our attention to Dōgen's scheme, however, this is not the case. In our analysis of affectivity we will make certain to consider both of the qualities of affecting and being affected in a person qua body. We have seen an instance of bilateral interplay in Dōgen's statement the entire/pervasive body hears the voices, in which the interrelationship of affectivity is obtained between "the entire/pervasive body" and "the voices." The difference between the body according to Kant and the body according to Dōgen is that in Dōgen's scheme, the entire human body is capable of being affected, not simply the physical sensory organ. Moreover, we can trace "that which does the affecting" in a person qua body back to the function of *saṃskāra* as the ground of potential, formative energy out of which affecting comes forth, though its power to give rise to affecting appears only dimly to our everyday empirical ego, except in a violent eruption of emotion. Since this power is generated beneath the empirical ego, most of the time we are unaware of its origin, unless we encounter an extreme situation. Since the empirical ego is the sole performer in our everyday consciousness, our sensory perceptions are also interlaced with, and activated by, the power of affectivity coming from the potential formative energy (saṃskāra). In light of the preceding observation, the practice of just sitting is a method of transforming the manner through which this interlacing and activation of saṃskāra functions. By just sitting, the nature of affectivity is also transformed both in respect to one's body and his/her ambiance, or both in respect to affecting and being affected. This is, for example, the reason why Nyojō thought that *shinjin totsuraku*[18] meant, at least in part, to discard the five kinds of desires (related to the five sensory organs). We demonstrated how this can be achieved when we analyzed the meaning of nonthinking, and we used as our illustration, the way in which the meditator responds to sounds.

Insofar as epistemology based upon sensory perception is concerned, it would be adequate to stop at our analysis of the affectivity as it bears upon sensory perception. From Dōgen's point of view, however, this is inadequate since it does not carry us any closer to truth. One must go deeper than an analysis of affectivity as it relates to sensory perception, to the ground that supports the foundation of sensory perception. This leads us to an analysis of a special kind of affectivity, namely, the elimination of the five kinds of barriers (*gogai*). In Nyojō's understanding, this affectivity constitutes half of what he meant by *shinjin totsuraku*.[19] The five kinds of barriers mentioned here are (1) avarice (*musabori*), (2) anger (*ikari*), (3) a darkening of mind and a heaviness of the body, as in sleep (*konchin suimin*), (4) restlessness and annoyance (*tōkai*), and finally (5) doubt (*tamerai*). For the purpose of our present analysis, we can view these dark emotions collectively as negative affectivity by which is meant that all are generally inconducive to the realization of the state of being a true person.[20] Or to use Zen terminology, the negative affectivity prevents a person from showing his "original face." In light of the concept of somatic appropriation, we may say that negative affectivity is transformed into a positive force in such a way that the original face or "authentic self" is somatically appropriated. The claim here is that negative affectivity "clouds" the proper functioning of both the mind and the body, and must be eliminated. The belief that it is possible to eliminate negative affectivity is founded upon Dōgen's contention that this negative affectivity is not an essential but an "accidental" property of beings, that is "accidental dust." Moreover, this is implied in his thesis that everything undergoes generation-extinction, for nothing in his scheme has an essential property which persists through time. Also, in light of our previous observation, this is a reiteration of the practical goal of eradicating "the root of all mental functions, although the "root" in the present context is specified as "negative affectivity."

If *shinjin totsuraku* is understood according to Nyojō as the elimination of negative affectivity, we can surmise that Dōgen's own experience of casting off the body and the mind must have transformed the manner in which negative affectivity functions in his everyday existence since it relates to the somatic act of supersensory synthetic function. Since, as we observed, negative affectivity does not have its origin in the "transparency" of everyday consciousness, but rather is issued from the body, particularly from the function of the dispositional tendency with its potential formative energy (saṃskāra), the transformation which Dōgen underwent must involve the region deeper than that of the empirical ego. In order to substantiate this observation, let us cite a few interpretations of this topic offered by Dōgen commentators. Akiyama Satoko, a depth-psychologist, supports this interpretation when she argues that a partial meaning of Dōgen's confirmatory experience is to "abandon the unconscious psychological self."[21] The term, "unconscious psychological self," though it is derived from a different conceptual model than that of Dōgen, may be equated with the dispositional tendency with the potential, formative energy (saṃskāra) insofar as both do not readily surface to our everyday consciousness. Similarly, Umehara Takeshi observes that the experience in question is "a state of freedom in which one has left behind all of the human captivations (*toraware*) (or 'negativity affectivity' in our terminology) of his body and mind."[22] From Nyojō's point of view, to leave behind "All human captivations" likely means to eliminate the five kinds of desires and five kinds of barriers. In contrast, while Takahashi Masanobu recognizes Nyojō's sense of eliminating the desires and the barriers, he interprets the experience in a more restricted but more concrete sense, namely, that it involves attaining a state of freedom by casting off the dominant force which has tenaciously taken root deep in the individual mind. It is not inconsistent to view this dominant force as having some bearing with "the five kinds of desires and the five kind of barriers,"[23] since what Takahashi means by "the dominant force" is a binding "hang-up" which takes a particular configuration in each individual (i.e., habits or pattern of psychological disposition), and which prevents him from attaining a state of freedom. This interpretation reflects Nyojō's other articulation of *shinjin totsuraku*, namely, to eliminate at least one of the five kinds of desires and/or one of the five kinds of barriers.

It must be apparent from our discussion that there are significant differences in interpretations by Akiyama, Umehara and Takahashi. One camp of interpreters (Akiyama and Umehara) claims that it is the negative affectivity in its entirety which is an object of elimination, while the other (Takahashi) claims only that there is a specific negative affectivity. This difference should be interpreted as a difference in the degree to which negative affectivity can be purged through the experience of casting off the body and mind. In other words, there is a "depth" to this experience, understanding the depth to mean a power of transforming the meditator. If we take the elimination of one of the five kinds of desires or five kinds of barriers as an initial stage, we can take the total elimination of desires and barriers as the ultimate goal of the aspirant. What is certain, however, is that all three commentators mentioned above agree that Dōgen's experience of casting off the body and the mind refers to a region that is deeper than the empirical ego, and hence the transformation that occurs as a consequence of the "elimination" of negative affectivity must alter the nature of the region in which the empirical ego functions. Furthermore, we can surmise that as a result of this, fundamental change in the region of the empirical ego with respect to the act aspect of supersensory synthetic function, must undergo a transformation as well. But what does the general or the specific transformation of negative affectivity into its positive counterpart mean in relation to the act aspect of the supersensory synthetic function? And what is the epistemological implication of this transformation?

The experience of casting off the body and the mind is a somatic transformation of negative affectivity into positive affectivity. This is why, for example, satori is described most of the time as a euphoric, and even an ecstatic experience; it is "dharma bliss." In this sense, the transformation yields an unequalled level of energy which had otherwise been undiscovered and untapped in our everyday existence—a consequence of the removal of the "binding," dominant force which had taken root deep in the psyche (or broadly speaking, the mind). Once this transformation has taken place, in proportion to the extent of the transformation, the affectivity becomes charged with a power and an acuteness that otherwise would have been unknown. Sensory perception, empowered and refined by positive affectivity, becomes capable of detecting "subtleties" which had previously gone undetected. Here is one of the reasons for using the term supersensory function. The status of the external world does not change, for the stillness of samadhi "does not disturb a speck of dust, nor does it distort a phenomenon [sō],"[24] but the manner in which it appears goes through a radical modification. According to our interpretation, this occurs in the immobility of samadhic awareness because the entire/pervasive body has turned into an affective sensorium such that it knows no limits of its lived space.

At the same time, through the transformation of negative affectivity into positive affectivity, the empirical ego is released from the "bonds" which had unknowingly constrained the meditator's sense of self and circumscribed his/her frame of reference. The energy which wells up from the depths of his/her being shatters the high ground of the empirical ego. And the empirical ego, to use Deutsch's terminology, becomes "unbound,"[25] it has "emptied" itself. In thus becoming unbound, the empirical ego realizes that the selectivity operative in everyday perception, is all too human; it is no longer a selectivity infested with, and motivated by, the ego-desire. It enters into the domain of objectivity—an objectivity which has been achieved through the eradication of subjectivity. Once he is unbound, the person qua body has a lived feeling of spatial spread and permeation, from which a somatic act shoots out as an instance of supersensory synthetic function in judgement via an attunement.

In order to see how this somatic act characterizes the mode of judgement which obtains in the experience of casting off the body and the mind, we shall now refer ourselves to an analysis of the felt inter-resonance.

FELT INTER-RESONANCE

Tamaki notes insightfully that the experience of casting off the body and mind is an instance of what I rendered here as the felt inter-resonance.[26] Using Tamaki's observation as a point of departure, then, we will analyze the experiential meaning of the felt inter-resonance with a view to bringing out more clearly the sense of somatic act which forms, as I contend, a mode of judgement via an attunement in samadhic awareness. The corresponding Japanese term for felt inter-resonance is *kannō dōkō,* which is made up of the four characters, *kan* (feeling) + *nō* (response) + *dō* (paths) + *kō* (to intersect). The rendition for this Japanese term as felt inter-resonance is purposely epistemological, as well as phenomenological. Both of these terms, "epistemological" and "phenomenological," should be understood in the broadest sense as designating a description obtaining in samadhic awareness. This approach is guided by our overriding concern, namely, to elucidate the epistemological perspective brought forth by means of somatic transformations via the practice of just sitting.

Traditionally, the term, *kannō dōkō,* has been given an ontological interpretation. For example, in *Dōgen: Meicho,* Tamaki explains that the term means "an intersectioning of paths between the feeling of sentient beings and buddhas' response," in which there is said to be an interpenetration between the self's existential ground and the Buddha that is transcendent (*chōetsusha taru hotoke*).[27] Since Tamaki does not clarify what he means by "transcendent," we shall take the liberty of interpreting this term in two senses: first, in the sense of being outside of, and going beyond our everyday consciousness, and secondly, in the sense of designating the things external to this consciousness, namely, the shaped things, abundant and invigorating in the natural world. When applied to Tamaki's explanation, the first sense of the term suggests that that which is transcendent does not appear to everyday consciousness which has not been transformed into samadhic awareness via a process of just sitting. In turn, this means that it does appear, however, to samadhic awareness, and therefore, from the elevated perspective of samadhic awareness, what is experienced to be transcendent in everyday consciousness can no longer be regarded as transcendent. It follows from this that once samadhic awareness is in effect, the second sense of the term also requires a redefinition, for the manner in which the shaped things in the natural world relate themselves to samadhic awareness is believed to be significantly altered. In order to capture this sense of modification, I propose to render the term, *kannō dōkō*, as felt inter-resonance. For the purposes of our interpretation, this translation is advantageous, since it casts in clear relief the characteristics of affectivity obtaining between the somatic act and the natural world, which will enable us to specify in more concrete terms a mode of judgement via an attunement. If this approach is on track, an "ontological" interpretation of the experience of *kannō dōkō* should also be implied.

With this preliminary interpretation of *kannō dōkō* we shall now turn our attention to Dōgen's experiential account of what we call the felt inter-resonance. Describing a lived feeling in samadhic awareness, Dōgen writes:

> If a person sits properly in samadhi even for a time, with the three karmic activities [of intention, speech, and action] imprinted in the buddha-seal, the entire dharma-world all becomes buddha-sealed, and the entire space becomes exhaustively satori.[28]

The three basic karmic activities of intention, speech, and action characterize in a Buddhist view the basic mode of being a person as he/she relates himself/herself to the other beings and things of the world. When these basic activities become commensurate with those of buddhas, that is, a melding of experience in which the meditator immediately realizes himself/herself, this realization, it is claimed, extends to beings other than the self and extends its influence to those other beings. In Dōgen's own words, "the entire space exhaustively becomes satori." For him to assert this, there must be a lived feeling within a meditator's body-image that reveals that his/her inner world envelops and extends to the entire space, the world of shaped things, with the intrinsic qualities of this lived feeling fulfilling the gap between them. Such a world is bright and shining. When this occurs, the meditator feels that "a subtle, intimate path of mutual assistance"[29] is established between the beings in the natural world and himself or herself, which is something totally other than the way in which the shaped things had appeared before. Moreover, this lived feeling has nothing to do with the meditator's own intentional perception because it occurs in "the stillness of samādhi [and] beyond [human] fabrication."[30] That is, the meditator has somatically appropriated the mind that opposes the working of the body, and the act aspect of supersensory synthetic function has become a somatic act. Hence, there is no fabrication on the meditator's part: he/she simply feels wondrous and blissful. According to Dōgen, this lived feeling is not restricted to a spatial spread but also includes all temporalities. He writes:

> Even though sitting in *zazen* involves just one person for a time, it performs buddhas' teachings and offers his guidance all of the time, throughout past, present, and future in an inexhaustible dharma-world, since it *subtly intermingles* with a myriad of dharmas and is perfectly in touch with all temporalities.[31] (emphasis added)

The lived feeling of spatial spread as well as "being in touch with all temporalities" is due to the meditator's lived feeling of "subtly intermingling with a myriad of dharmas." This "subtlety" refers to a dynamic moment concurrent with an arousal of feeling which usually escapes our notice. Moreover, this subtlety is closely tied to mastering the rhythm of breathing. The "subtle intermingling with a myriad of dharmas" may, therefore, be interpreted as follows. The breathing during meditation establishes a certain relation between the meditator and the natural world through its incoming and outgoing psychophysical energy or vital breath [*ki*].[32] The vital breath comes in from the natural world and it returns to the natural world from the meditator. When meditation deepens, this bilateral exchange between the meditator and the natural world creates a harmonic rhythm and a rhythmic harmony through "a subtle, intimate path of mutual assistance." When this interdependence is lived, the meditator can be said to have entered into a consummate state of meditation, perhaps identical with what Dōgen calls the immobile sitting, in which the meditator is said to "think of not-thinking." An experiential correlate accompanying this consummate state is an awareness on the part of the meditator that he/she is passively enabled to breathe instead of an awareness that he/she is an active agent performing breathing. Think of not-thinking, as we have observed, goes beyond "the measure of thinking," although it does not exclude it. The immobile sitting goes beyond the measure of thinking, precisely because a subtle, intimate path of mutual assistance is created independent of the measure of thinking.

When this consummate state of meditation is firmly established, an "inter-resonance" emerges in the invigorating lives between the meditator and the shaped things of the natural world. The meditator qua body is attuned to the natural world through a complete consummation of the somatic appropriation. Once this inter-resonance is achieved, the shaped things, either sentient or insentient, begin to present themselves to samadhic awareness as being intimate with the being of the meditator. Hence, Dōgen observes:

> At such a time, the land, the trees and the blades of grass, the walls and fences, the tiles and the pebbles in the dharma-world of ten directions all perform the work of buddhas.... Those *co-habitating* with them, and speaking *the same language*, are mutually endowed with the limitless buddha efficacies.[33] (emphases added)

That is, there emerges a sense of complete inter-resonance—a bilaterality between the meditator and the natural world in which they are mutually responsive to each other. The meditator has achieved an affective state to such an extent that he/she feels that the shaped things in the natural world are no longer foreign to him/her, for he/she realizes that he/she has been intimately "co-habitating with," and "speaking the same language" as the shaped things in the natural world. "Co-habitation" may be taken as a description of the meditator's intimate "being-in" the natural world, while speaking the same language refers, among other things, to his/her acquisition of a natural rhythmic, vital breath, through which the insentient beings (which includes the entire range of organic, vegetative life in Buddhism) express themselves. It is the *resonance* of this vital breath that becomes the means of communication, since the root of all languages is grounded in the resonance of vital breath, a psychophysical energy. Elsewhere, Dōgen states:

> A language of the total lands is intimate with...the mind, and the words; it is closely intimate with them, without any fissure.[34]

In light of this explanation, the statement we observed previously becomes intelligible: the insentient beings are capable of hearing the insentient beings preaching dharmas. Since the meditator has acquired the same language as the insentient beings, he/she can comprehend and appreciate their "speech," which is filled with the invigorating energy of life.

These two lived feelings, co-habitating with the insentient beings, and speaking the same language, give rise to a bilaterally intimate feeling which, Dōgen believes, is unified by features of the lived experience in deep samadhic awareness. He writes:

> If you sincerely practice [just sitting], putting the four elements and five aggregates in full operation, you will attain the way. If you sincerely practice, putting the trees and blades of grass, the walls and fences in their full motions, you will attain the way. For "the four elements and five aggregates" and "the trees and the blades of grass, and the walls and fences" participate in the *same* [practice], sharing the same nature [*dōsei*]. They share the same mind and life, [*dōshin dōmei*] and the same body and momenta [*dōshin dōki*].[35]

Attaining to the way in Zen Buddhism is equivalent to attaining satori; it is a realization of buddhahood. Therefore, the "sameness" between a person qua body and the insentient beings with respect to their body, mind, life, nature and momenta refers to the concept of "buddha-nature"; a bright pervasive force or energy which a Buddhist believes is present in each and every being in the world. Dōgen says, "seeing the mountains and rivers are seeing the buddha-nature."[36] Accordingly, the body, mind, life, nature and momenta come to be characterized in terms of buddhahood as bearing the seal of buddha-nature. They are buddha-body, buddha-mind, and so on. These elements are characterized by a single unifying concept of buddha-nature, for Dōgen held a firm belief in the "right buddha dharma." Moreover, this buddha-nature acted as the frame of reference for Dōgen's philosophical-religious experience, and he practiced accordingly. During the early stages of the process in which just sitting is cultivated, Dōgen must have had a series of hallucinatory experiences of a buddha-image appearing before him. For Dōgen, it was a natural connection to make between the buddha-nature and the elements of body, mind, life, nature and momenta, and therefore, he characterizes these elements in terms of it.

We may detect a "metaphysical" or an ontological overtone in the way in which Dōgen identifies a sameness in both the human being qua body and the insentient beings with respect to their mind, body, life, momenta, and nature. Indeed, Dōgen's language easily lends itself to a metaphysical interpretation. For example, we can argue that, since a sameness exists in the human being qua body and the insentient beings, and this sameness grounds their beings metaphysically, there is in essence no difference between them. If we remove the term metaphysical from this characterization, it is not intrinsically in disagreement with Dōgen's own understanding. That is, if we continue to assume as we have throughout this chapter, that this sameness is a lived feeling derived from a deep meditative state vis-à-vis a felt inter-resonance, it is evident that the term metaphysical, meaning "going beyond physis," is inappropriate to describe the sameness which is said to exist between the human body qua body and the insentient beings. However, if it is necessary to linguistically identify this sameness, we may use Yuasa's terminology, and call it metapsychical, since the sameness of mind, body, life, momenta and nature are disclosed in a deep meditative experience of casting off the (everyday sense of) the body and the mind.

Having briefly examined Dōgen's experiential account of felt inter-resonance, we are now in a position to articulate characteristics of the somatic act which give rise to the experience of felt inter-resonance.

THE SOMATIC ACT

As we have demonstrated, the experience of casting off the body and the mind transforms the negative affectivity to a positive one. As a consequence of this transformation, the entire body pervasively becomes an affective sensorium in the paramount sense of the term, and this is simultaneously accompanied by a transformation of the body-image. The body-image that we have in our everyday existence is lived from within the boundary of the skin. In the process of transformation that occurs through casting off the body and the mind, this body-image is changed into a lived feeling which expands beyond the physical delineation of the skin to embrace the shaped things of the natural world. A somatic act is an act that is issued from this transformed image of one's body, from the body as an affective sensorium. Accordingly, a "vector" of the somatic act expands in proportion to the depth of the somatic transformation which accrues a positive affectivity.

Through a somatic transformation, the somatic act is charged with the positive affectivity, and this positive affectivity yields a powerful, yet subtle energy that is generated in the depths of the empirical ego. Moreover, this energy influences the incoming and outgoing vital breath or psychophysical energy, by bringing it into harmony. The movement of the incoming and outgoing vital breath is bilateral, and moves from the person qua body to the natural world, and vice versa. An intrinsic feature of the somatic act, then, is charged with the energy of harmonization, and this energy we have termed the power of attunement. Accordingly, the somatic act functions in proportion to the degree to which it is endowed with the power of attunement. This was the meaning of depth, and consequently, the depth of the experience is a measure of the degree of this attunement.

The attuning power that is present in the somatic act is generated by the bilateral movement of the incoming and outgoing vital breath that joins the person qua body with the natural world. Through this bilateral movement, a certain affectivity is established between the person qua body and the natural world. This affectivity we have termed the felt inter-resonance, and the experience of felt inter-resonance owes its genesis to the transformed body-image which accompanies a heightened, positive affectivity. The concept of affectivity is bilateral and constituted by the momenta of affecting and being affected. This may be interpreted that when affectivity obtains, there is an exchange of the respective qualities or features between that which is affecting and that which is being affected. Moreover, affectivity takes place only when what is affecting and what is being affected share, in some sense, *common* qualities or features. This is a logical requirement for the affective experience to obtain. The somatic act as affecting reaches the shaped things in the natural world and a target of a somatic act in the natural world is in turn felt to reach the depth of being, that is, a somatic act as being affected.

In this respect, the somatic act is a supersensory synthetic function, which relates a person qua body to the natural world, and the somatic act is a basic connecting link between them. Being a synthetic function, it may also be considered an act of judgement. However, this judgement does not originate in cogito or in the empirical ego. For this reason, if we understand the "intentional" to mean that an act is issued from cogito or the empirical ego, it is not intentional in character. Rather, the somatic act has its origin of function in the depth of empirical ego, in the somaticity of a person. Accordingly, the "act" is said to be somatic. The term, depth, as it is used in the phrase, "the depth of empirical ego," is employed in order to suggest a dimension of awareness which is brought forth by means of somatic transformations via the practice of just sitting.

CHAPTER 7

Dōgen and the Body in Action

INTRODUCTION

We have seen in the preceding chapter an example of an epistemological perspective obtaining through a somatic act which in turn is achieved by somatic transformations. We have characterized the phenomenon appearing through this transformation as "felt inter-resonance." But, if we were to conclude our analysis of Dōgen's philosophy without exploring its practical application to the external world particularly in terms of action, we might give the impression that what we have been discussing in the previous three chapters is an instance of "Oriental Quietism" in that whatever Dōgen has to offer is confined to the interiority of a meditative self and is, therefore, irrelevant to the more practical concern of actionally relating oneself to the world. In order to dispel this kind of mistaken evaluation, we now turn to an analysis, first, of the world as it appears to Dōgen from the perspective of felt inter-resonance, or rather to an analysis of the way in which he characterizes the natural world by means of this perspective. This will, then, prepare us to understand how the body in action is characterized through Dōgen's perspective of felt inter-resonance in interaction with the world. This discussion will serve to bring the concept of somatic act out of the domain of meditation, that is, a samadhic awareness, into the domain of samadhic action, where the samadhic action designates action performed through samadhic awareness.

DŌGEN'S IDENTIFICATION OF MIND WITH OBJECTS

There is a common, intellectual belief (*doxa*) that the mind is immaterial while the body is material with a tendency to view

155

the former as being superior to the latter, but Dōgen maintains that the mind *is* the objects (mostly natural objects).[1] Although this contention is derived from a larger position he maintains concerning the oneness of the body and the mind, what does Dōgen means when he says that the mind is the objects? Logically there seems to be two interpretations we can offer to Dōgen's identification of the mind with the object: (1) to absorb the mind within the object, which is a (naive) realist and empiricist position (and by extension, materialist position as well), or (2) to absorb the object within the mind, which is a subjective idealist position. Let us first briefly examine the implications of these two positions.

If we interpret Dōgen's statement that the mind is the object according to the first interpretation, namely, that the object absorbs the mind, is Dōgen contending that since the human living body is a synthetic unity between the material and the immaterial, the material part of our human body is identical with, or the same as, the materiality of the body? If so, the sense of identity or sameness between the mind and the physical object is maintained vis-à-vis the materiality of the body. In this case, is Dōgen contending that the identify between the mind and the physical object is of numerical and quantitative identity? However, if we follow this interpretation, the mind is left out of this equation, or is reduced to the material. Obviously this is not what Dōgen means when he maintains that the mind is the objects. On the other hand, if we interpret Dōgen's statement that the mind is the object in the sense that the mind absorbs the object, the materiality of an object is left out of consideration, and simply becomes an object of mind. This interpretation does not recognize the objective status of an object. It is not what Dōgen means by "mountains, rivers, and lands," either. When we reject these two interpretations, what other interpretations are there to understand Dōgen's contention that the mind is the objects? What does he means by the identification between the mind and the objects? In order to respond these questions, we must analyze the experiential basis that enabled Dōgen to make this identification.

In order to account for the experiential basis of Dōgen's identification of the mind with the objects, we must be clear about the meaning of the terms which are identified. We shall begin our analysis by first examining Dōgen's concept of objects, and then his concept of mind, after which we explore the meaning of, and the experiential basis for, Dōgen's identification of mind with objects.

What then does Dōgen means by mountains, rivers, and lands, or in short, what is ordinarily considered to be objects. He states:

> Those things, such as mountains, rivers, and lands, are neither being nor nonbeing, neither small nor big. They are not [the objects of] attainment nor [the objects of] non-attainment, neither knowledge nor non-knowledge. They do not change in satori or in non-satori.[2]

Although Dōgen urges us to accept this position with a resolute faith in "studying the way through one's mind,"[3] for our purpose here we might venture a philosophical exposition aided by the results of the previous three chapters. We might attempt to understand the position, advanced in the foregoing quote, against the background of Dōgen's major belief in constant generation-extinction, whose force claims everything that is, and examine how objects are understood in the context of this generation-extinction. An example of Dōgen's idea about generation-extinction is found in the following:

> In personally studying the coming and going, there is a life and a death in going as well as in coming. There is coming and going in birth as well as in death. Coming and going fly away, and fly in, using the total world as their wings. The total world *qua* true human body transforms one's body well by turning the brain, with life and death as its head and tail.[4] (emphasis added)

When the whole world is characterized as embodying the characteristics of an incessant coming and going, such a world assumes a dynamic character. This dynamism, when translated into human terms, acquires actional, practical character because practical knowledge is gained by actionally engaging the object. This leads Dōgen to assume an agnostic attitude towards objects, which is expressed in the foregoing quote as: "the mountains, rivers and lands" are "neither knowledge nor nonknowledge." This is so, Dōgen argues, because they are "neither being nor non-being, neither small nor big." They arise as a consequence of the fabrication of human mind, which prevents the objects from announcing themselves in their own right. Dōgen cautions to those who may think that the status of object thus recognized may change after having a satori or an enlightenment. He states: "They are not [the objects of] attainment nor [the objects of] non-attainment. They do not change in satori or in non-satori."

Therefore, for now, I propose to understand Dōgen's agnostic attitude toward the objects as predicated on the assumption that the value of these objects lies in their being actionally engaged by a somatic act. Dōgen's rejection of being and nonbeing and his rejection of the knowability of being in respect to mountains, rivers, and lands, is based upon, and stated from, the standpoint of "emptiness" (kū). According to this standpoint, nothing in the world has a substantial self-nature which persists through temporal change. Particular objects acquire a *seeming* ontic status, and therefore the knowledge which we can have of them is only a seeming (practical) knowledge, because particular objects are ephemeral, generated from the vast and complex matrix of the conditioning process of generation-extinction. For this reason, the standpoint of emptiness goes hand in hand with the thesis of generation-extinction. Consequently, when objects are understood in the light of generation-extinction, they are not substantial entities maintaining their identities through time. If they are not substantial entities, that is, neither being nor nonbeing, it follows that they are not the objects of *theoretical* knowledge either, since for an object to be known in toto, it must be given to us exhaustively, for example, both in its temporal and spatial dimensions.[5] But a possibility for such a knowledge remains simply a construct, or at best a methodological stance. If we accept this interpretation, it does not follows, however, that Dōgen is also denying the knowability of objects in terms of its practical utility.

In the context in which we have been discussing Dōgen's philosophy, his understanding of the concept of the mind includes, among other things, a thinking function, an emotive/affective function, and a remembering function. This understanding is based upon the functions of the mind, much as Plato understood the "mind" in terms of its various "faculties." Furthermore,

Dōgen mentions various attitudes of mind which are developed in the course of achieving the experience of felt inter-resonance (*kannō dōkō*), such as the mind aspiring to the unexcelled, perfect knowledge, (*hotsubodai shin*), the mind of the past buddhas (*kobutsu shin*), the mind uncovered (*shaku shin*), the everyday mind (*heijō shin*) and the mind as it is understood in the phrase "triple world is one mind."[6]

Judging from the fact that Dōgen mentions the experience of felt inter-resonance in this connection,[7] the concept of the mind which enables him to make an identification with the objects is believed to be grounded in the experience of felt inter-resonance. Let us see how this interpretation bears out. Dōgen observes:

> Clearly bear in mind: what is called "mind" [*shin*] is the mountains, rivers, lands, and the sun, the moon and the stars. However, if you carry this statement one step further, it becomes inadequate. If [on the other hand] you stop short of it, it becomes excessive. The mind *qua* mountains, rivers, and lands is mountains, rivers and lands.[8]

The obvious difficulty in attempting to interpret the above passage comes in understanding the experiential basis upon which Dōgen identifies the mind with mountains, rivers, and lands, and so on, or more generally, identifies the mind with particular objects existing in the natural world. Dōgen advances two rather cryptic arguments in order to support his position; (1) a rejection of the (naive) realist and empiricist position (and by extension the materialist position as well). This is argued as "if you carry this statement [i.e., the identification of the mind with objects] one step further, it becomes inadequate," and (2) a rejection of the subjective idealist position. This position is formulated as "If [on the other hand] you stop short of it [i.e., the identification of the mind with objects], it becomes excessive." By rejecting these two positions, Dōgen attempts to establish that the particular object *qua* mind finally becomes simply particular object as he states, "The mind *qua* mountains, rivers, and lands is mountains, rivers and lands." This position is entailed by the fact that the mind becomes empty, or to put it epistemologically, it becomes exhaustively transparent. When it becomes empty of the subjective, ego-constitution of an object, the object in turn presences itself in toto in its pristine condition. That was, for example, the meaning and the consequence of "casting off the mind," or more positively, it was the meaning of "samadhi of oceanic reflection" where the mind is likened to a crystal clear mirror without distorting the objects which are reflected on it.

Now, let us interpret the above observation directly in light of the experience of felt inter-resonance. In this lived experience of samadhic awareness, the empty mind resonates with a particular object. In order for this to occur, there must be a bilateral interplay between the mind and the particular object engaged by the former. This bilaterality is actionally realized through the somatic act, an act requisite for obtaining the experience of felt inter-resonance. It is accomplished, among other things, through the externalization of the mind vis-à-vis the expansion of the body-image accompanying the samadhic awareness, where the mind is empty of any discriminatory positing act. As we recall, the object-body is appropriated within the subject-body in this expansion of body-image, where a somatic field is created. In this somatic field, there is a felt inter-resonance between the mind qua the samadhic awareness and the object engaged by the latter. This suggests that the object becomes enveloped vis-à-vis the expansion of body-image pertinent to a given somatic field. When this enveloping takes place, the object which otherwise stands, because of its materiality, opposed to the mind is incorporated within the somatic field of the samadhic awareness. When this incorporation takes place, the materiality of the object does not present the barrier for samadhic awareness to become resonant with the *raison d'être* of an given object. When this occurs, the materiality of an object recedes into the background of samadhic awareness, and is transformed into an animating and animated object within this awareness. Here we witness an echo of animism in Dōgen's experiential background.

The mind experienced from this standpoint may best be characterized by the descriptive term, "total or exhaustive transparency." The use of this term is suggested by the experiential statement: "The total world in ten direction is one transparent pearl [*ikkamyōju*]"[9] since "nothing is concealed in the total world."[10] In order for Dōgen to predicate "the total world" with "one transparent pearl," the experiential ground assumes the state of exhaustive transparency. Moreover, in the experience of felt inter-resonance, there is an intimate affectivity; as the somatic act engages objects, it intimately relates itself to them, because "there is no obstruction" in the act.[11] Because there is no obstruction, the objects that are engaged by it surrender themselves in toto and in pristine condition to the act. This is understandable only if we presuppose that an object recedes into the background of samadhic awareness, and is transformed into an animating and animated object within this awareness.

According to our interpretation, the characterization of Dōgen's concept of the mind as total or exhaustive transparency, is actional and bilaterally relational, or in other words, it is at once mind qua objects and the objects qua mind where there occurs an interfusion or interpermeation of animating energy, which arises as an instance of felt inter-resonance between them. The mind and the objects both gain their respective values by actionally relating to each other. There is no axiological difference between the mind and the object. Neither can, for example, escape the working of generation-extinction, or in human terms, life-death.

We have some indication of the above mentioned bilateral reciprocity when we find Dōgen describing the relationship between the total world and the self as a dynamic, incessant activity. He writes:

> The total world in ten directions is incessant activity in which chasing things becomes a self [*jiko*], and chasing a self becomes things [*mono*]... Since chasing things becomes a self, the total world in ten directions is incessant activity.[12]

This bilateral reciprocity between the self and the things is also applicable to the relationship between the mind and the objects, when we understand the self to be an integrative function of the mind. However, from Dōgen's perspective it would be a mistake to limit this bilateral relation *merely* to noesis-noema with its phenomenological correlativity, a correlativity between a noetic act and its corresponding noema. We have emphasized the word merely in the preceding sentence in order to indicate that Dōgen does not exclude from his understanding of objects the realization that objects are *analyzable* as noematic contents, for he states that "Coming and going are simply one or two thoughts [nen]. One or two thoughts are mountains, rivers, and lands."[13] Even though objects in the natural world are analyzable in this manner, they are not exhausted by the analysis.

As a matter of fact, Dōgen's concept of the mind is more comprehensive than the act of the mind itself. This is evident from Dōgen's comment upon the Zen dialogue between Nandai and Kayashata regarding how to understand the tinkling sounds of a bell.[14] Upon hearing the bell tinkled, Nandai asked Kayashata: "Is it the wind that tinkled or is it the bell which tinkled?" Kayashata responded: "It was neither the wind nor the bell, rather it was my mind which tinkled." Commenting on this dialogue, Dōgen rejects both positions as indication of "erroneous understanding." He says:

> Kayashata states, "It was neither the wind nor the bell [that tinkled], rather it was my mind which tinkled." At the very moment when there is an act of hearing, there is a generation of thought, and he took this generation to be mind. How could the resonance of a bell be occasioned without the mind thinking? Since hearing takes place due to this act of thought, which must be essential for hearing, Kayashata uttered "[My] mind tinkled." This is an erroneous understanding.[15]

In the fascicle cited here, Dōgen does not offer his own understanding of the problem, but elsewhere he states:

> You should not understand that there is no benefit in hearing dharmas unless it is *occasioned* by a discriminatory conscious mind [shin ishiki]. Those whose minds become extinguished and their body extinguished should receive the benefit of hearing dharmas. Those who have no-mind and no-body ought to receive the benefit of hearing dharmas. All buddhas and patriarchs have experienced these [different] temporal occasions, and have become buddhas and patriarchs.[16] (emphasis added)

Dōgen's reference to the act of "hearing dharmas with no-mind and no-body" carries the same meaning as the experience of "casting off the body and mind," or attaining nirvana which forms, according to our interpretation, a somatic act generative of the experience of felt inter-resonance.

As we have seen, what Dōgen rejects is, generally speaking, a subjective idealist position (e.g., Berkeley, Kant, and Husserl), which Dōgen argues is "excessive." He says "If you stop short of it (i.e., the identification of the mind with objects), it becomes excessive." According to our interpretation, what is criticized as excessive is due to the fact that the subjective idealist position "absorbs" everything within the mind, within its subjectivity. Take the example of Kant; he schematized the functions of the mind neatly using transcendental categories, but in so doing, he ignored the fluid bilaterality, mostly via affectivity, between a bearer of experience and the objects, and as a consequence, fossilized the bearer of the experience. Along with this, the subjective idealist position does not take into account how the mind functions in bodily action. Of the three critiques Kant wrote, one deals with "pure reason" while the other deals with "practical reason," methodology that borrows from the Greeks two separate methods of investigation, *theōria* and prāxis, in which the former always take precedence over the latter.[17]

This separation of theōria and prāxis also applies to a naive realist position. Referring to the identification of the mind with the objects, Dōgen criticizes the realist, arguing: "If you carry this statement one step further, it becomes inadequate." By using the word, "inadequate," Dōgen is perhaps suggesting that the naive realist position does not recognize an actional involvement of the mind, designating a reality solely to the objects themselves. The epistemological subject here is the one who sits comfortably in his "armchair" passively observing the objects external to him. This criticism of the realist's position seems to follow also from Dōgen's concept of the mind as actionally bilateral. Dōgen asks us to reflect upon the working of our minds:

> Is it [i.e., the mind] inside or outside? Is it coming or going? At the time of birth (or generations), does it increase a point or does it decrease? At the time of death (or extinction), does one speck of dust disappear or does it not? Where are you to place [the ground of] generation-extinction and the views concerning it?[18]

The last rhetorical question anticipates the answer "no-where," and to the rest of the preceding questions, Dōgen expects us to answer "neither." What is of particular relevance to our present analysis is the first question: "Is it [i.e., the mind] inside or outside?" Inside and outside correspond respectively to the subjective idealist position and to the (naive) realist position (and by extension, empiricist and materialist). Yet, for Dōgen to conceive of the mind as either "inside" or "outside," as we have just seen, is an extreme position which lacks a proper understanding of how the mind functions. Dōgen conceives of the mind as a total transparency, and when it engages objects, these objects become actionally transparent as well, since its engagement is performed by a somatic act generative of the experience of felt inter-resonance.

However, when mind qua objects is actionally engaged, Dōgen claims that it becomes simply the objects themselves. He makes this point as follows:

> In addition to this [i.e., the mind qua the mountains, rivers, etc.], there is no "triple world is only one mind," nor is there "dharma-world is simply a mind." They are simply the walls, the fences, the tiles and the pebbles.[19]

This position appears to echo the position shared by the empiricist position, namely to relegate reality solely to the objects. But Dōgen has already rejected this position. What we must recognize in Dōgen's position is that there is a transformation of the mind into no-mind, or empty mind. In other words, the transition from the mind qua objects to mere objects indicates a transition from a meditational posture to an acting posture. In the meditational posture, the object engaged by such a mind is transparently revealed without the fabrication of the ego-constitution of the mind. The intrinsic act itself is identical between the meditational posture and actional posture, because it is the somatic act that runs through both the meditational posture and the acting posture. When the somatic act is actional, the mind qua objects becomes the *actional* objects, not the objects of cognition, but the objects of being "played at." In this context, somatic act may be understood to be an embodiment of "samadhi-at-play," that is, a samadhic awareness realized in samadhic actions.

A TRUE HUMAN BODY

In the preceding section, we have interpreted Dōgen's identification of the mind with the particular objects of the natural world, and in so doing, we have had a glimpse of how the somatic act as an epistemological concept can also function as an actional concept. In short, this glimpse revealed to us the fact that the somatic act is not merely epistemological, but is also actional in character. Implicit in understanding the concept of the somatic act in this manner, then, is the idea that what is primarily considered to be "epistemological" is rooted in the function of the body, and this function which we have termed the "somatic act," is an active integrator in the process of knowing pragmatically. In any case, our move from the somatic act as epistemological to the somatic act as actional corresponds to the shifting of our perspective from the meditational posture to the acting posture. In the present section, we shall discover that the bearer of the somatic act in both senses of the term as we have defined them above, is what Dōgen calls the "true human body" (*shinjitsu nintai*). In so doing, we shall point out a few essential characteristics of the concept of the true human body, namely, (1) a presencing, and (2) a total functioning.

According to our interpretation, Dōgen's contention is that the body which is naturally given to us at birth and grows biologically toward death is not a true human body. Dōgen conceives of the true human body as achieved, or appropriated through "studying the way." He writes:

> Studying the way through the body is to study the way with one's body. It is studying the way with the raw chunk of meat. The body comes from studying the way. When [the body] comes from [studying] the way, it becomes the true human body [*shinjitsu nintai*].[20]

Generally speaking, the concept of the true human body may be understood to be the body that has been transformed through personal self-cultivation, which is a type of habit-formation, and which is accompanied by a change in the body-image, since the nature of the body-image is shaped by the kind of training or cultivation that one goes through. Specifically, as we have observed, this personal self-cultivation meant for Dōgen the practice of just sitting. He states that the true human body is achieved through studying the way, and it is important that we recognize that the concept of the true human body is a practical, existential consequence of the experience of casting off the body and the mind, and of the process of "deepening" which accompanies it. Accordingly, we can identify the concept of the true human body as a concept that emerges primarily from the process of "the extinction of the four elements and five aggregates," a negative working of which Dōgen initially accepted as the concept of the human body.

A qualification of the term "human body" by means of the adjective, "true," must be understood as obtained after the initial experience of somatic transformations, primarily the transformation that occurs as a result of what we termed "negative affectivity" in the preceding chapter. Dōgen states:

> You will twirl and accommodate the *extinguished* four elements and five aggregates as your eyes and your hands. On this track [of extinction], you will make progress and will encounter [buddhas] with the *extinguished* four elements and five aggregates. At such a time, it is inadequate to say that one's pervasive body [*tsūshin*] has turned into eyes and hands. It is still inadequate to say that one's entire body [*henshin*] has turned into eyes and hands.[21] (emphases added)

The linguistic expression of the experience of casting off the body and the mind is negative in a sense, since the phrase does not concern itself with *what* one acquires after this experience has taken place. In the above passage, however, Dōgen supplies this missing element: "twirling and accommodating the eyes and the hands." The term, "accommodation," may be reinterpreted as somatic appropriation, and "twirling" as a utilization of the somatically appropriated body. Corresponding to "somatic appropriation" and its utilization is the symbolic use of the terms "eyes" and "hands." Of the five sensory organs, the eyes are the most acute in their discrimination, and they are often used in Buddhism metaphorically to describe the highest form of wisdom such as "buddha-eye" and "heavenly eye." Conversely, hands are the most mobile in the limbic system. We can interpret eyes and hands accordingly, as parts of the body which symbolically designate the consummation of both the intellective and the somatic capacities of a person. Dōgen characterizes a person who possesses these qualities as a person in whom "both practice and understanding correspond to each other." In this context, the term, "consummation" may be understood to refer to the pervasive function of the somatic act in which there is "nondependence" and "nonopposition."

These two terms nondependence, and nonopposition, may now be understood to describe the intrinsic tendency of the somatic act, and this use expands upon our application of the terms to designate the relationship between noematic contents. In fact, our earlier interpretation of nondependence and nonopposition as noematic content in samadhic awareness is made possible only if we presuppose that the somatic act is operative in samadhic awareness, since in order for an attunement to obtain via somatic act, there cannot be "dependence" or "opposition" between the terms of attunement.

With this understanding of twirling and accommodating the eyes and the hands, Dōgen claims that when a certain level of satori is attained, "it is inadequate to say that one's entire body [*henshin*] has turned into eyes and hands," much less that "one's pervasive body" [*tsūshin*] has similarly been transformed. Previously, we interpreted the statement twirling and accommodating the eyes and the hands to mean an expansion of the body-image. Among other things, Dōgen seems to be suggesting that a mere expansion of the body-image is "inadequate" unless it is put into action. Consequently, Dōgen's term, "inadequacy," may be understood as referring to the absence of an "acting posture," which demands a move from the meditational posture. To use Dōgen's terminology, this requires one to enter into "the invigorating path of leaping out of the body."[22] This interpretation of shifting from a meditational posture to an acting posture may be further substantiated when we recall Dōgen's criticism of both the subjective idealist position and the (naive) realist position in placing the mind, respectively, inside and outside.

Along with his criticism of these positions, Dōgen rejects the attitude of Zen meditation which places its emphasis on "pointing to man's mind," and "becoming a buddha by looking into one's nature": he argues that "In these statements, there is no invigorating path of leaping out of the body nor is there a disciplined pervasive body."[23] Apart from the obvious reason that Buddhism does not maintain that there is such a thing as persisting self-nature, the reason why Dōgen criticizes these statements is that the meditator confines himself to the interiority of the self, and does not actionally demonstrate the efficacies of satori or an enlightenment. If we are accurate in our preceding observation, then we have established a rationale from which we can contend that the true human body is, indeed, a bearer of the somatic act. In this connection, we must be careful to point out that when the intrinsic tendency of nondependence and nonopposition is translated into actional terms, which characterizes the true human body as a bearer of somatic act, it becomes nonobstruction. That is, in its operation the somatic act carries an intrinsic power to assimilate what is presented to it; it has the power to carry everything into the harmony that is achieved in the somatic act in its meditational posture. Dōgen states that, among other things, this intrinsic tendency to nonobstruction forms the closely interwoven fabric that makes up the concepts of the "transparent world," the true human body, and the "total body." He states it as follows;

> The total world in ten directions is one transparent pearl [*ikka myoju*]... The total body [*zenshin*] is a pair of right dharma eyes. The total body is a true human body. The total body is one word. It is transparently illuminating. The total body is the total mind [*zenshin*]. When one is a total body, there is no obstruction for it; it is graciously smooth and tumbles [freely].[24] (emphasis added)

In this passage, Dōgen provides a series of identifications among one transparent pearl, the total world, the total mind, the total body, and a true human body. Unless we first have a clear understanding of what Dōgen means by these identifications, we cannot hope to go beyond a simple comparison. What remains particularly obscure is the idea of actional freedom, expressed by the last statement of the quotation: "When one is a total body, there is no obstruction for it; it is graciously smooth and tumbles [freely]."

Dōgen's claim is that there is no essential difference among these various *designata*. In order for Dōgen's claim to be a valid one, there must be an experiential ground in the same way that it was necessary for his identification of the mind with the particular objects in the world. However, it should be evident from our foregoing analysis of the experience of felt inter-resonance that these identifications are made in view of this felt experience. Assuming that our analysis has demonstrated satisfactorily that this experience underlies the ground for these identifications, we shall indicate briefly the nature of their interconnection.

The transparency of the total world is grounded in the appropriation of "right dharma eyes," within the body, and the right dharma eyes are acquired through the practice of just sitting. These eyes through which the world is seen, are crystal clear, are exhaustively transparent because they *are attuned to* the things which are seen. At the same time, the world provides the eyes with the particular objects to be seen by virtue of the actional bilaterality which obtains between the mind and the total world, but it is also a transparent world, for Dōgen says that the total world is experienced as a one transparent pearl. In other words, the particular objects of the total world are a source of affecting, and these objects become affected through the somatic act, thereby enabling the somatic act to penetrate the heart (*kokoro*) of the particular objects of the world. In this context, "penetrating the heart of things," may be understood to mean, among other things, the process by which the somatic act locates a particular object properly, with a crystal clear transparency, within the complex matrix of the conditioning process of generation-extinction. Consequently, we are led to believe that both the world and the eyes are mutually transparent since "nothing is concealed in the total world" in the samadhic awareness. These eyes are part of the true human body. Consequently, the identification of the eyes with the total body indicates an instance of the oneness of the body and the mind. The eyes as the highest form of wisdom are functionally integrated into the total body. Eyes and hands, which we identified previously as symbolizing a consummation of the intellective and the somatic modalities of the true human body, are integrated into the action which the true human body performs in the invigorating path of leaping out of the body. When this takes place, the actional objects which are transformed from the mind qua particular objects in the world present no obstacle. Dōgen says: "When one is a total body, there is no obstruction for it." The concept of the total body as it is appropriated through the practice of just sitting, means experientially that there is no "fissure" between the mind and the body. In light of the present context, the mind in its bodily intention is integrated into the dynamic movement of the body for a readiness to action. This integration is based upon the lived feeling of the agility and the mobility of one's hand taking over one's body. The total body in this instance is no longer a body which resists the bodily intention of the mind.

When this total body is in effect, the concept of true human body encompasses an aspect of "presencing" as one of its intrinsic features. Dōgen states:

> The time of nonstop generation-extinction is "who undergoes generation-extinction?" "Who undergoes generation-extinction" is the person of attainment with this body [ōi shinshin tokudosha], that is, to *presence* one's body [sokugen shinshin].[25] (emphasis added)

Dōgen's mention of "generation-extinction" with respect to its experiencer, "who," is significant in our understanding that the true human body presences itself through its intrinsic tendencies of nondependence and nonopposition, since Dōgen thereby indicates how presencing takes place in the midst of this dynamism of generation-extinction. In a qualified sense, the who of the true human body nullifies the inevitable course of generation-extinction, for who is not an everyday person self-conscious of its action, at least insofar as the action performed by who does not leave a "residue" in the complex of generation-extinction. That is to say, since the somatic act of the true human body sees "no obstacles," it unfolds its actions freely against the transparency of the total world, which, in turn, makes its presence felt in its surrounding ambiance. In other words, in presencing, the true human body creates *a field of presence* through its actions, and thereby distinguishes itself from the surrounding ambiance. Here, we have a glimpse of what samādhi-at-play may mean. The important point which we should bear in mind, however, is that somatic act of the true human body bears as its essential quality a dynamism of presencing.

Along with this dynamism of presencing, we must also keep in mind, when we are considering the characterization of the somatic act of the true human being, the manner of its operation in giving rise to the presencing act of the true human body. Dōgen uses the term, "total functioning" (*zenki*) to describe this manner of operation. He says:

> Life is not coming, nor is it going. It is neither presencing nor becoming. In spite of this, life is a presencing of *the total functioning* [*zenki*], and so is death.[26] (emphasis added)

The negation of generation-extinction (i.e., neither "coming" nor "going," neither presencing nor "becoming") when set beside its affirmation seems contradictory. This recognition of two (ontological and epistemological) orders is in keeping with the Mahāyāna Buddhist tradition, of which Zen is one of its offshoots. In light of our interpretation, Dōgen attempts to dissolve this contradiction by bringing the samadhic awareness into the realm of the samadhic action, or by making a move from the "stillness" of the meditational posture to the dynamism of the actional posture. In making this move, Dōgen is deeply cognizant of the contingent fact of human existence qua body, and to use Wittgenstein's metaphor, his way out of the "fly bottle" lies in action. Logical contradiction cannot be resolved within the same domain of discourse, unless one dialectically leaps from it. Dōgen chooses to dissolve the apparent contradiction between affirming and negating generation-extinction through recourse to action, for action does not admit the division between affirmation and negation; it is impossible to negate an action in words. To counter one action, another action is required. Take the example of nodding or shaking one's head for approval or disapproval, or in our terms affirmation or negation. When one nods one's head as a sign of affirmation, this affirmation is performed in action. Similarly, when one shakes one's head as a sign of negation, this is also performed in action. I have said that nodding one's head or shaking it is a sign, because it carries within itself an act of either affirmation or negation. Consequently, when we maintain the interpretation that Dōgen dissolves the above mentioned contradiction in actional terms, we recognize that this concept of action must be understood in the widest possible sense, in the sense, for example, of "Suddenly, a fire arises."

Now that we have clarified the disparate standpoints, we can turn our attention briefly to the meaning of Dōgen's term, total functioning. The adjective, "total," must be taken in the sense of nothing is concealed in the world, that is, it must be understood to mean a exhaustive transparency of everything experienced. Moreover, when this meaning of total is combined with the word "functioning," the resultant phrase implies a dynamism of the world characterized by the constant process of generation-extinction. Consequently, in its largest sense, the phrase, total functioning, means that each and every thing in the world is living to its fullest in the matrix of the process of generation-extinction, although the truth of this statement is, unfortunately, concealed from most of us who stay in the domain of everyday experience.

When we translate one definition of the term total functioning into human terms, it acquires special meaning. That is to say, if one were to perform any action in the manner of Dōgen's total functioning, one must be, so he claims, "a total body and a total mind." The term, total, as in total functioning, may be interpreted to mean a lived experience of actional oneness between the body and the mind; that is oneness not only in the sense of the stability of being, but also in the sense of a graceful flow of becoming. That is to say, there cannot be any fissure between an epistemological and an actional subject in the execution of an action. In addition, when the term, total, is used to describe a somatic act, it suggests a controlled and composed quality in the comportment of one's body without this control falling into the reign of self-consciousness. Moreover, total functioning characterizes a true human body in its ability to simply respond to a task that is to be performed in accordance with the demand of its execution. For example, speaking analogically about fish and birds, Dōgen says:

> When a fish swims the water, there is no limit to the water, and when a bird flies the sky, there is no limit to the sky, When a demand is great, the use [of swimming or flying] is great, and when it is small, the use is small.[27]

The idea expressed in this quote is a realization of actional nonduality. Dōgen doesn't state that "a fish swims *in* the water" nor does he say that "a bird flies *in* the sky." Absence of the preposition "in" in describing the activity of a fish or a bird amply demonstrates the idea of realization of actional nonduality. This idea of actional nonduality may be explained as follows. Without the sky, the bird cannot fly, and without the water, fish cannot swim. Therefore, the water swims the fish and the sky flies the bird. Dōgen's idea of the water or the sky shows a marked contrast, for example, with the Newtonian concept of space, which is simply a lifeless container.

The actional nonduality does not mitigate the *raison d'être* of respective being involved in action. But instead there is a full recognition of each being engaged in action. This realization of actional nonduality presupposes the experience of felt inter-resonance in which the experiencer does not encounter an opposition and dependence among the things experienced.

In the total functioning of the true human body, there is, then, the discernment of a situation. However, this "discernment" is not simply cognitive in character, nor is it somatic. It is rather achieved through the integration of both the intellective and the somatic aspects of a person, an integration that is the result or the appropriation of the body. To use our earlier terminology, this discernment is grounded in the attunement of the true human body to the current situation. And since the true human body is attuned to the situation, its discernment of the precise condition of the situation enables the somatic act of the true human body to respond to the task in proportion to its demands, neither excessively nor deficiently. Such an act, in other words, executes its action "rightfully."

CONCLUDING REMARKS

In part 2 we have focused on Dōgen's philosophy of the body and have analyzed the practice of "just sitting," while attempting to respond to the overriding questions posed in the beginning of this inquiry. We have concerned ourselves with theoretically articulating the process of the body's transformation vis-à-vis the practice of just sitting while holding in view an epistemological perspective which opens up through such a transformation. In particular, we specified in Chapter Four this transformative process as an existential, practical movement from an I to a who, effecting the everyday existence to change into samadhic existence, and characterized this transformation, taking place against the theoretical background of generation-extinction, as a process of "uncovering" the accidental dust. When this was translated into experiential correlates, we interpreted it to mean a transformation from the dependence and opposition of *dharmas* to its nondependence and nonopposition.

In chapter 5 we have delved into the analysis of the practical procedure involved in just sitting in order to learn in more concrete terms how the experiential correlate of nondependence and nonopposition is achieved. While discussing this issue in consideration of the preparation, the attitude, and the goal of just sitting, we have analyzed the experiential meaning of "immobile sitting" vis-à-vis the samadhic awareness that accompanies it. This samadhic awareness was interpreted to be an instance of achieved body-mind oneness. Since this is understood to be an achievement, it has provided us with a theoretical justification for understanding the practical and existential transformation of everyday existence into samadhic existence. When this transformation was examined in light of the mind-body problem, we learned that it further correlates with the transformation of dualism into nondualism, that is, mind-body oneness. To demonstrate the validity of this interpretation, we discussed Zen's contention that theory and practice must be one, that is to say, the theoretical formulation of Zen experience must be verified first by practical lived experience.

In chapter 6, we delved directly into Dōgen's confirmatory satori experience of enlightenment, which is linguistically expressed as casting off the body and the mind. We have interpreted it to mean, using the phenomenologist's category, a disappearance of the distinction between subject-body and object-body, or more positively, an appropriation of the object-body within the subject-body. The experiential correlate to this appropriation, we argued, was based on the felt inter-resonance between samadhic awareness and its object of engagement. We have argued and demonstrated that the mode of judgement operative in the experience of felt inter-resonance is somatic in character in contrast with the act of *cogito* associated with our everyday, ego-consciousness, where we proposed to understand "somatic" to mean somatically induced awareness.

In chapter 7, we have taken our investigation out of the context of just sitting to see whether or not the above mentioned felt inter-resonance also serves as a basis for the body in action, which we termed "samadhic action" to contrast it with "samadhic awareness." This move was motivated to dispel a criticism that whatever obtains experientially in samadhic awareness is an instance of Oriental Quietism. In this endeavor, we first analyzed Dōgen's identification of the mind with objects, where we learned that it presupposes a samadhic experience of felt inter-resonance. This understanding has guided us to articulate what it means for the body to act vis-à-vis the experience of felt inter-resonance. We have analyzed it in light of Dōgen's concept of true human body and interpreted this concept to mean an achievement, wherein understanding and action are correlative with each other—a further specification of Zen's contention that practice and theory are one. When this correlativity is lived, we have characterized it as an actional realization of nonduality.

At this juncture, it seems appropriate to provide a transition to part 3. In the preceding two parts, we have focused on three first-rate Japanese thinkers, Ichikawa Hiroshi, Yuasa Yasuo and Dōgen Kigen, to learn how these thinkers understand the concept of the body. Each has formulated, from their own perspective, a unique concept of the body, with an overall effect of modifying our persistent idea of the body as a material substance. This idea has been the dominant common sensical understanding of the body, particularly becoming strong in the West ever since Descartes declared the separate realities of mind and body. In agreement with Descartes' mind-body dualism, the West has developed a persistent tendency to devaluate, or in extreme cases, to disregard the important function which the body plays in our everyday existence, and has sometimes ended up treating it as no different from a *lifeless* material substance. Notwithstanding, the secularized West has made numerous untiring attempts to elevate the human body to the status of "beautiful face," "nice figure," and "muscle man." As one would notice immediately, this is at the level of object-body, perhaps with a flare of sexual overtone. This is a deplorable situation. Contrary to this popular image of the body we recognize as we have shown through the analysis of Dōgen's concept of the body, that the modality of our everyday lived body can transform into a higher, samadhic modality of awareness and action by training or cultivating the body, even to the point of discovering a sacred and divine in this process.

Keeping the above remark at the background of our investigation, we would like to develop in the next three chapters of part 3 a *new* philosophical theory of the body, which is called "attunement," by *creatively* thinking through the fruits of the investigation which we have gained from the previous two parts. Because the theory of attunement is new, it is a departure from the previous two parts, although it is not discontinuous from them at least insofar as the theory of attunement incorporates, though under different terminologies, the insights discovered in the previous two parts.

There are a few underlying motives in proposing a new theory called attunement. It is offered as an instance of comparative philosophy where "comparative philosophy" is used to mean an intellectual endeavor of thinking creatively across the boundaries of philosophical, cultural, and ethnic traditions with the view to going beyond these traditions. By focusing on this theory of attunement within the context of comparative philosophy, part 3 offers an alternative perspective to the various theories and ideas developed within Western philosophical traditions. In particular, the theory looks into the meaning of mind-body problem vis-à-vis the phenomenon of attunement and the status of knowledge indicative and reflective of this experience. Though far from being a full-fledged philosophical theory, the theory of attunement, when properly understood, demands a rethinking, among other things, of what it means to acquire knowledge, and eventually what it means to become a human.

PART 3

A Theory of Attunement

CHAPTER 8

Preliminaries and a Theory of Attunement

"The body is a great reason."
——Nietzsche, *Thus Spoke Zarathustra*

INTRODUCTION

Our philosophical investigation now turns to sketch "a theory of attunement" as a thought-experiment which has been suggested through our preceding study of Ichikawa, Yuasa and Dōgen. Methodologically, this theory of attunement will not be bound by the conceptual framework and terminologies of the preceding parts, although this does not mean that it will not be guided by their "spirit." Whenever appropriate, I shall attempt to indicate the conceptual origin of all the terminologies that will be utilized in articulating the theory of attunement.

This theory of attunement purports to articulate the mode of *engagement* that obtains actionally as well as epistemologically between a person and his/her living ambiance,[1] where we *for now* understand the concept of "person" to be an entity of psycho-physical integration, and "the living ambiance" to be the totality of shaped things, either animate or inanimate, including a person with *anima*.[2] Engagement in this formulation is used to designate an actional as well as epistemological orientation of the person toward both an external and an internal world. It is to be observed that the manner through which the person engages its living ambiance or the manner through which living ambiance engages the person depends upon the lived experience of his/her mind and body. For this reason, the theory of attunement will be advanced as an epistemological paradigm which will hopefully serve as an alternative to the so-called mind-body

179

dualism, when it is viewed as a metaphysical theory. Moreover, since the theory is concerned with articulating the *modes* of epistemological and actional orientation toward living ambiance, it attempts to demonstrate the nature of the relationship obtaining between the person and his/her living ambience. The term "attunement" may for now be understood to be a *descriptive* term for the nature of this relationship.

In proposing to understand the theory of attunement in this way, the following implications are naturally suggested. In the Western philosophical tradition, epistemology has been understood to be a systematic articulation of either the relation obtaining between the mind *qua* knowing subject and the external world (e.g., empiricism), or the constitution of an object by a knowing mind (e.g., idealism). As we can see, both of these theoretical attempts have been construed disregarding the somatic aspect of a knowing subject. If we understand the totality of the external world to be the sum of the shaped things, inanimate or otherwise, including a person with anima, the personal body as a shaped thing must become a medium through which the living ambiance is known and understood. Moreover, when we understand the person to be an integrated whole of psycho-physical being, it is apparent that the traditional Western approaches to epistemology are unilateral, for it takes *either* the psychical *or* the physical to be the parameter of the possibility of knowledge.[3] Idealism of any sort absorbs everything knowable within the subjectivity, within the mind of a person, while empiricism, presupposing the mind to be a *tabula rasa*, has relegated the reality solely to the external world. Moreover, both of them are primarily concerned with the so-called external perception, as if the force and the meaning of internal perception arising from the psyche have nothing to do with the external perception for its formation. In contrast to these traditional ways of approaching epistemology, the theory of attunement will argue that the epistemological foundation lies in the bilaterality obtaining between the person and his/her living ambiance, while taking into consideration the "depth" (or internal perception) of the living human body. This will be advanced primarily in consideration of "affectivity" that obtains between the person and his/her living ambiance, since affectivity which is rooted in the body touches the innermost being of the person.[4]

Since the traditional Western approaches to epistemology, as they are observed in the preceding, are concerned with the knowing subject without taking into account the function of the personal body in gaining knowledge, the human as an epistemological subject and the human as an actional subject have been considered as separate, and hence belonging to separate domains of philosophical investigation. This separation is motivated in the Western philosophical tradition by a presupposition that *theōria* always takes precedence over *prāxis,*[5] relegating the theoretical to epistemology and the practical to ethics of action, or conduct. This kind of presupposition, when applied to an examination of the concept of self, eventually leads to a formation of "divided self," or "split personality," because the theoretical or the intellectual always runs ahead, leaving the practical behind, the prāxis which inevitably involves a bodily engagement and bodily modification such as emotions, desires and passions. The divided self or split personality indicates an imbalance between the modality of the mind (i.e., the theoretical, or the intellectual) and the modality of the body (i.e., the practical, or the affective). In contrast to this attitude, the theory of attunement proposes to understand both the theoretical and the practical, both the actional and the epistemological, under a single phenomenon of attunement obtaining between the person and his/her living ambiance.

In order to accommodate the above implications, the theory of attunement assumes a philosophical position which recognizes various degrees of psychophysical integration of the person. This may be alternatively stated as follows: the theory in question assumes a philosophical position of "provisional dualism" in which the mind and the body are *provisionally* or *tentatively* regarded as separate and distinct,[6] although they are integrated as a whole to the extent that both the mind and the body are not disjunctive; they are maintained in the person as a cohesive whole under normal, healthy conditions. This philosophical position characterizes our everyday mode of existence. The theory does not maintain, however, that this provisional dualistic tendency is the final position that characterizes the nature of the person. It recognizes a transformation from this provisional stance to the nondual stance. Epistemologically, this will trans-

late into recognizing a transformation of everyday ego-consciousness to extraordinary samadhic awareness, in the sense
that these terms were defined in dealing with Dōgen.

Broadly speaking, this transformation may be conceived of
as a special kind of habit-formation: the formation of a habit
that destroys the provisional dualism operative in our everyday
mode of existence. This was, for example, how Yuasa understood the meaning of Eastern self-cultivation (See chapter 3).
Since it is conceived to be a habit-formation, this transformation
pertains to the body, rather than to the mind, for habit-formation in its aspect of sedimentation or embodiment is not primarily cognitive in character. Since we take the practice of meditation
as pivotal to this transformation, which is a somatic aspect of a
person, this special kind of habit-formation involves the somaticity of a person. We shall understand therefore that this transformation is primarily somatic in character: it is the somatic transformation that enables a person to transform himself/herself
from the provisional dualistic stance to a nondualistic stance.
Alternatively, this somatic transformation may be conceived of
as achieving *a higher degree* of psycho-physical integration than
the one available in our everyday mode of existence. Since this
transformation is effected by the practice of meditation, there is
no separation between theōria and prāxis, for meditation is an
engagement of a whole person.

To put it differently, this special habit formation is effected
by existentially retrogressing toward the *altus* of the personal
body. It is toward the altus, I maintain, because our preceding
investigations of the experiential status of "felt inter-resonance"
points in this direction.[7] Through the investigation of Dōgen we
have been led to believe that a true sense of knowing is "concealed" in the altus of the human body, concealed in the sense
that our everyday mode of consciousness is incapable of disclosing or uncovering the true sense of knowledge. I choose the Latin
term, altus, to indicate that our investigation is directed toward
the depth and height of the lived experience of our body, since
the term has both meanings.

To conceive that there is such knowledge, we are here presupposing that the human body embodies a ground or a source
of intelligibility, though it is concealed from our everyday ego-

consciousness.[8] It belongs to the invisible dimension of the everyday ego-consciousness. This was, for example, exemplified in Yuasa's concept of "unconscious quasi-body circuit." "Knowledge" thus disclosed or uncovered deserves the name of "somatic" knowledge, in contrast to "cognitive" knowledge. It is called somatic to indicate its origin: it is through the somatic transformation via meditation that a true sense of knowledge is acquired. In view of the inseparability of theōria and prāxis which the theory of attunement takes as its stance, the knowledge in question is both actional and epistemological in character. Therefore, knowledge without a possibility of being instantiated by prāxis, or knowledge that is not based upon prāxis is automatically excluded from our investigation.[9]

When we conceive of "somatic knowledge" in this manner, the theory of attunement is also contending that it is in a certain qualified sense more primary than, and therefore a foundation for, a cognitive knowledge.[10] To indicate this sense of primacy and its foundational nature, I want to discuss briefly the sense of priority claimed in respect to somatic knowing over so-called cognitive knowledge. The priority is preontological in nature, if we understand ontology to mean the study of the region arising from "thinkability" in Parmenides' sense, or from "understanding" (*Verstand*) in Heidegger's sense made explicit in his *Being and Time*. Or, put simply, if ontology is the region arising from Cartesian cogito, somatic knowing is preontological, since it precedes temporally and logically the region of thinkability. This suggests that the region of our investigation lies in other than the everyday mode of understanding or thinkability. Or, it is, we might say, ontological in the more rigorous sense if the theory of attunement, as it promises, reveals a foundation for the ontology hitherto unconcealed, that is, a region of beings arising from the investigation of the personal body. We might designate such a region as the *somatic region*. The theory of attunement attempts to investigate this somatic region. The somatic region is to be distinguished from the body qua body in that it is made into an object in order to understand the latter. Ideally, though, the body qua body should coincide with the articulation of the somatic region. In such an instance, we would have a complete knowledge of our personal body.[11]

Corresponding to the appropriation of a higher degree of psychophysical integration—the account of which the theory of attunement accommodates within itself and which is recognized via somatic transformations—the manner through which a person relates himself/herself to the external world is also altered. This is because the somatic transformations bring forth a higher degree of psychophysical integration in the person. Consequently, when these transformations are seen in light of the somaticity of the personal existence, it will be argued within the theoretical structure of the theory of attunement that there are, at least, three distinct types of psychophysical integration discernible in the person in proportion to the degree of his/her integration. Of the three psychophysical integrations, the first one is that which characterizes our everyday mode of existence in which there is a provisional dualistic tendency between the mind and the body. This dualistic tendency can be translated as embracing a "tension" between the mind and body we live in our everyday life.[12] Because of this tension between them, operative in our everyday mode of existence, we shall refer to this mode as "tensional," or more abstractly, "tensionality." The process of transforming the dualistic mode of existence to the nondualistic mode of existence will be referred to as "de-tensional" in the sense that the person goes out of, or de-conditions, this tensional mode by means of the somatic transformations. This, then, is the second sense of somatic modality with which we shall be concerned to articulate. We have seen clearly the instance of this mode when we dealt with Dōgen's concept of "just sitting." As an ideal state in which this de-tensional process is completely mastered, we can conceive of such an accomplishment that is instantiated in our daily attitude of knowing and acting. We may call this state "non-tensional" in the sense that the tensional mode of personal existence which characterizes our everyday mode of existence is overcome and hence absent. We have had a slight glimpse of this when we dealt with the concept of somatic act characterizing Dōgen's mode of engagement with the world.

To recapitulate the preceding introductory remarks concerning the theory of attunement in a propositional form, we may state its thesis as follows: "Appropriation of somatic knowledge is in proportion to the degree of attunement which obtains between the person and his/her living ambiance, and the degree of attunement is in turn correlative with the degree of psychophysical integration achieved in the person." In order to witness the development of this thesis, let us now turn our attention to preliminaries on the theory of attunement.

PERSONAL BODY: A CONTINGENT BEING

Before we attempt to articulate the theory of attunement, a preliminary remark concerning the starting point upon which the theory of attunement will be founded must briefly be indicated. This will help us to see where the theory of attunement finds its basic orientation, a very beginning point. Therefore, the validity and plausibility of the theory hinge upon its acceptance. The specification of this beginning point calls for an articulation of the nature of the personal body, the concept which has been employed up to this point without an adequate clarification of its meaning.

As long as we remain in what Husserl called "natural attitude," which is the only perspective available to us insofar as our everyday experience is concerned, the endowment of a body is an indispensable qualification for personal existence. It is inconceivable that a human exists without his/her body; to exist means to exist embodied, somatically. This marks a person as a finite being, because he or she is subject to constant generation-extinction. Moreover, it is a biological fact that a human makes his/her emergence into this world by means of his/her body. Our exit from this world is also characterized by the disappearance of our body: no historical figure has survived his/her bodily death. This suggests that a personal body is characterized by its onceness; it only lives once, insofar as "this" world is concerned, or insofar as its body is concerned. Furthermore, this onceness in terms of birth and death implies that it is an individual being, distinct from the other things shaped, and since such a being is suspended between life and death, it is an unstable being, generating psychologically an anxiety, as Heidegger pointed out in his *Being and Time*. Being individual, a personal body enjoys various perspectives unique to itself; its unfoldings are characterized by a "place" (*basho*) where a person is situated, the nature of such a

place assuming a multiplicity of different kinds; a historical, cultural, interpersonal, affective, spatial, and the like, situation.

When the personal body is seen philosophically in light of its
finitude, onceness, individuality and perspectival determination,
all this amounts to recognizing that a person is a contingent
being. Heidegger, for example, in his *Being and Time*, characterized this contingency as being "thrown" into this world. This
"thrownness" has a meaning only if it presupposes a spatial
dimension, both of that which is thrown and that into which it is
thrown. In Heidegger's case, the former is *Dasein* or personal
existence and the latter the "world." Although Heidegger does
not make an explicit reference to the concept of the body in his
Being and Time, it seems to follow that if his Dasein is characterized in terms of thrownness, it must be understood primarily in
light of the personal body. That is to say, Heidegger's Dasein has
a meaning only if it is understood as a person spatially situated.
This is further in accord with his characterization of Dasein as
"being-in-the-world," the preposition "in" obviously indicating
a spatial dimension, "the world." The reason that Heidegger
chose "the world" as a spatial place into which Dasein is thrown
is because his Dasein discovers itself through understanding
(*Verstand*), which is a cognitive function of the person. In contrast, we say it is the ambiance into which the personal body is
thrown in order to indicate an immediacy of its discovery. Heidegger's concept of the world is conceived by conceptually
expanding the circumference of the ambiance, which, incidentally proves that his Dasein is primarily a cognitive subject. At any
rate, we must recognize with Heidegger that the person is a contingent being thrown into an ambiance, which is characterized
by the endowment of his or her body.

If we accept this observation that the personal body is a contingent being, the following consequence, among other things, necessarily seems to follow. Namely, the consequence that anything that
is construed conceptually with respect to an ontological primacy
over the region of personal body, or what we call a somatic region,
is secondary, if not false, because such an endeavor *presupposes*
the contingent fact of the thrownness of personal body: it would be
a conceptual fabrication to disregard this contingent fact. It would
be, to use Heidegger's terminology, a "forgetfulness of Being." It is

through attunement, then, that we come to understand the nature of our being, and the theory of attunement articulates the structure necessarily involved in understanding the attunement.

This contingency of our personal body, which has emerged through the analysis of Heidegger's concept of thrownness does not mean, however, that the personal body comes into this world without any determination. It is the insight of Buddhism to insist that the personal body is dispositionally determined, although such a determination is not absolute but relative. That is, personal likes and dislikes, as we saw in the analyses of Dōgen's concept of the body, are nonetheless deeply rooted in the personal body. It is this sense of dispositional determination that we said we would examine when we remarked that the theory of attunement analyzes the altus of the body, for the dispositional determination is concealed therein and remains opaque for most of us. Seen in this light, the theory of attunement may be conceived of as an attempt to discover a necessity in the contingent fact.

ENGAGEMENT:
FUNDAMENTAL MODALITY OF THE PERSONAL BODY

Once we are led in this manner to recognize that the person or the personal body is a contingent being thrown into its living ambiance, a structural relationship between its body and ambiance becomes a crucial concern for understanding the nature of our being or, as we said, somatic region, for it is through such a structure that the personal body as he or she is situated in the ambiance can be made intelligible. What, in other words, is the most fundamental manner through which the personal body is related to its living ambiance? In asking this question, we are looking for a category that is comprehensive enough to include all the modes of the personal body, that is, the somatic modality, and at the same time, that is true to them all. To respond to such a demand, we can just reflect upon how the personal body maintains itself as such. It is, I contend, an engagement. By virtue of the fact that the personal body is a thing shaped, beautifully or otherwise, it has to make "contact" with the ambiance: the contact here does not have to be restricted to the sense of the tactile, but to be taken as a general manner of a personal body's being in the ambiance in the sense of assuming somatically pre-reflective attitudes toward the external world. When I am standing, I am standing *before* I "see" reflectively my self making a contact with the ground. That the personal body invariably makes contact with the ambiance means, generally speaking, then, that it is *engaged* in the ambiance. Engagement is a manner through which the living personal body relates itself to the ambiance through its activities or just being in the ambiance. It is then a universal fact, insofar as the personal body is concerned, that it is engaged in an ambiance, for there is no instance of the somatic modality otherwise revealed and lived.[13] The English expression, "being-engaged-in," however, is somewhat unfortunate, because it is syntactically expressed in the passive voice. For this reason, we might philosophically think of the two generic aspects of engagement, namely, "engaging" and "being-engaged" as constituting engagement. In terms of the experiential correlate of these two aspects, they correspond to the *affective* residue of a particular engagement, respectively, for example, when one feels engaging a thing other than himself or herself and when one feels being engaged by it.

To use the term, engagement, as a general term for the somatic modality of a personal body is felicitous; it has an advantage of mitigating the subject-object distinction, for "to see" and "to be seen" in respect to the personal body becomes a distinction without difference. For example, when a person places oneself in a particular form (*kata*) of engagement, for example, shaping oneself in the form of a breast stroke in swimming, the essential "form" of breast stroke is lived from within, as well as observed from outside. The form of engagement, in other words, becomes a parameter to verify or falsify the meaning of experience. Engagement functions as a principle of verification of the truth or falsity of an experience.[14] A person does not "know" what it is to swim unless he/she actually swims.

A personal body verifies, in other words, the meaning of engagement only when he/she places himself/herself in the "same" form (kata) of engagement with other people. Put still differently, a possibility of establishing an inter-subjective and inter-corporeal ground lies in assuming the same engagement among a group of people. This should hold true at least as far as the first-hand knowledge is concerned, which is the first order of "knowing." The point that the theory of attunement emphasizes is that engagement is a universal fact for a living, personal body, without which it is meaningless to assert that it exists.

Engagement includes even "doing nothing" for engagement as such, as we understand the term, does not have to be engaging to the extent that the person loses himself/herself in an engagement. If engagement is the most universal way of characterizing a manner through which the person relates to his/her ambiance, we can safely regard it as the most fundamental mode of one's existence. The theory of attunement for now postulates that engagement is the most fundamental designation for a structural relationship obtaining between the personal body and his/her living ambiance.

By virtue of this fact, for example, the ambiance into which our body is thrown enables us to acquire a meaning in experience. The ambiance becomes a place in which an engagement takes place. Only through this somatic modality can we exist in the ambiance. Seen in this manner, the personal body and its living ambiance are correlative terms. A recognition of this correlativity prevents us from falling into a one-sided view concerning the ontogenesis of the "meaning" of experience. A certain camp of idealism contends that the generation of "meaning" should be sought in the meaning bestowing activity of cogito, while a certain camp of empiricism maintains that the meaning is to be derived from the material object qua object. The truth of the matter lies in the middle way, that is, in the correlative bilaterality between the person and his or her living ambiance.

Needless to say, there is a multiplicity of different kinds of engagement. Consequently, when we say that engagement is the most fundamental, universal way of characterizing a structural relationship obtaining between the personal body and his or her living ambiance, it is too general and becomes vacuously true of all the somatic activities and its modes of existence. For this reason, the term, engagement, is too vague for the purpose of first showing that there is an intelligible structure in the living, personal body and secondly elucidating the somatic knowledge indicative of the former. We need, in other words, another term that qualifies the term, engagement, while retaining the sense of engagement we have just discussed, in such a way that an episte-mological aspect of engagement can be made more explicit. For this purpose, I propose the term, attunement, to capture an episte-mological aspect of engagement.

ENGAGEMENT AS THE BODY'S ATTUNEMENT

Even if we concede to the theory of attunement that the structural relationship obtaining between the personal body and its living ambiance is characterizable in terms of engagement, it may seem still questionable why this engagement, when seen as a way of capturing an epistemological aspect, must be viewed in terms of attunement. This is because, insofar as engagement is concerned, it is an "attuned" engagement; no engagement is primordially out of attunement. To maintain such a position, the following argu-ment may be mounted first by way of further unpacking the meaning of thrownness. Biologically, thrownness has its founda-tion in sexual intercourse. So if one were to ask from where the person is thrown into this world, the answer, biologically speak-ing, is from our mother's womb. We can keep on asking where our mother came from and our mother's mother and so on to the point where we reach the very beginning of human life.

Such an endeavor may be conceived of as a *horizontal* pur-suit of human genealogy in the sense that it goes back on the lin-ear track of temporality. This will not provide us, however, with the existential meaning of thrownness. And those who are philo-sophically minded may not be satisfied with this answer, particu-larly if we want to see our "original face before our parents were born." This suggests that we must question the biological foun-dation from a philosophical point of view. In contrast to the hor-izontal pursuit, we must attempt to question the biological foun-dation of thrownness in terms of the *vertical* orientation, that is, toward the altus of personal body in the sense of existentially retrogressing into it.

Thrownness, as we have just seen, has a meaning only if we presuppose it to be somatic in character: its somaticity marks the entrance into this world, or more concretely, into the immediate ambiance. Thrownness in light of the above biological consideration may be reinterpreted as a recognition of the de facto and incipient event of a particular personal body. However, if thrownness is the singular characterization of our somatic emergence into a particular ambiance, we would be lost in the midst of its ambiance. The ambiance, notwithstanding, does not present itself as a place inconducive to living. It is not a dangerous place. Epistemologically interpreted, this means that the ambiance does not present itself as chaos. That it is not presented as chaos implies that we can intellectually conceive that there is a principle of ordering, or at least, an intelligibility inherent either (1) in the personal body, (2) in the ambiance or (3) in the interrelationship between the two. If it is in the body alone, the presentation would be a mere delusion without requiring a being of ambiance as an occasion for presentation, for such a presentation would be a creation of the person. Moreover, this position mitigates the fact of our somatic thrownness, for thrownness would become meaningless. If on the other hand, it is in the ambiance alone, the presentation to a personal body becomes meaningless, for presentation is always a presentation of something to something else. This leaves us with the middle way, the third alternative as the position we should assume, namely, that the intelligibility lies in the interrelationship or co-arising between the personal body and his or her ambiance.[15]

These observations, however, do not directly demonstrate that there is an intelligibility in the co-arising between the personal body and its living ambiance. It simply demonstrates that the presentation in question is other than being chaotic. But what is "other than being chaotic"? Does it mean that there is another kind of chaos, more encompassing in nature than the one we have entertained? No, as long as it is chaos, it is ruled out as a possibility of an orderly presentation. It must be other than chaos. What then is other than chaos? What in other words is the opposite of chaos? It must be, at least, an ordered pattern capable of being discernible. That is, it must be an intelligible order of patternment that makes a presentation actual and actually meaningful insofar as the personal body is concerned. This leads us to conclude that the intelligibility lies in a co-arising between the personal body and its living ambiance, for we have ruled out the two alternatives, namely, (1) that the presentation is in the personal body alone, and (2) that it is in the ambiance alone.

This means, among other things, that either the personal body emerges into the ambiance already equipped with a adaptive capacity to the ambiance, or it acquires an adaptive capacity at the time of its birth, so that the ambiance does not present itself as chaos. If either possibility is denied, a chance of adaptation to the ambiance, for example, insofar as a newly born baby is concerned, is eliminated, let alone the survival of the baby. Regardless, however, of which position we accept, it is de facto a case that a newly born baby not only survives but also adapts itself to its ambiance, provided that care proper to child rearing is administered. Here, the theory of attunement is not concerned with the degree of adaptability. What it is concerned with is the bare minimum requirement for a baby to adapt itself to the ambiance. The theory takes this adaptive capacity of a newly born baby as a ground and a possibility for obtaining attunement. In this respect, the personal body is not only a being-in-the-ambiance thrown into it but also it is thrown attuned. If this is correct reasoning, we might say that attunement, using Heidegger's terminology, is a fundamental mode of being in the ambiance. Everything else is secondary or at least derivable from this position.

In our contemporary age, we witness only negatively the truth of the theory's contention that the personal body is endowed originally with an adaptive capacity to the living ambiance. That is, we witness it in terms of psychosomatic disorder. For example, Selyé's stress theory endorses our contention. According to him, "stress" is defined as an *over-adaptation* of living organisms to the ambiance (i.e., a general adaptation syndrome). This over-adaptation occurs in the personal body, according to our interpretation, because the degree of psychophysical integration is not brought to a higher degree of integration. To put it differently, the personal body in its everyday mode of existence cannot properly select, and incorporate within itself, what is conducive to health: it assimilates within itself indiscriminately everything that is presented to it, without being able to change the negative elements of the ambiance to the positive ones, "positive" here to be understood as conducive to maintaining the psychophysical balance of the personal body. Since this over-adaptation takes place unconsciously, primarily in the body, we find a case of psychosomatic dysfunction only when it is brought to a level of awareness, that is, only when a psychosomatic dysfunction has become fairly advanced.

However, one may reject the example used to justify the introduction of attunement as a further characterization of the term engagement with an epistemological meaning indicative of the relationship that obtains between the personal body and its living ambiance on the grounds that this way of understanding does not seem to be philosophical enough, let alone epistemological. This is perhaps because the example employed is an experience either forgotten or outside of the standpoint of ego-consciousness. This is in effect an objection to the position held by the developmental psychologist who would maintain that the consciousness we associate with an adult's life is an emergence not observable at the time of birth but later "developed" in infancy. But this objection may be mitigated, if we remember Ichikawa's argument, namely, that the functions of the body underlying the function of consciousness prepares and regulates the latter. Ichikawa used an example of walking. Is there an obstruction between the legs and the ground they cover, provided the legs in question are not in need of medical care? In walking, one is not consciously controlling every muscle fiber involved in executing this action. Because there is no obstruction between the walking and the ground, that is, in our terminology, there is an attunement between them, walking is actualizable.

Admittedly, the examples cited for advancing the contention of the theory of attunement may not exhibit a fullest sense of somatic knowledge, for they simply point out that there is an intelligible principle emerging through the personal body. In fact, because of this primitive nature of intelligibility, philosophical activity as a reflective endeavor to understand the nature of our being can be erected upon this primitive intelligible source, claiming it to be a higher order of intellectual undertaking. However, such an endeavor is carried out, in most cases, upon and through our everyday mode of existence—hence the concealment of the intelligibility of our personal body—without considering the possibility of somatic transformations which enables us to see afresh the everyday mode of existence.

CHAPTER 9

A Sketch of a
General Theory of Attunement

THE FORMAL CONDITIONS OF ATTUNEMENT

What then is "attunement"? We may first note its formal conditions, "formal" to be understood as an intrinsic condition without which attunement cannot obtain, insofar as it is expressed in a propositional form. The term, attunement, is a two-place predicate; it indicates a relation of two entities or two groups of entities. For example, we can meaningfully assert that "an x is attuned to a y" where x and y are the members of the same domain of discourse. Theoretically, any two entities can be instantiated for the relation of attunement to take place in this formulation, an x is attuned to a y. Such a condition, however, would make the theory of attunement too powerful, for anything whatsoever can be instantiated in the places where x and y occur. Therefore, we shall impose an existential restriction in view of the preceding discussion, namely, that the domain is to be restricted such that its members are comprised of the persons and their ambiance. They are then the structural components of attunement. The ambiance as noted previously, is a general term designating the totality of the shaped things found in it, which is comprised of inanimate, animate entities, including persons with *anima*. Needless to say, to choose these two entities from many other possible combinations reflects my interest, an existential concern, the philosophical justification for which we have labored in the preceding chapter.

Along with this existential restriction, we must now note the criterion by means of which we can assert meaningfully or truthfully that an x is attuned to y. This criterion, as we have seen previously, is the somatic modality of "engagement." The grammaticality of the statement an x is attuned to a y therefore depends upon whether there obtains an engagement between an x and a y. This criterion is introduced first to indicate a generic origin of attunement in the fundamental somatic modality of engagement, and secondly to determine the meaningfulness, or truth or falsity of the statement an x is attuned to a y. Engagement as we have already seen serves also as a principle of verification, that is, to use a mode of engagement to verify whether or not a personal body undergoes the same kind of attunement. For example, it is false to assert, according to the theory of attunement, that the person is attuned to the act of swimming if he/she has not or is not engaged in swimming. On the other hand, it is true to assert that the person is attuned to dancing if he/she has undergone or is in the process of undergoing the practice of dancing, for example, a hula. Verification comes from the intrinsic nature of a particular engagement, which is observable to the person as well as to the other persons who have gone through the particular engagement.[1]

With the conditions that both the existential restriction and the criterion of verification in terms of engagement are operative, we can then recapitulate that attunement designates a structural relationship obtaining between the personal body and his/her ambiance. This may be formulated as: "The personal body *is attuned to* y where y is an entity (or a group of entities) in the living ambiance." The theory of attunement purports to elucidate this structural relationship, that is, to articulate the constitutions of somatic knowing operative between the personal body and its living ambiance in terms of its structural organization.

This structural relationship is propositionally expressed as an x is attuned to a y. Notationally, we might designate it as xAy, where the x is a grammatical subject and the y is of that which is predicated in terms of the relation of attunement. As a logical possibility, we can think of the converse of this relation, namely, that "the y is attuned to the x," that is, yAx. A question arises whether xAy and yAx are logically equivalent, "logical equivalence" here understood as meaning that the substitution of x with y in respect of their occurrences in the above formulation does not change the status of attunement, for example, it does not degenerate into some other relation that might hold between x and y. If they are logically equivalent, understood in the sense noted, we say that x and y hold a *strong* instance of attunement.

We might say that a strong sense of attunement establishes a bilateral inter-corporeality. On the other hand, if x and y are not interchangeable, we say that they hold a *weak* instance of attunement. In this case, we can think that a unilateral inter-corporeality is established. The demarcation between the strong and weak senses of attunement becomes useful if we want to deal with particular entities in the totality of the ambiance, for example, between two animate entities. If, for example, two persons, A and B, go through the "same" engagement *at the same time*, a strong instance of attunement holds with respect to both A and B. But on the other hand, if A goes through an engagement now and B goes through the same engagement later, that is, both A and B go through the same engagement, but at different times, a weak sense of attunement holds only in respect to A. (But, if B goes through the same engagement as A which the latter has gone through before, we might say that a strong sense of attunement could obtain between A and B, insofar as A *understands* what B goes through.) The difference, then, between the strong and the weak senses of attunement lies in whether or not the same engagement obtains between two entities at the same time.

In our articulation of the theory of attunement, however, we shall be concerned only with the weak sense of attunement, because if the weak sense of attunement is proved to be operative, it would naturally follow that the strong sense of attunement would also be the case. Consequently, what follows is the elucidation of the weak sense of attunement. In light of the plan of our project, this means that our investigation proceeds from this point on by articulating the theory of attunement from the experiential perspective of the person.

THE EXPERIENTIAL MOMENTUM OF ATTUNEMENT

Having thus briefly stated the formal conditions of attunement, the next issue that concerns us in sketching the theory of attunement is to specify the experiential *momentum* of attunement that satisfies its formal conditions. This is important for if the theory of attunement does not have an experiential correlate to the formal conditions, it would be the work of mere fancy or empty speculation. The experiential momentum of attunement is predicated on the contention that engagement is the most fundamental somatic modality obtaining between the personal body and the ambiance.

What then is the experiential momentum that gives rise to attunement? Such a momentum, I submit, is a coming-together between the personal body and his/her living ambiance. "Coming" in the experiential momentum of coming-together designates a fluid bilateral movement between the personal body and the living ambiance, and "together" indicates a fruition of this coming. Fruition, epistemologically speaking, is a fruition of somatic knowing in the sense that both the personal body and the living ambiance come to reach a *common* quality (or qualities) that are made explicit through the experiential momentum of coming, by means of the emanation of invisible psychophysical energies (*ki*) which are issued both from the personal body and an entity in the living ambiance. In this respect, the momentum of coming may be conceived to be as temporally enabling that which is concealed to announce itself. Care must be taken, however, in understanding this experiential momentum of coming-together: coming and together are not *separate momenta*, consecutively taking place, for example, first coming and then together. This is indicated by a hyphenation connecting coming and together as coming-together. When an attunement obtains, both coming and together occur with one stroke. They are an inseparable momentum for the experiential correlate to attunement.

The coming here should not be taken as a physical locomotion, but rather it is an orientation "towards" in the sense that the personal body and the ambiance engage each other. The physical locomotion in terms of the body's activity is not certainly excluded from the coming intended here, but what is epistemologically significant at this point is the structural specification of the experiential momentum for attunement. Naturally, if we think of the coming in terms of physical locomotion, inanimate, shaped things cannot certainly "move" themselves toward the personal body. Even in this instance, an inanimate object provides an experiential momentum for the personal body in such a way that both the personal body and the inanimate object come to reach epistemologically as well as actionally a common quality (or qualities). Therefore, what is important in advancing the concept of coming-together as an experiential momentum for attunement is a recognition of the bilaterality between the personal body and the ambiance as a necessary condition for obtaining an attunement between them, which becomes a momentum for somatic knowing. On the other hand, if either a personal body or his/her living ambiance do not engage each other through the experiential momentum of coming-together, the possibility for obtaining an attunement between them disappears.

Coming-together is then a designation for this engagement between the personal body and the ambiance, bringing out a "fruition of" such an encounter which would become an instance of somatic knowing, and which could culminate in a demonstrable somatic knowledge. We might here point out that this fruition is realized as an attunement of the *seemingly* distinct entities, that is, the personal body and an entity in the living ambiance. The theory of attunement takes this fruition which could culminate in demonstrable somatic knowing as an essential reason for the living ambiance not presented as chaos—a restatement of the discussion we had in the preceding section concerning the intelligibility qua co-arising between the personal body and the living ambiance.

Accordingly, we have discovered that the personal body and his/her living ambiance are brought together to form a fruition through the experiential momentum which is a movement of coming-together. This is the generation of new being. Formation of a new being is a generation of somatic knowing. In fact, this coming-together is a necessary condition for somatic knowing, which refers to a mode of somatic engagement, that is, how a particular personal body is oriented to the living ambiance, and how he or she has mastered his or her orientation to it. In order to clarify the meaning of somatic *knowledge*, the theory reminds us to take note of the fact that knowledge, etymologically speaking, is a togetherness, that is, *con* and *science*, which reflects, incidentally, also the etymological origin of the term, "consciousness." According to the theory of attunement which considers the experiential momentum of coming-together between the personal body and the living ambiance as paradigmatic for somatic knowing, the term consciousness in the sense of con + science designates the bilaterality between the personal body and the living ambiance, the fruition of which culminates in knowledge (science). Here we have a slight glimpse of the claim we have made concerning the priority of somatic knowledge.

In thus proposing to understand coming-together as the experiential momentum for attunement, it is not, however, advanced without an assumption. We have implicitly assumed that the personal body is essentially an *openness towards* the living ambiance. If the personal body was closed off by nature within his or her own interiority, the fruition which is brought forth through the experiential momentum of coming-together could not occur insofar as it relates itself to the living ambiance. An attunement that might obtain in the closedness of the personal body, albeit in a formal and vacuous manner, is a minimum one leaving the person only in the world of imaginative thinking, eventually leading him/her to a solipsistic world. In this respect, we can envision philosophy to be an intellectual, theoretical endeavor to clarify the presuppositions inherent in our everyday ego-consciousness. At any rate, we must note in order to show a consistency maintained in the theory of attunement that this assumption of "openness toward" was couched within our contention that the personal body is originally endowed with an adaptive capacity, for the concept of adaptability requires for its meaning that one entity is *open* to another entity, and within the context of the theory of attunement, it means that the personal body must be open toward the living ambiance for an adaptation to take place, particularly in the form of somatic knowing.

But what does it mean to understand coming-together as the experiential momentum for attunement? What have we gained in proposing to understand "knowing" in terms of the fluid bilaterality obtaining between the personal body and the living ambiance? These questions call for an articulation of the implications which can be drawn from the theory of attunement, insofar as the latter has been discussed up to this point. We have maintained that the term, attunement, is descriptive of the *relationship* obtaining in the fluid bilaterality between the personal body and the living ambiance. This means that we have shifted the locus of the traditional epistemological investigation away from both the mind as an epistemological *subject* and the shaped thing as an epistemological object. The subject-object bifurcation occurs when we focus in our analysis either upon the mind as an epistemological subject or upon the shaped thing as an epistemological object as our primary way of understanding the epistemological issue. This follows from our observation that there occurs a fluid bilaterality between the personal body and the living ambiance through the experiential momentum of coming-together. A corollary to this avoidance of the subject-object bifurcation is the rejection of an active-passive dichotomy also as a primary conceptual scheme to view epistemology, a dichotomy which has been believed to be operative in the constitution of the meaning of our experience, perhaps first made explicit by Kant. This dichotomy occurs primarily because our everyday ego-consciousness qua the espistemological subject has been regarded as the locus of knowing.

Having thus indicated a direction from which to overcome the traditional Western attitude towards epistemology, we have yet to specify more positively the conceptual relationship between the phenomenon of attunement and somatic knowing. We have observed that somatic knowing is a fruition of attunement. We must now observe that the *locus* of somatic knowing lies in the personal body. This is due to the fact that the person as a contingent being is individual. Somatic knowing then takes place in the personal body. However, it is reflective of the *degree* of attunement which obtains between the personal body and an entity in the living ambiance. To put it another way, the degree of attunement is correlative with the power of appropriation which a particular person embodies, whose conceptual origin can be traced back to the original adaptive capacity of the personal body, where the power of appropriation may be conceived of as an expression of sustained, concentrated efforts. Although more has to be said about the nature of embodiment, particularly, in relation to the degree of psychophysical integration of the personal body, let us for now conclude that the phenomenon of attunement is appropriated as a form of somatic knowing in the personal body in proportion to the degree of attunement obtaining between the personal body and an entity in the living ambiance.

In connection with this, we must also observe that the phenomenon of attunement is *self-certifying* to the extent that it is appropriated within the personal body. "Self" does not mean, however, that the self of a personal body carries out the act of certifying on its own. If this were the case, we could not distinguish in the appropriation of somatic knowledge, for example, the cases of self-deception from those which are not. By virtue of the experiential meaning of attunement, a possibility of "self-deception" is excluded, that is, the phenomenon of self-deception occurs when the personal body is out of attunement. Therefore, the self in self-certifying is not the *ego* of the personal body. Rather, the phenomenon of attunement has as its intrinsic quality the power of self-certification. The self in the sense of "naturally" or "automatically" refers to the intrinsic quality of the phenomenon of attunement. (We can trace its conceptual origin in the adaptability of a personal body.) It is a confirmation achieved through the experiential momentum of coming-together in the sense, as observed earlier, that both the personal body and the living ambiance come to reach a common quality (or qualities). This suggests that the phenomenon of attunement is an instance of confirmatory experience. For this reason, we stated earlier that the engagement as the fundamental modality of the personal body serves as a principle of verification for the meaning of experience.

In sketching the experiential momentum of coming-together I have avoided to characterize it in terms of consciousness, and its derivative terms such as "preconscious," "pre-reflective." The reason for this avoidance is to guard the theory from falling into the pitfall of the rigidity of mind-body dualism, since consciousness and its derivatives are understood, unless otherwise redefined as "incarnate" or "somatic" consciousness, primarily in terms of the mind. Therefore, I have used a broader terminology, the person or the personal body.

THE SOMATIC FIELD

To say that coming-together is a condition for somatic knowing in respect of the weak sense of attunement is to recognize a source of energy emanating from the personal body in engagement as well as from the living ambiance, for without this, coming cannot take place. In other words, everywhere in the world is filled with the invigorating activities of life-energy (*ki*). For this reason, we could assert in the previous section that coming-together is a bilateral movement or orientation towards. In order for an x to bring a coming as part of experiential momentum, we must acknowledge the source of its energy, the energy which spreads centrifugally from the personal body to the living ambiance, and at the same time, the energy which comes into the personal body centripetally from the invigorating ambiance, as a consequence of which an interfusion of the energies is formed, which we identify under normal, everyday circumstance, as having a quality or feature in our experience. Owing to this interfusion, the bilaterality between the personal body and the living ambiance is established in the experiential momentum of coming-together. This interfusion accounts for its experiential correlate, the phenomenon of attunement.

The emanation of an energy from the personal body is a divine gift in the sense that it calls for a recognition of its pervasive presence in the living ambiance which embraces the personal body as a contingent being, for it shares the same "natural" elements which comprise the totality of physical nature, as we saw in the analysis of the Buddhist concept of the body. In more secular terms, it originates from the personal body as a biological organism with its own quanta of life-energy. To say that it originates from the biological fact is a recognition of the mystery of life insofar as our current knowledge of biology and medical science is concerned. In either case, however, we must recognize that this energy belongs to an invisible dimension of the personal body, for our everyday perceptual consciousness cannot detect its working to its fullest operation. This was for example the meaning of Yuasa's fourth circuit, the "unconscious quasi-body."

Having said this, we must yet point out that the person has a glimpse into this dimension of energy through his/her act of breathing and eruptions of emotion. I mention here the instance of breathing, for it has a great correlation with a being of the personal body: when, for example, the person is in anger or generally, in great excitement and/or agitation, the breathing is rapid and irregular. On the other hand, when the person is in a calm state, the breathing is rhythmic and regular, as for example in the case of dreamless sleep. In either case, the act of breathing is carried out automatically and naturally in the field of our everyday existence, that is, under normal circumstances, or to be more precise, insofar as it is performed by means of the involuntary nervous system. At the same time, however, breathing can be controlled consciously or voluntarily to perform its act either slowly or faster. This suggests that the conscious act of breathing challenges the involuntary function of breathing, and hence how we experience the living ambiance. This dual aspect of breathing suggests that what is considered to be "automatic" or natural is a function which is confined within the autonomic nervous system, which opens up the vast regions of the involuntary functions of the body. The conscious act of breathing then comes to mean the appropriation of this involuntary region of the body, particularly the affective aspect of the person. This in turn will affect and alter the manner through which the external perception functions, for example. We shall see a further specification of this point when we deal in the next section with an "affective style" of the personal body.

For the above stated reason, almost all the meditation methods practiced in Eastern religions stress the importance of regulating one's breathing. We saw an instance of this when we dealt with Dōgen's concept of "just sitting," a partial meaning of which was to transform negative affectivity in general to positive affectivity. When this transformation takes place, an appropriation of the involuntary system of the body occurs as well, as Yuasa demonstrated through his concept of body-scheme, particularly his concept of the emotion-instinct circuit. When we generalize this fact, we come to understand that the personal body is a tangential point connecting the visible and invisible dimensions of the person.

That breathing can be altered in this manner suggests that the energy pervasively present naturally in the living ambiance as well as in the personal body is psychophysical in nature, because the basic activity of both the macrocosm qua the physical nature and the microcosm qua the personal body are the same. It further suggests that it is a bridge, a mediating point between the psychical and the physical of the person. That it is a mediating point means that it can communicate to the psychical aspect of the person as well as to its physicality, since by definition, being psychophysical means that it is neither psychical nor physical per se, insofar as it is energy.

To contend that there is energy of this sort, we are drawing an implication from the fact that a personal body, is a psychophysical integration in nature, although its degree of integration in the field of our everyday existence may vary from person to person, assuming what we earlier referred to as "provisional mind-body dualism." In light of this provisional mind-body dualism, then, the above observation suggests that the seemingly disparate status of both the mind and the body can be brought to a higher degree of integration through breathing exercise. If this observation is proved to be true, what is further implied with regard to the *what* of the person is that it is other than psychophysical, at least, a synthetic entity *higher* than the psychophysical, such as buddha-nature or *Tao*. At any rate, the recognition of the emanation of energy points towards a possibility of discovering an essential nature of the person, its potentiality, its depth concealed behind the visible materiality of the body and things shaped in the ambiance.

In regard to our observation that an emanation of energy is recognized in the experiential momentum of coming-together the theory of attunement also points out that the emanation of energy creates a field, "somatic field," in the sense that the personal body makes its presence felt in the living ambiance, as it announces itself or moves itself in the ambiance by means of a particular mode of engagement demonstrating a qualitative dimension of the person, whose experiential correlate is mostly in terms of "affectivity" which the personal body carries. Within this somatic field, the physical delineation of the body or the physical presence itself becomes secondary, for this physical presence is overlaid by the kind of qualitative aura that is being created in the bilateral interfusion between the personal body and the living ambiance. For example, in characterizing the type of persons close to us, we do not identify them primarily in terms of the physical delineation of their body, or physical "features," but we identify them by the tonal ambiance which is expressed through the "shape" of their physical being. For this reason, the physical shape recedes into the background of a somatic field, since this somatic field displays a *qualitative* presence of a particular personal body. It is primarily qualitative in nature. Needless to say, this generation of field is concurrent with the experiential momentum of coming-together in that the latter is observed to be a movement-towards.

In this somatic field, the so-called "objective" space and time become, for example, incorporated within the field, and a unique spatialization and temporalization become engendered within it in accordance with the nature of engagement that the personal body has learned to embody as an instance of habit-formation, or a sedimentation of a habit. Take an instance of a master dancer performing his/her dance. We do not identify him/her with the physical delineation of his or her body when he/she performs. Rather, we take his/her body in action to be an expression of something other than the physical. His/her engaging performance creates his/her own spatiality and temporality—spatiality through the movement of his/her body and temporality through the rhythm that the movement creates. In light of this, the somatic field which we have observed as emanating from the particular person may now be characterized as embodying a rhythmic fluidity. Therefore, the somatic field is not delineated experientially as well as phenomenally by a rigid boundary. Each person creates his/her own temporality and spatiality, and experientially, there is no single objective time and space. That is to say, there is a multiplicity and multidimensionality of temporality and spatiality which the person creates, the scope and depth of which naturally is reflective of the kind of attunement which obtains in a particular somatic field. It is perhaps needless to say at this point that the creation of these unique modes of temporality and spatiality holds only insofar as the personal body assumes an engagement.

In close correlation with the generation of temporality and spatiality, this somatic field displays various tonalities ranging from "sacred" to "profane" depending upon the kind of engagement which a personal body has learned or sedimented. We may be able to enumerate many more which can be classified within this range of tonalities, according to salient features which a particular somatic field displays. However, we may just point out that each somatic field engendered has its tonality with its own intensity and scope (consider a case of charisma).

We may see an instance of tonality with its own intensity and scope of somatic field for example in the thirteenth century Noh critic Zeami, particularly in his concept of freedom, wherein we discern the ascending movement of appropriation of "flowers" in proportion to the degree to which an actor learns performing techniques.[2] A beginning actor who has not yet learned various performing techniques, when he is allowed to perform on stage, shows "awkward" movements, and the tonality of his somatic field would indicate a status of "ham" actor. In contrast, a master actor who has learned all the performing techniques along with a proper attitude of nonperforming mind, would display the status of "moving sculpture" in his somatic field. Naturally, not every engagement the personal body assumes can be labelled as embodying this excellence. There would be a hierarchy in the excellence in performance. Likewise, every somatic field that the personal body engenders can be mapped in accordance with the salient features which are experientially and phenomenally present in a particular somatic field.

Although the phenomenon of the somatic field which we have just sketched above does not seem to have a direct and an explicit bearing on the epistemological aspect of the theory of attunement, we must yet point out that since all the engagements that the person or the personal body performs occurs in this somatic field, it is evident that the concept of somatic field is essential to understand what and how a particular engagement transpires. A spatiality or a lived space which a personal body creates in close correlation with a mode of engagement would alter, for example, the perception of a shaped thing in the ambiance.[3] Similarly, a temporality, or a lived time which a personal body creates would transform the perception of the living ambiance, for example, one part may be accentuated more in the perceptual field than another as displaying a more meaningful aspect of a shaped thing.[4]

AFFECTIVITY: FEELING-JUDGEMENT

The psychophysical energy which is given to the personal body with its infinitely available *quanta* of life-energy, when it is enacted by the experiential momentum of coming-together, turns into affectivity. Affectivity is essential for the experiential momentum of coming-together, for it renders every experience personally meaningful. When this ceases to accompany the experiential momentum, the person also fails to find any meaning in his/her life with an imminent possibility of becoming a living corpse, because affectivity is a source of *animation* for the personal body. Since it pertains to animation, affectivity is essentially the expression of anima.[5]

Given this observation, an important issue for the theory of attunement is first to specify the ontogenesis of affectivity in the personal body and then examine it in light of the bilaterality of affectivity as it is constituted in the experiential momentum of coming-together. The theory argues that this affective bilaterality co-functional in the experiential momentum may be characterized as "feeling-judgement." In other words, the phenomenon of attunement, when it obtains between the personal body and an object in the living ambiance, is characterized by feeling-judgement which is formed through an "affective resonance" in the phenomenon of attunement. This affective resonance, we may understand, is the basis for that which gives rise to a common quality (or qualities) in the bilateral experiential momentum of coming-together when an attunement obtains. In order to argue for this position, we shall then briefly analyze the experiential meaning of affectivity as it relates to the theory of attunement first in terms of the source of affectivity, and then in terms of its feeling-judgement."[6]

Affectivity has its source in the adaptive capacity of the personal body, an element we introduced previously as a basis for recognizing that the phenomenon of attunement is epistemologically fundamental to the being of the person. This source lies, however, concealed in the body, in the *altus* of the body, because the alleged "transparency" of everyday ego-consciousness is incapable of detecting its origin, much less the principle of its operation, especially when consciousness is directed to the external ambiance. This follows from our previous remark that affectivity is the ex-pression of anima; anima as such is concealed from the alleged transparency of our everyday ego-consciousness, although personal likes and dislikes are indicative of the source of affectivity. To be more specific, this concealment is a concealment from the *ego* of the personal body. Reflections upon one's likes and dislikes, however, enable the person to have a *glimpse* into the working of anima, and the person discovers that anima through its expression of affectivity is the source for impulse, passion, sensation, mood, emotion, feeling, perception, and thinking. In short, it is the source for all the animation of the "life of consciousness."

Even though anima in its total functioning is concealed from the everyday ego-consciousness, the alleged transparency claimed in respect of our everyday ego-consciousness is in turn unknowingly or subtly affected by anima, via its expression of affectivity. The ego of the personal body is held together by the host of its inherent affective likes and dislikes. In other words, the ego is permeated by its own affective likes and dislikes. This pervasive permeation renders each ego of the personal body individually unique. A philosophically significant point in this observation is that the ego is unaware of this pervasive permeation. This was, for example, effectively demonstrated by Ichikawa in *Seishin to shiteno shintai* where he describes phenomenologically the dependency of cogito upon the (subject-)body for its functioning and survival. Specifically, he demonstrated it when he shows among the mood, the emotion, the feeling, the perception and thinking, that there is, in the order mentioned, a proportional degree of affective influence from the base of the subject-body, from what Ichikawa called "an obscure, hazy horizon of *cogito*."[7]

That the personal body in its everyday mode of being-in-the-ambiance is unaware of the working of affectivity does not mean that every person or personal body demonstrates the same "configuration" of affectivity. Neither does it mean that every personal body is endowed with the same configuration of affectivity. On the contrary, anima provides each personal body with a particular affective configuration which we identify as a personal character. That the person is endowed with its unique configuration of anima is due to the fact that the personal body is an individualized contingent being, carrying the "seeds" of past history which transcends the individuality of the personal body. This was the meaning of the Buddhist concept of saṃskāra as a potential, formative energy which configures a dispositional tendency of each personal body.

Generally speaking, however, this personally individualized configuration of anima may be thought of as embodying the two conflicting dispositional tendencies; (1) one is light (*hikari*) and positive in its experiential correlates and (2) the other shadow (*kage*) and negative in its experiential correlates. Since the light tendency is positive in nature, it carries a set of such inclinations as inclinations toward creativity, happiness and ecstatic illumination, all that is luminous. In contrast, the shadow tendency is the opposite of the positive; its inclination is the source of destruction, unhappiness, death—all that is opposite to the luminous. The contrast between the light and the shadow may seem to be an arbitrary distinction, but the personal body seems to know intuitively this demarcation when, for example, it falls into the "depressive" (shadow) or "ecstatic" (light) moments *without* or *in spite of* a transparent "reason." I add in spite of here, because it is always possible to "rationalize" a phenomenally discernible set of "causes" for falling into a certain state. This suggests, among other things, that the activity of anima is mostly independent of our everyday ego-consciousness.

Insofar as these conflicting tendencies are tendencies, they are not the fixed determination, although we must recognize numerous variations or combinations of these two conflicting tendencies. Nonetheless, in the numerous combinations of these two conflicting tendencies is always a predominance of one over the other. The *ratio* of light and shadow tendency in the personal body is more or less set, which resists a reconfiguration of the ratio. This ratio is a *ratio cognescendi* for the personal body. By virtue of this ratio, the person is always under the sway of "affective mood" in one way or another, which is not a particular "mood" as one would say, "she is moody," but rather it is a general manner for the person to present himself/herself to the living ambiance. In fact, a particular mood into which a personal body falls is indicative of the larger constitution of affective mood. It is his/her affective style. Since affectivity is the source of anima-tion, the person cannot but exist in a certain affective style. What this suggests *inter alia*, is that in order to obtain objective knowledge, one must eliminate the influence of affective style, or neutralize it so that knowledge thus obtained can be free from personal affective style. This is, for example, a reason that somatic knowledge calls for a somatic transformation, because the affective style is deeply rooted in the personal body, while the so-called "cognitive" knowledge does not bother to dispel it and yet it claims "objectivity." This will be the topic we shall explore later when we deal with the "de-tensional" mode of the personal body. For now, what is important for the theory of attunement is to recognize the contributing factor of affective style in the constitution of the meaning of experience.

When we apply the above observation of affective style to Merleau-Ponty's concept of "body's intentionality," for example, we must modify it in such a way that this affective style will be incorporated within his concept of body's intentionality. For Merleau-Ponty, the body's intentionality is a *basic* intentionality in the sense that it functions as "general synthesis" for all the phenomena of the life of consciousness.[8] The body's intentionality is necessary for making the life of consciousness lived, by rendering every experience meaningful. Merleau-Ponty's contention is that the body's intentionality establishes an invisible intentional-arc (i.e., the experiential momentum of coming-together in the terminology of the present theory) between the personal body and its intentional object. In formulating the concept of body's intentionality in this manner, he fails to mention the influence which the body's intentionality receives from the affective style of the personal body, as if the formation of the intentional-arc by means of the body's intentionality is not colored or tinted by the affective style. If our preceding observations are correct, it follows that the body's intentionality is predetermined as to what it captures through the intentional arc, that is, as to what constitutes a meaningful noema by means of an affective style in the body's intentionality. Unless we conceive of it in this manner, we cannot, for example, account for the fact that supposedly "the same" object, when presented to many persons, receives different descriptions. This must suggest that different affective styles are operative in the formation of the body's intentionality which casts an invisible intentional arc to an intentional object.

In order to think out the issue of the affective style contributing to the formation of the meaning of experience, in particular, how somatic knowledge is formed, we must now turn our attention to a clarification of the concept of affectivity. Up to this point, we have concerned ourselves with the concept of affectivity as dispositional tendencies with its potential formative energy, or the affective style of the personal body. This sense of affectivity serves in fact as preparatory to the next sense of affectivity which is crucial for the theory of attunement, especially in respect to the phenomenon of feeling-judgement.

Earlier, we observed that the experiential momentum of coming-together is a bilateral relationship holding between the personal body and the living ambiance, and this bilaterality is understood as reaching a common quality (or qualities) between the personal body and the living ambiance. In thus recognizing the bilaterality in respect to the quality which is brought forth in the experiential momentum of coming-together, the affectivity as dispositional tendencies of the person plays a crucial role as to how the quality obtaining between the personal body and its living ambiance, appears to, and is judged by, the person. Now, when we understand the affectivity as an aspect of the bilateral relationship between the personal body and the living ambiance, we have here the second sense of the concept of affectivity.

Let us first observe through an analysis of the concept of affectivity that there is indeed an *affective* bilateral relationship obtaining between the personal body and the living ambiance. Logically, the concept of affectivity (in the second sense of the term) demands that affectivity is grounded in the bilateral interplay between what does the affecting and what is being affected. In fact, to eliminate one of the terms in this formula renders the concept of affectivity vacuous. "Bi-lateral interplay" may be understood to be a dynamic exchange in the role in "affecting" and "being affected" due to an affective resonance, that is, that which does the affecting can be turned into that which is being affected. This is to say that in order for x to be an affective agent, it must be both active and passive, both affecting and being affected. This analysis reinstantiates the earlier contention that the bilaterality between the personal body and the living ambiance not only arises in the experiential momentum of coming-together, but also they come to reach a common quality (or qualities) between the personal body and an object in the living ambiance.

What becomes a crucial concern for the theory of attunement, in recognizing the affective bilaterality between the personal body and the living ambiance, is a *paradigmatic* understanding of this phenomenon insofar as it concerns the person, that is, as to how this phenomenon appears to, and is judged by, the person. I use the term paradigmatic understanding in order to exclude from our investigation the individual instances of what affective bilaterality is, can be, and will be engendered as in our everyday life. This should be a task for philosophical psychology, although such a task is immensely important in understanding each person, for its "configuration" of affectivity naturally endowed to each personal body has many varieties. For philosophical psychology, for example, it would be a major task to investigate how the affective bilaterality which obtains between the personal body and the living ambiance, affects or influences the affectivity as the intrinsic dispositional tendencies or the affective style of the person, or vice versa, when this occurs in an individual case of the experiential momentum of coming-together.

For our purpose of articulating the theory of attunement in respect of the affective style in the experiential momentum of coming-together, we must, at least for now, be satisfied with a paradigmatic understanding of the affective bilaterality which obtains between the personal body and the living ambiance, especially in respect to how this affective bilaterality appears to and is judged by the person. This is an issue of how to characterize and analyze this phenomenon of affective bilaterality as it pertains to somatic knowing for the personal body.

I propose to characterize this affective bilaterality as feeling-judgement when it is experienced by the personal body through an affective resonance. In feeling-judgement the locus of this experience is the personal body as a whole, as an affective sensorium, which functions as an epistemological as well as actional apparatus. It is, in other words, a holistic function. Individual sensory perceptions are only particular instances abstracted from this holistic function in order for the personal body to *attend* to a specific aspect of an object that is engaged through the experiential momentum of coming together. In feeling-judgement they are only an aspect that contributes to the formation of somatic knowing.

What then is feeling-judgement? The hyphenation between "feeling" and "judgement" indicates that, when attunement obtains, two faculties of the personal body function concurrently within the person with the affective sensorium functioning as a basis for them. Feeling in feeling-judgement is used to indicate the affective aspect which is influenced by intrinsic dispositional tendencies of the personal body, while judgement designates an aspect of understanding in agreement with the quality (or qualities) which is brought forth through the experiential momentum of coming- together. "Understanding" in this sense is a further specification of the concept of affective resonance. As a consequence of this fruition of coming-together, it results in a somatic knowledge. Understanding here as an aspect of judgement does not mean, however, a purely cognitive operation of judgement, because a whole of the personal body, as we observed, is operative as an affective sensorium.

This may be shown by contrasting feeling-judgement with intellectual judgement. The intellectual judgement takes the subject-predicate form in which the process of forming this judgement involves an epistemological subject which is allegedly divorced from the body of an experiencer. In contrast to this, feeling-judgement does not take the subject-predicate form. It is rather pre-predicative, because there is no *intellectual* distinction in feeling-judgement between the personal body as an experiencer and an object experienced. In other words, there is an attunement in feeling-judgement between them. Therefore, the act of feeling-judgement is not the act of cogito proper, if we understand it to be "thinking" which is operative in the momentum of forming an intellectual judgement. Rather, the act aspect of feeling-judgement is indicative of the manner in which the personal body assumes and orients himself/herself towards an object that is engaged. To put it differently, knowing-that and judging-that are one and the same momentum in feeling-judgement. This was the meaning of feeling-judgement being a holistic function. For example, when one gets burned by a fire, there is no distinction between knowing that one has been burned and judging that one has been burned. It is a spontaneous and immediate somatic response. Although we must point out that "spontaneity" and "immediacy" depend upon the manner of orientation which the personal body has acquired, or appropriated through habit-formation. In other words, there is a range of spontaneity and immediacy in feeling-judgement, for example, between natural response and a cultivated one. "Natural response" with respect to spontaneity and immediacy has its ground in the *adaptive* capacity of the personal body, while "cultivated response" is a refinement and an enlargement of the natural response. For example, when one practices *karate*, assuming a certain form for a block is spontaneous and immediate in proportion to the degree to which one has mastered the art of karate. In this case, the feeling that one is spontaneous and immediate in assuming the form of a block is correlative with judging that one has assumed a "right" form of a block. This correlativity is an intrinsic quality of feeling-judgement which, as we saw earlier, is the basis for attunement to be self-certifying as well as engagement serving as a principle of verification of truth or falsity of the fundamental modality of the personal body which is engagement.

When we understand the concept of feeling-judgement in this manner, it is apparent that in the formation of somatic knowledge through feeling-judgement there is no distinction between an epistemological subject and actional subject, for somatic knowledge is knowledge that can be attained *only* through the utilization of one's body, or to be more specific, through engagement which the person undertakes. Somatic knowledge appropriated through feeling-judgement includes an appropriation of skill, theatrical performance, athletic movements, learning to play a musical instrument—all that involves the engagement of the body.

Granted that somatic knowledge is operative in this manner through feeling-judgement, a question naturally arises whether or not this somatic knowledge qualifies as more a sublime form of knowledge such as religious truth, philosophical truth, in short, knowledge in the paramount sense of the term. If it does not, the theory of attunement which embodies feeling-judgement as an integral structural component for the theory of attunement may seem trivially true. In order to dispel this kind of impression, we must now deal with an analysis of sedimentation as a special form of habit formation, and distinguish essential and nonessential forms of sedimentation.

SEDIMENTATION

A single instance or occurrence of coming-together generative of somatic knowing is, however, ephemeral owing to the dynamic character of the experiential momentum of coming-together, which is indicated by the gerundive form of the verb, "to come." It does not usually constitute a redemonstrable knowledge, although the ephemerality of a single occurrence of the experiential momentum of coming-together may be considered sufficient in some cases for an appropriation of somatic knowledge. An apparent reason that a single occurrence of the experiential momentum is sufficient for obtaining somatic knowledge must be due to the fact that it can imprint an indelible mark in the innermost region of anima of the personal body. In this respect, somatic knowledge thus gained may be considered to be an extraordinary experience. To this class of experience belongs, in its negative experiential correlate, all that is traumatic, and in its positive experiential correlate, all that is euphoric, both having their origins respectively in the "light" and the "shadow" affectivity of the personal body. The contrast between "positive" and "negative" is used here to demarcate the experience which enhances and enriches a quality of the person from the experience which impoverishes and deteriorates a quality of the person. For extraordinary experiences to be appropriated as somatic knowledge with a single occurrence of the experiential momentum of coming-together, especially when they occur naturally, they do not require a repeated occurrence of more or less the same experiential momentum of coming-together. For this reason, we shall for now exclude extraordinary experiences from our analysis.

Most experiences that the person undergoes in the everyday field of existence slip through his/her fingers, as it were, and the person ends up empty handed, when there is only a single occurrence of the experiential momentum of coming-together. They slip by the person unnoticed for experience to be qualified to be somatic knowledge since somatic knowledge in its fuller sense of the term is that which is appropriated in the personal body. This is because the person is buried in the everydayness of his/her existence with a set of habits which regulates his/her life. A set of habits which the person possesses may be considered to be a matrix of habituated somatic knowledge. Any experience that appears to the person *outside of* this matrix will be presented as novel. The point that we would like to call to our attention is that somatic knowledge as a constant and redemonstrable property of the person cannot be obtained nor claimed by means of a mere single occurrence of the experiential momentum of coming-together, unless it happens to be an extraordinary experience, for the personal body is constantly changing, in the field of his/her everyday existence, his/her mode or direction of its orientation towards his/her ambiance, like a monkey in the zoo.

Somatic knowledge that is redemonstrable is sedimentational in character. The term "sedimentational" refers to a process of acquisition in which somatic knowledge is appropriated in the personal body through the repeated occurrences of more or less the same experiential momentum. A single occurrence of the experiential momentum of coming-together with its ephemerality, comes to be secured steadfastly only by means of the sedimentational process in which a particular person resolutely undergoes in the course of his/her life.

The very possibility for a person to have a capacity for appropriating various forms of sedimentation lies in, or is grounded upon, the adaptive capacity of the personal body *originally* endowed to him/her, for adaptability enables the personal body to *attune* himself/herself to whatever is presented. Sedimentation in this sense is a process of *attuning*. What interests us here in regard to the theory of attunement is an analysis of the phenomenon of sedimentation which enhances and enriches the quality of the person, just like Aristotle in *Nichomachean Ethics* thought that personal "virtues" are acquired through a process of habit formation.

As it is mentioned in the preceding, sedimentation in the sense that the personal body attempts to attune himself/herself to whatever is presented is possible because of the adaptive capacity of the person. It is therefore appropriate to regard the fruition of the sedimentational process as "*somatic* knowledge." For this reason, the attuning process of sedimentation is not, strictly speaking, performed by the act of cogito, but it is rather somatic in character. Insofar as "I want to learn x" is a conscious phenomenon that has surfaced from the modification of the body, this desire of "wanting" is grounded in the personal body. However, not all the possibilities of wanting which must eventually be realized in an engagement—that which is the universal and fundamental mode of being-in-the-ambiance—that the personal body could assume can be realized and incorporated as the fruition of sedimentation, owing to the inherent limitation of the body as a finite being. This means that among the multiplicity of possible engagements, sedimentation takes place with the principle of selectivity for the personal body. The principle of selectivity is configured by the ratio of likes and dislikes unique to, and characteristic of an individual personal body—part of the meaning of the original capacity of adaptability of the personal body.

However, within the range of multiplicity of engagements which are agreeable to personal likes and dislikes, whatever the person chooses to learn can result in redemonstrable somatic knowledge, whether it be a practice of karate or the practice of meditation. A diligent application of the same form (*kata*) of engagement is essential in this endeavor. Consider a process of learning a new skill, say, of using a brush for calligraphy (*shodō*). At first, a person must learn to hold a brush right. What this means is that when a perspective shifted from a person learning to use a brush to the perspective of a brush, the brush *demands* that it is to be held right. A person should not hold a brush in the same way, for example, that he/she would hold a screwdriver. The brush, in other words, demands a conformity to the right form of handling for its most efficient use. To state it with the terminologies we have devised for the theory of attunement, it can be translated as follows. The personal body *attends* self-consciously to the right form of handling a brush. This means, at the initial stage of learning to hold a brush right, there is a minimal degree of attunement obtaining between the personal body and a brush, for there is an epistemological as well as actional *gap* between them—a discrepancy between the movements of the body and those of the mind that arises from "self-conscious attention." Insofar as there is this gap, the affective resonance is minimum between a hand attempting to hold a brush and the brush itself. In order to have the most efficient use of the brush, the personal body must respond to, and fulfill the demand which the right form of holding the brush imposes upon the personal body, so that the above mentioned gap will no longer exist between the personal body and the brush. When this is mastered, the personal body no longer attends self-consciously to holding the brush right. The feeling-judgement operative in this instance would be that the brush is no longer an object that opposes in its function the personal body. In this instance, we can say that a higher degree of attunement obtains between the personal body and the brush, insofar as it is concerned with a simple task of holding a brush right—higher compared to an initial stage of learning to hold a brush for calligraphy. Both the personal body and a brush "come-together" through the experiential momentum of holding a brush right. This is an appropriation of the use of a brush for the person, and at the same time, for the brush to be incorporated within the personal body in this manner, it acquires a "life" as a brush. In this sense, the use of a brush becomes a "second nature" for the person, and it allows him/her to create its own lived body-space, for example, his/her "hand" extending, as far as the tip of the brush.

Generally speaking, then, an appropriation of a sedimentational process means, *inter alia*, a transformation of the lived body-space, or lived body-image. When we substitute the use of a tool in learning a new skill with learning an athletic performance, say, gymnastic movements which involve a training of one's own body, the essential process which accompanies this training is the same as learning to hold a brush, for both processes require a "coordination of the body." On the surface, what is to be "coordinated" appears to the movements of the physical body in gymnastics, and in the use of a tool, an efficient *hand*ling of a tool. That is, in the case of learning gymnastic movements one's body as a tool for expressing gymnastic beauty, that is, the body as that which is to be appropriated, goes through various degrees of appropriation. This suggests, among other things, that the person goes through various degrees of psychophysical integration in the sedimentational process. This shows that the coordination of the body is in effect a coordination of physical movements with the movements of the mind.

When this sedimentational process is applied to the mind-body issue, it implies that the mind and the body are *provisionally* distinct in our everyday mode of existence. The mind and the body in the everyday field of existence are provisionally dualistic. Otherwise, there cannot be a progression of appropriating a higher degree of psychophysical integration. When a person initially learns gymnastic movements, an intention of turning one's body in a certain way cannot be executed in its corresponding physical movements. With a diligent practice, however, there occurs a transformation from an awkward "coordination" of the bodily movements to a perfect "ten" in the bodily movements. This implies that the provisional dualism operative prior to the sedimentational process is not the final characterization of the person.

An interesting question arises whether or not all the sedimentational processes, be it training in karate or gymnastics, or the practice of meditation, are the same with respect to the nature of appropriation, that is, with respect to a kind of psychophysical integration which accompanies the sedimentational process in general. It would seem that we must introduce here a distinction between "essential" sedimentational process and "nonessential" sedimentational process. We may understand for now nonessential sedimentational process to be that sedimentation process in which there is a refinement of the *voluntary motor-movements* in the sense of coordination of the physical body. On the other hand, we may understand the essential sedimentational process to be, though not exclusive of a refinement of the voluntary motor-movements, that sedimentational process in which the coordination of the body pertains to the affectivity of the personal body, that affectivity which is concealed from the everyday perspective of the person. To use Yuasa's terminology, the essential sedimentation pertains to the emotion-instinct circuit. In light of this distinction, the difference between the essential and the nonessential sedimentational process then is whether or not the sedimentational process touches the *innermost* region of anima and transforms the mode of its function as it relates itself to the state of the personal body. Or to put it differently, the psychophysical integration in the case of essential sedimentational process is concerned with a transformation of the altus of the body, particularly, the shadow region of the affective component of the personal body, while in case of the nonessential sedimentational process, this transformation does not occur. In light of the concept of this transformation, the difference between the essential and nonessential sedimentational processes may be regarded as lying in the difference in the degree of, and hence also the nature of, the psychophysical integration. Since the former involves a *radical* transformation in the sense of affecting the innermost region of anima, while the latter does not, the degree of psychophysical integration is much higher in essential sedimentational process than it is in nonessential sedimentational process. By virtue of this difference, the transformation of body-image, or the lived body-space which accompanies both cases, is believed to be radically different, as well. We touched upon the transformation of the body-image, or lived body-space when we dealt with Dōgen's experiential account of "felt inter-resonance." What follows from these observations is that the nature of somatic knowledge which is achieved through the essential sedimentational process is radically different from the one achieved from the nonessential sedimentational process—radical in the sense of shattering the supposedly valid ground of the life of an ego of the person. We saw in the analysis of Dōgen's concept of just sitting this shattering of the high ground by means of "casting off the body and mind." In the final analysis, this difference between the essential and nonessential sedimentational processes leads to a recognition of the total transformation of the person. Because of these salient features of essential sedimentational processes, what concerns us in the next chapter is the essential sedimentational process.

Up to this point, we have sketched the structural components of the theory of attunement; (1) the formal condition for attunement, (2) the experiential momentum of coming-together for obtaining attunement, (3) the somatic field in which attunement occurs, (4) affectivity as feeling-judgement in the experiential momentum, and (5) sedimentation which increases the degree of attunement. Our concern in the following section is to articulate the different modes of engagement relative to the psychophysical integration of the personal body, and specify the nature of attunement which obtains vis-à-vis each different mode of somatic engagement. This will also serve to clarify a transformation from the provisional dualism operative in our everyday existence to nonduality which obtains in samadhic awareness. This now leads us into an investigation of the stratification of the somatic modality of engagement.

CHAPTER 10

A *Stratification of Engagement*

INTRODUCTION

Up to this point, our discussion has been concerned with specifying the theory of attunement with a view to articulating its structural components. In so doing, we have assumed that engagement as the fundamental and universal mode of being-in-the-ambiance for the personal body in his/her relation to the living ambiance (in terms of the experiential momentum of "coming-together") is fixed and constant. But if this engagement admits of transformations through the process of essential sedimentation, the manner through which the personal body engages, and is engaged by, the living ambiance through the experiential momentum of coming-together undergoes a radical modification, and hence so does the degree and the nature of attunement which obtains in the bilateral relationship between the personal body and its living ambiance.

Here, we encounter a need to discuss the stratification of engagement. By "stratification of engagement" is meant a specification of the different *manners* or *modalities* of engagement through which the experiential momentum of coming-together takes place, correlative with the degree of psychophysical integration of the personal body. A manner or modality of engagement may alternatively be conceived of as indicative of an "orientation-towards" which the personal body assumes in relating itself to the living ambiance. Orientation-towards indicates *a locus from which* the personal body engages, and is engaged by the living ambiance. Since it points toward the *locus* of the person, this issue of stratification of engagement has a direct bearing upon an analysis of the degrees of psychophysical integration of the person, which in turn gives us an opportunity to discuss the mind-body issue within the conceptual framework of the theory of attunement. Consequently, an analysis of the stratification of engagement enables us to witness a transformation of the provisional dualism operative in the field of everyday existence to a nondualistic position of samadhic awareness. We shall see this transformation being effected by means of what we called in the previous chapter the "essential sedimentational process." This stratification of engage-ment also enables the theory of attunement to demonstrate a *proportionality* of attunement obtaining between the personal body and the living ambiance. In fact, we shall see that the degree of attunement obtaining between the person and his/her living ambiance is proportionate with the degree of psychophysical integration of the person.

In order to execute these contentions, the theory of attunement will develop three different concepts designating three different modalities or orientation-towards of engagement, each of which purports to reflect paradigmatically the kinds of experience which the personal body undergoes in accordance with the degree of its psychophysical integration. These three conceptual designations are (1) "tensionality," (2) "de-tensionality," and (3) "non-tensionality." Although we shall pursue a detailed analysis of what these terminologies mean, we may for now understand tensionality to be an everyday standpoint, de-tensionality to be "going out of" an everyday standpoint, and non-tensionality to be free from an everyday standpoint which is achieved through an essential sedimentational process, or to use a more broad category, through a de-tensional modality of engagement. When we understand the senses of these terminologies as indicated above, what has been discussed up to this point regarding the theory of attunement receives further specification in respect of its actual instantiation.

TENSIONALITY

An underlying assumption in advancing the theory of attunement thus far, especially in articulating an experiential momentum of coming-together as an intrinsic condition for obtaining attunement, is that the personal body remains in the natural standpoint (Husserl's starting point) or everyday mode of existence (Heidegger's starting point). Hence, we have not taken into the purview of the theory of attunement a degree of psychophysical integration which plays an essential role in this theory. By bringing our analysis to bear upon the stratification of engagement, we shall be faced with an impending question—the question which enables us to discover an essential characterization of the natural standpoint or everyday mode of existence. What then characterizes the modality of engagement that corresponds to, or is reflective of, this standpoint? What, in other words, is the modality of engagement that is unique to this standpoint?

I propose to analyze such a modality in terms of what I call "tensional" or its nominal form tensionality. It may be surmised that these two terminologies, tensional and tensionality, must be related to the common term, "tension," in its psychological as well as its physical sense. However, the psychological as well as physical connotation is unwanted as a primary way of characterizing what this term means, since we are concerned with a philosophical theory of attunement, particularly, its epistemological-actional aspect, although they are not excluded as forming its derivative meanings. What is a philosophically primary way, then, to understand the term, tensional or tensionality when we say that the engagement as it pertains to the everyday standpoint or to the natural standpoint, is a tensional engagement? Earlier, we observed that there is an orientation-towards as a constitutive element in the experiential momentum of coming-together. This orientation-towards has its pivot in the depth of the personal body, that is, in the person as an epistemological-actional apparatus and it is generated by *adding tension* to this apparatus from within.[1] Adding tension is analyzable to "add tension," which in turn, synthetically becomes "attention," or its derivatives such as "to attend," "to be attentive," and "attentively."

Let us further analyze how this adding tension turns into attention (and by implication its derivative terms) in light of the conceptual framework of the theory of attunement which has been articulated up to this point. The power that supplies an energy to add*ing* tension, as we observed earlier in connection with affectivity, comes from the psychophysical energy with which the personal body is originally endowed in his/her adaptive capacity. This power of adding, when it is seen in light of the analysis of affectivity, is colored by an individually configured affective style of the personal body. Adding tension, thus equipped with the psychophysical energy which is realized as an affective style, functions as a *vector* in the somatic field which is brought forth through the experiential momentum of coming-together. A vector in the somatic field is consequently realized as attention. To put it differently, the personal body *attends* to an object in the living ambiance, which is a consequence of the psychophysical energy being enacted, along with the affective style, by the experiential momentum. To attend to something means to *attend self-consciously*. When we interpret tensionality as adding tension in the sense of attending self-consciously, the personal body *as the epistemological-actional locus of an affective sensorium shifts its focus* to consciousness that is aware of itself, that is, to self-consciousness. Hence, by focusing upon the self which carries with it a host of somatic modalities such as desires and passions, the self of the personal body becomes a dominant parameter by means of which everything experienced is measured. Here, we have then a developmental characterization of how tensionality is derived from adding tension from within the personal body, allowing the person to form attention, or enabling the personal body to attend to, or becoming "attentive to" an object in the living ambiance, with its self turned into a dominant parameter against which everything experienced is measured by it.

Needless to say, this articulation of tensionality in the sense of attending self-consciously as a way of characterizing the being-in-the-ambiance for the person in the everyday field of existence does not apply to epistemological-actional acts that are performed by habits, when we understand habits to be those actions which do not require an effort, or in light of what we have just observed, a self-conscious attention. Most experiences in the everyday field of existence are undergone within the matrix of habits which the personal body has appropriated or incorporated within itself. They fly by the person unnoticed. An obvious inapplicability of tensionality in the sense of attending self-consciously to the actions performed by habits, is that when it is translated into the terms of the theory of attunement, the matrix of habits is appropriated in the personal body as the body of *somatic knowledge*. Somatic knowledge as appropriated through attunement, as we recall, does not require an intellectual judgement of which attention is an intrinsic part. Furthermore, we must also note another fact of the everyday existence which is not appropriate to characterize in terms of tensionality in the sense of attending self-consciously. This is the sleep state, or states analogous to it. Tensionality in the sense of attending self-consciously pertains only to waking moments of the person. We must therefore refrain from characterizing both the matrix of habits and the sleep state[2] as being tensional.

What then are the experiences in the everyday field of existence which qualify for the modality of tensional engagement in the sense of attending self-consciously? Our preceding analysis suggests that any experience in the waking moments which falls outside of the matrix of habits, appropriated as somatic knowledge within itself, would be characterizable in terms of tensionality. Experiences which are outside of the matrix of habits are *novel* experiences, in which an interest is aroused in the person. Naturally, this includes any experience in the process of being appropriated, or in a process of sedimentation, a habit formation, on the way to a fuller sense of somatic knowledge.

Having now delineated the applicability of the term tensionality in the sense of attending self-consciously, we can then formulate this finding as follows: "the personal body *tensionally* engages, and is engaged by the living ambiance." Insofar as the person is concerned, this would translate, according to our analysis, into: "the person self-consciously attends to the living ambiance." What does this modality of tensional engagement in the sense of attending self-consciously reveal to us concerning the degree of psychophysical integration of the person?

The above question calls for a philosophical analysis of the meaning of attending self-consciously in light of the conceptual framework of the theory of attunement. In order to unpack this issue, we shall ask the following question: what does attending self-consciously mean to the personal body? This question may be approached from two perspectives. First, we might characterize that "attending" is an act performed by the personal body, and self-consciously indicates a manner of this act of attending. This approach further calls for specifying the relationship between the personal body and the self. Since we interpret a self to be a surge from the altus of the personal body, and hence it is not an entity distinct from the personal body, we shall abandon this approach. Second, we might analyze the phrase attending self-consciously to mean that "consciously" qualifies a manner of the act of attending, while the manner of this act *is referred back* to the self as a bearer of the act of "attending consciously." Since the second approach enables us to contrast the theory of attunement with those of the traditional Western epistemological theories, we shall approach the question from the second perspective. What then is this self which is referred back through the act of attending consciously?

The self surges as a bearer of the act from the altus of the personal body which, as an extended thing, is a continuum, through and in which this surge occurs. This surge of the self on the way to the act of attending brings with it *unknowingly* a host of somatic affectivity, a determination of either positive or negative experiential correlate, what we called earlier "affective style." We say unknowingly because this surge is a preconscious operation, or the self in question is not yet realized fully as a reflexive self. The reflexivity of the self emerges when the self engages an experiential momentum in which an object is contrasted with this self. Even though the self in question does not carry reflexivity at this stage, it embodies a germ for reflexivity. This is a *negative momentum*, in the sense that "I am *not* an x" where x is an entity other than the self. This negative momentum is a *refusal* to identify itself with anything other than itself. Insofar as it is a refusal, it is rooted in a negative affectivity. This negativity, when encountering a thing other than itself, brings forth a reflexive momentum to the self, because negativity gives rise to a distinction between what is negating and what is negated. At the same time, it establishes the self to be an individual being with its reflexivity as a consequence of an operation of the negative momentum, that is, it refuses to be identified with any thing other than itself, which is, in turn, correlatively determined by the contingent fact that the personal body, *inter alia*, is a shaped thing like any other thing in the living ambiance.

With this refusal for identification, the self, as we have analyzed, establishes itself to be an individual being with reflexivity. Since it is individual, it attempts to discriminate itself through its reflexivity from any other thing in the living ambiance. In other words, it awakens (an emergence of consciousness) itself to the fact that every experience that it undergoes bears a mark of "mineness." The personalization of experience therefore becomes a salient feature of the self realized as a consciousness. Here, we have a philosophical ontogenesis of the concept of "self-consciousness."

When we analyze the self in attending self-consciously in this manner, the meaning of attending as an act of a self that is a bearer of this act is cast in clear relief. This attending is charged with the somatic affectivity, and logically embodies a negative momentum of I am not an x. Hence, the act of attending that is an intrinsic feature of the self has a power of discriminating itself from what is attended to. In thus discriminating itself from what is attended to, the act of attending as an experience is *personalized*. Insofar as this self is concerned, any experience it undergoes, consequently bears the mark of "my" experience.

Now, what does this analysis of attending self-consciously mean to the personal body? When we analyzed the derivation of attention from add tension, we pointed out that the personal body *shifts* its epistemological-actional focus to consciousness that is aware of itself, that is, to a self-consciousness. This shifting leaves the personal body as an affective sensorium, as a locus of epistemological-actional apparatus, in the background of the experiential momentum of coming-together. In turn, this shifting allows the self of the personal body to surge and advance forward in the foreground of the experiential momentum. To put it differently, the self by virtue of a surge into attention is transformed into an epistemological subject allegedly *divorced* from the personal body. That is, the self becomes merely an epistemological subject, instead of its original status as an epistemological-actional subject. This is how the standpoint of self-consciousness as an epistemological subject is established as a starting point for epistemological method, for example, Descartes' *cogito*. Along with this, if we use the sensory apparatus of the average person, and universalize it, we reach the epistemological theories of the Western philosophical tradition, whether it be idealism or empiricism.[3] At any rate, when this self is functionally coupled with the external sensory perception, the dualistic tendency between the self as an epistemological subject and the body as its object (and by extension, the physical matter) is clearly established, and the self assumes itself to be a paradigm for knowing.

With this analysis of self-consciousness in reference to the surge of attention it looks as though we have exhausted the ground for the possibility of knowledge. But this is deceptive. When we turn to an analysis of the personal body in this discussion of tensionality in the sense of attending self-consciously, the body which is left out in the preceding analysis discloses the following fact. The body which has receded into the background in the experiential momentum of coming-together in virtue of the surge of the self as attending receives an affective *residue* that arises from the bilateral experiential momentum occurring between the personal body, especially in terms of the self, and an object in the living ambiance—the affective residue which finds its expression for an average person only in dreams and/or in psychosomatic disorders. What this suggests is that, in spite of the dominance over the body which the self claims in "attending to an object," the personal body co-functions as an epistemological-actional apparatus, as an affective sensorium. The difference between the functions of the self and the body in this respect is that the self possesses an explicit function as an epistemological subject, while the body is degraded to an *implicit* function as an affective sensorium.[4] By virtue of the fact that the body functions implicitly, it can easily be tossed into an oblivion in the experiential momentum of coming-together where the self takes a seeming predominance over the body. This does not mean, however, that the body ceases to function as an epistemological-actional sensorium, for it receives an affective residue, albeit only implicitly. This explicit-implicit bifurcation occurs when we takes the self, connected with external sensory perception, as the parameter for obtaining (explicit) knowledge. This is, in fact, an aspect which Western epistemological theories have emphasized. There is, however, no logical reason to emphasize an explicit order of knowledge while deemphasizing or ignoring the implicit order, when both are orders of knowledge. Needless to say, this implicit-explicit bifurcation is rooted in the dualistic tendency which we observed as arising from the surge of the self in attention from the altus of the personal body. What this suggests, *inter alia*, is that the self in question has not appropriated the body into its explicit order.

This is exemplified by our earlier illustration that an initial stage of learning a new skill or a new athletic performance is met with a resistance on the part of the personal body: one can not move his/her body as his or her mind dictates it. Consequently, we must conclude that the dominance of the self as establishing an explicit order of knowledge is a *seeming* strength of the self. It has yet to appropriate the implicit order of knowledge qua body within the explicit order of knowledge qua self.

The fact that the self is incapable of appropriating the implicit order within the explicit order implies that the self is an *inherent limiting* condition for somatic knowledge, when we understand somatic knowledge to be that knowledge which is appropriated within the personal body through its epistemological-actional apparatus. As a matter of fact, this implication was already disclosed albeit implicitly when we observed that the self functions only as an epistemological subject, instead of an epistemological-actional subject.

When we recognize the self to be an inherent limiting condition for appropriating somatic knowledge, we must ask what degree of psychophysical integration is operative in this tensional modality of engagement—tensional as is defined in the sense of attending self-consciously. Preparatory to responding to this question, it is useful to examine the tensional modality of engagement in light of the structural components of the theory of attunement, which we have sketched in the previous chapter.

Insofar as the self of the personal body as an epistemological subject engages an object in the living ambiance in the mode of attending self-consciously, there is nonetheless a certain degree of "attunement" obtaining between them, that is, to the degree to which the capacity of a self as an epistemological subject engages an object. In turn, the object is engaged by the self qua epistemological subject only insofar as it is an epistemological object, understanding here "epistemological" as pertaining to explicit knowledge which is based primarily upon external sensory perception. To be more specific, the object is an epistemological object insofar as the sensory apparatus of the personal body is capable of receiving the manifold of an object, for example, the visual organ in its natural endowment has a certain fixed range of visibility. Outside of this range of visibility, the object does not reveal itself epistemologically to the self of the personal body, Thus, the attunement which obtains vis-à-vis the sensory apparatus of the self is delimited by its naturally endowed capacity.

As a parenthetical remark which will guide us to a further discussion of stratification of engagement, we might note the following. What the above analysis suggests is the bilaterality as a condition for obtaining an attunement is operative by "carrying the self to an object," which Dōgen, for example, rejected as an inauthentic way of living. The object is "seen" insofar as the self bestows a meaning upon it. Therefore, the object thus constituted is not an object as it is in its natural state. It is fabricated by the self qua epistemological subject. In order for an object to be revealed in toto, it is apparent that the self must assume a different mode of engagement than the tensional one, the tensionality in the sense of attending self-consciously. This implies that it must attend to an object *unself*-consciously. We shall deal with this issue in the next section when we discuss the de-tensional modality of engagement.

In the preceding analysis we have pointed out an aspect of bilaterality vis-à-vis the tensional modality of engagement between the self as an epistemological subject and an object which is engaged by it. This is an explicit aspect of bilaterality in the tensional modality of engagement. No doubt, this consequence is entailed by the seeming strength or predominance of the self over the body. But, now, in addition to this explicit aspect of bilaterality, we must yet note another aspect of bilaterality which is equally operative in the tensional modality of engagement. This is an implicit aspect of bilaterality concurrently functional with the explicit bilaterality. This implicit aspect of bilaterality is formed by means of the personal body as an affective sensorium, as an epistemological-actional apparatus, which is experientially realized as an affective residue. This affective residue is present in every experiential momentum of coming-together, whether it is brought to an awareness or not. In proportion to the degree of the strength or predominance of the self, when the self is not reflected upon, this affective residue is faded into the affective sensorium. Conversely, in proportion to the degree of the predominance of the body as an affective sensorium, the affective residue is increasingly felt within the personal body which is an affective sensorium. In the latter case, however, we no longer have a case of the self attending self-consciously. It is an instance which has already been incorporated within the matrix of habits that belongs to a particular person. Consequently, when we want to determine the degree of attunement obtaining in the tensional modality of engagement, we must weigh a relative dominance between the self qua epistemological subject and the body as an affective sensorium.

This may be discussed in light of the concept of "feeling-judgement" operative in this modality of engagement—the feeling-judgement which is an intrinsic constituent in the theory of attunement. We characterized that feeling-judgement is pre-predicative in the sense that it is immediate and spontaneous, and that knowing-that and feeling that are one and the same in the formation of this judgement. In any feeling-judgement, the pre-predicative aspect always remains immediate and spontaneous, but the proportion between knowing-that and feeling-that will be reflected upon in a relative predominance of the self qua epistemological subject and the body as an affective sensorium. Insofar as the experience of the self in the sense of attending self-consciously is concerned, the feeling-judgement is formed such that knowing-that takes precedence over feeling-that. This follows from our observation that the self as an epistemological subject attends to an explicit order of knowledge, and that it *appears* to dominate the body as an affective sensorium in relating itself to the external living ambiance.

This "appearance" has two subtly distinct senses (1) as a phenomenon of consciousness and (2) as a contrast to "isness." In light of the first sense of appearance, the self *believes* that the self-certifying nature of attunement is proportionate to the feeling-judgement such that knowing-that alone appears to secure a basis for the validity of experience, without however fully incorporating feeling-that. In this formation of feeling-judgement where knowing-that plays a more important role than feeling-that, there is always a chance of *proto-doubt* as an expression of affectivity creeps into the alleged "transparency" of the judgement formed by a seeming predominance of knowing-that in feeling-judgement. "Certainty" in other words is not grounded in the somaticity of a person, namely, by the feeling-that which is equally an integral aspect of feeling-judgement, hence the use of the term proto-doubt.

That this is a belief arises from the fact that the self *forgets* that it is somatically constituted, that it is colored by its own affective style. To put it another way, the feeling-judgement constituted primarily by means of knowing-that does not fully incorporate within it an aspect of feeling-that. This is an implication that can be drawn from the fact that the self in the sense of attending self-consciously has not appropriated and incorporated the implicit order within the explicit order of knowing. The person in this tensional modality of engagement consequently embodies *a provisional disparity* between its mind and its body. The term "provisionality" must be emphasized to indicate that this disparity is not the final characterization of the person. The degree of psychophysical integration in this modality of engagement reveals only a *natural* integration, that is, as a correlate to the adaptive capacity of the personal body.

For the personal body in this tensional modality of engagement to experience a fuller degree of psychophysical integration (and therefore, by implication, a fuller sense of verification and self-certification of knowledge), it must transform the belief, thus formed through knowing-that, to knowledge. In case of the self attending self-consciously, the belief that the self understands its epistemological object can be verified only when it is put into a concrete physical action, that is, only when the self in the sense of attending self-consciously is put out of action and the personal body as an affective sensorium, as an epistemological-actional apparatus takes precedence over the self. This now leads us to an analysis of de-tensionality. De-tensionality is an existential, practical project of "going out of" the tensional modality of engagement. Since it is practical and existential, our articulation of this modality is only a second order enterprise, and as such it should not be confounded with its first order. What follows is only a reflective approximation of the first order enterprise.

DE-TENSIONALITY

The next stratum in the stratification of a modality of engagement about which we must concern ourselves is a characterization of disengagement from the tensional modality of engagement which we have just analyzed in the foregoing section. We shall designate this process by the term, de-tensionality. De-tensionality is an essential sedimentational process, the prefix, "de" expressing the sense of going out of. It is a practical, existential process of going out of the tensional modality of engagement with a purpose of transforming the tensional modality of engagement into an ideal state of attunement. The term "ideal" here should not suggest that it is beyond the common sensical reality, pointing to an eidetic (*eidos*) world, although it is certainly a departure from it.

Husserl, for example, attempted a similar project in *Ideas* in terms of suspending judgments (*epoché*) concerning the belief we have of our "natural standpoint" followed by a series of "transcendental phenomenological reductions."[5] He applied this method to the act of cogito in an attempt to bring out a "pure" (or eidetic) realm of the functioning of cogito, believing that it would enable us to understand the universal structure of consciousness across the boundary of culture and tradition. His contention was that these reductions do *not* affect the natural standpoint. And as such, it is a thought-experiment. Heidegger, on the other hand, envisioned in *Being and Time* a movement within the everyday standpoint from the inauthentic mode of existence to the authentic mode of existence, and he believed that this movement is effected by resolutely realizing personal existence (*Dasein*) to be a "being-toward-death," where "understanding" plays an essential role.

To make a contrast with the above mentioned philosophers' projects, the concept of de-tensionality pertains to the personal body, not to cogito alone or to its modifications, and importantly, it is a practical, existential attempt to look into the "invisible" dimension of personal body towards its altus. And insofar as it is a practical, existential attempt it demands the person to go through transformations of the everyday mode of existence in which the relationship between the mind and body are *provisionally* dualistic in their operation. An avenue to this de-tensional modality of engagement is by means of what we earlier called "essential sedimentational process," specifically by means of the self-cultivative meditation, which is a practical attempt to place the personal body in a certain prescribed form (*kata*) of engagement. As such, it is still a modality of "engagement" in the sense which we defined it in the beginning part of this concluding part.

As a preliminary to understanding de-tensionality, we shall contrast its goal briefly with the tensional modality of engagement which we have discussed in the foregoing section and thereby we shall indicate a direction to which the theory of attunement points. We have analyzed the tensional modality of engagement operative in the field of everyday mode of existence in light of attending self-consciously. A direction which is suggested from this analysis, we noted *en passant*, for achieving an ideal state of attunement is to "attend unself-consciously." If we take this attitude of attending unself-consciously as an achieved goal of the de-tensional modality of engagement, the difference between the tensional modality and the goal of de-tensional modality may be regarded as follows. The former has as its basic orientation to the external ambiance attending *self*-consciously, whereas the latter attending *unself*-consciously. This recognition of this difference enables us to specify further that the de-tensional modality may be conceived of as a process aimed at transforming the orientation of attending self-consciously to that of attending unself-consciously.

The difference between attending self-consciously and attending unself-consciously still further corresponds, when seen epistemologically, to the contrast between the explicit order of knowing qua self as an epistemological subject and the implicit order of knowing qua body as an epistemological-actional apparatus, or as an affective sensorium. In view of this difference, the goal of achieving a de-tensional modality of engagement is a process of appropriating the implicit order of knowing within the explicit order of knowing. When this observation is applied to an analysis of the degree of psychophysical integration of the personal body, it suggests that this appropriation occurs when achieving a higher degree of integration. Moreover, when it is seen in light of the mind-body issue, it also suggests that in the process of this appropriation the provisional dualistic tendency operative in the everyday mode of existence, that is, the tensional modality of engagement, is transformed to a nondualistic position.

When we speak of the transformation of the attitude from attending self-consciously to that of "unself-consciously," or when we speak of appropriating the implicit order of knowing within the explicit order of knowing, what has to be kept in mind is that this transformation or appropriation is effected by means of what we earlier called essential sedimentational process, which involves an existential transformation of the personal body. Accordingly, we may for now think of the de-tensional modality of engagement to be an existential, practical process by means of which the above mentioned transformation and appropriation are effected. If we miss this point, the meaning of "de-tensional modality of engagement" will not be clearly demarcated, for example, from Husserl's project or Heidegger's project, and consequently it will not be understood properly.

But what is the meaning of attending unself-consciously? When we analyzed the tensional modality of engagement, we defined the self to be a surge from the altus of the personal body in the mode of attending. In light of this understanding of the self, the logical negation of this concept yields the concept of unself or "no-self," and we have a glimpse of what attending unself-consciously might mean. This is not an inappropriate way of understanding the unself, that is, as a logical negation of the self. However, this is somewhat misleading, because it obliterates and belittles a process of negation that is involved in reaching the concept of unself or no-self, or more generally, the goal of achieving the de-tensional modality of engagement. The point we must observe in this connection is that the logical negation of the self is implied as *a practical consequence* of the manner through which the surge of a self is somatically altered by means of the essential sedimentational process. If we grant that there is a transformation in the way that the self surges to the foreground of epistemological-actional apparatus, we can surmise that there is also a transformation in the manner of attending and being "conscious." Consequently, the analytical task of unpacking the concept of de-tensional modality of engagement is to describe the process whereby attending unself-consciously becomes an essential characterization of the person.

In order to articulate this philosophical meaning of attending unself-consciously, then, we must now provide a paradigmatic understanding of what de-tensional modality of engagement is, a practical process by which the personal body achieves the modality of engagement characterized as attending unself-consciously.

We noted in the beginning of this section that de-tensional modality of engagement is an existential, practical attempt to go out of the tensional modality of engagement which is operative in the everyday mode of existence. Specifically, this means for the personal body to disengage itself from the everyday engagement with the external living ambiance. To characterize this "disengagement" positively, it is *a progressive retrogression*[6] into the altus of the personal body, from which the self surges, carrying psychophysical energy and affectivity with itself, to the foreground of the epistemological-actional apparatus of the person. Epistemologically, this progressive retrogression means to minimize and eventually to halt the working of external sensory perception as we observed in discussing Dōgen's just sitting. In this sense, the experiential momentum of coming-together as it pertains to the external living ambiance is no longer operative. Therefore, almost all the characterizations we have provided on the structural components of the theory of attunement are temporally suspended as inapplicable to the de-tensional modality of engagement.

This inoperation of the external sensory perception is a practical consequence of the essential sedimentational process, specifically, the consequence of sedimenting the effect of assuming the lotus position, or its variations. We saw an instance of this sedimentational process when we analyzed Dōgen's concept of "just sitting." When the person puts his/her external sensory perception out of action, the experiential momentum of coming-together consequently obtains within his/her interior, namely, between what is considered to be one's self and one's body which forms provisionally the dualistic tendency in the everyday mode of existence. Therefore, that which engages and that which is engaged no longer takes place between two shaped things, between the personal body and a shaped thing in the external living ambiance. Rather, the engagement obtains within the interior of one and the same locus which is the personal body, within its interiority. A demarcating feature in this shift is that the personal body qua the life phenomenon enters into the purview of the experiential momentum of coming-together, which was not explicit in the former.

The inoperation of the external sensory perception prepares the person to dive into the "invisible" dimension of its being through the process of progressive retrogression—invisible here to be understood relative to that which is perceived by means of the external sensory perception. In fact, we might use "internal phenomena of consciousness" instead to avoid confusion with the description of what transpires in the experiential momentum of coming-together in its inoperation of the external sensory perception, for in the initial stage of progressive retrogression, the person in meditation encounters an incessant generation of "visible" images—images of the recent past, distant past as well as images of a near future and distant future, which are either this-worldly or otherworldly, or ideally both. For now, we can take these "visible images" as expressions of the affectivity, both light and shadow. What is important in recognizing the inoperation of the external sensory perception in the initial stage of progressive retrogression, is to keep in mind that engagement takes place within the interior of the person between what is conceived to be its self and its personal body.[7] When this is interpreted in light of a degree of psychophysical integration, the personal body stands at the threshold of achieving a higher degree of psychophysical integration, because the various images welling from within the personal body are gradually integrated into the constitution of a self. Here we have a glimpse of the meaning of appropriating the implicit order of knowledge within the explicit order.

A natural question arises at this juncture as to why the inoperation of the external sensory perception prepares the personal body to achieve a higher degree of psychophysical integration. The psychophysical energy which would otherwise be consumed through the activities of the external sensory apparatus is turned to an internal engagement in the course of the essential sedimentational process of progressive retrogression and this internal engagement obtains between the self and its body as a consequence of the inoperation of the external sensory apparatus. This is, for example, the reason why the person in meditation experiences an incessant generation of various images in its initial stage. An assumption here is that the energy in the personal body must be meaningfully discharged.

What is philosophically significant about the inoperation of the external sensory apparatus is that when meditation deepens, it effects, *inter alia*, an elimination or a disappearance of the lived experience of the object-body, because the lived object-body is experienced primarily by means of external sensory perception. This is for example what Dōgen meant partially by "casting off the body."

Since the concept of lived object-body is not like the Cartesian concept of the body which is divorced from *ego* or the self and which is elevated to the concept of bodyness vis-à-vis a thinking cogito, that is, since it is synthesized qua self, the elimination or the disappearance of the lived experience of the object-body further implies a transformation of the manner through which the synthetic activity of the self functions. In light of this observation, it is inadequate, and perhaps misleading, to say that the object-body is eliminated, or disappears as a consequence of the inoperation of the external sensory apparatus, for what is actually experienced is that this synthetic activity of the self judges that the object-body is no longer an object that *opposes* its function. In other words, it achieves axiologically the same status as the subject-body which has functioned as the locus of the self. A better way of characterizing this phenomenon is to say that the object-body is *appropriated* within the subject-body, the body which does not, as Ichikawa demonstrated effectively, have a definite physical delineation, but *extends* as far as imaginable. Here we witness one sense of transformation intrinsic to the de-tensional modality of engagement.

The appropriation of object-body within the lived feeling of the subject-body is experientially correlated with the effect of detentional modality of engagement. De-tensional modality of engagement is a practical process of learning to enter into samadhic awareness where the oneness between the subject-body and object-body is achieved. This oneness does not mean an undifferentiated consciousness, though it may be temporally occasioned by an obliterating ecstatic moments. Naturally there is an infinite degree of oneness that can be achieved in proportion to the mastery of art of going out of the tensional modality.

When the above mentioned appropriation of the object-body within the subject-body occurs, there is a significant change in the concept of the body-image as far as the personal body in deep meditation is concerned. The concept of body-image is that which is formed through a general function of synthesis of the self that brings together the subject-body and the object-body into a certain "image," insofar as the everyday lived experience is concerned. In contrast, we have just observed that the object-body is appropriated within the subject-body. In light of the concept of body-image, this appropriation of the object-body in samadhic awareness suggests that the body-image cannot be formed, if we understand that for a synthesis of body-image it requires both the subject-body and the object-body, and hence it would seem that it is a category mistake to talk about the body-image in this context. However, the concept of appropriation describes the manner of how synthetic activity of the self functions, for example, in the sense that the object-body no longer opposes the subject-body, axiologically achieving the same status with the subject-body. In this sense, since appropriation is a lived experience, it suggests that the object-body as a physically delineated thing comes to be realized not as a primary way of living it. Consequently, the physical delineation with its definite boundary is cleared so that the body-image which the self synthesizes is no longer *bound* by this physical delineation. In other words, the boundary of the body-image expands beyond the physical delineation of the object-body. We saw an example of this expansion when we interpreted the experience of Dōgen's "felt inter-resonance."

This should not suggest, however, that the change of the body-image is effected simply by virtue of the consequence of the inoperation of the external sensory apparatus. There is a more fundamental transformation taking place in the process of progressive retrogression; the change of the body-image is merely a consequence of this fundamental transformation. I use the term "fundamental" to indicate that this transformation pertains to the nature of what is considered to be the self. In particular, this fundamental transformation is concerned with the *synthetic* act of the self. Synthetic act in its functions has two inseparable momenta of reflexivity and judgement. When the self is in the process of progressive retrogression, these inseparable *momenta* of reflexivity and judgement are no longer of the external, living ambiance, but rather are of the *internal-invisible* living ambiance where the personal body also finds invigorating activities of nature, because it encounters its own life-phenomenon. This internal-invisible ambiance is presented to the self, though implicitly, in the personal object-body when these momenta in their synthetic act are directed toward the external ambiance, for it has receded in the background when the self as an epistemological subject functions in its negotiation with the external ambiance. But now, both reflexivity and judgement of the synthetic act of the self are directed toward the internal-invisible ambiance. Consequently, whatever is reflexively brought forth within the self through the function of judgement, particularly the affective style unique to each person with his/her individually configured light and shadow tendency, will be synthesized in the course of the progressive retrogression just as the external perception familiarizes the person with the external ambiance by means of the synthetic act directed toward the external ambiance.

We have observed that the self is a surge from the altus of the personal body, and that in this surge, the self brings with it a host of affectivity, that is, an individually configured affective style. The process of progressive retrogression is to go in a counter direction to this surge of the self, to the altus of the personal body. In thus going in an opposite direction, the individually configured affective style becomes an object of synthesis. In the course of this progressive retrogression, the self which considers itself as an incorrigible ground for negotiating the external ambiance encounters the *raw* materials of what make up the individually configured affective style, first through its negative components and then through the positive components, or a combination of both depending upon the affective style of the personal body. This gives an opportunity for reflexivity and judgement of the synthetic act of the self existentially to examine the relative worth of each element that comprises the individually configured affective style.

What is paradigmatically important in this encounter is an encounter with the negative momentum in the individually configured affective style, namely, the refusal to identify itself with anything other than itself, and this refusal is grounded in the proto-doubt which has been concealed in altus of the personal body. Reflexivity and judgement work on this proto-doubt which has a negative momentum of I am not an x. Since there is nothing appearing in the deep meditative state, the reflexive function brings forth nothing as its object, and the judging function judges nothing, for there is nothing to be judged, but rather become interfused with the things of the living ambiance. (This was for example the meaning of samadhic awareness.) Together with these *momenta*, the self qua its synthetic act realizes that this negative momentum is groundless. It comes to realize that this negativity is a play of proto-doubt. This negativity is a "delusion." As such, it is not worthy of maintaining it as part and parcel of the self. In other words, it is abandoned.

When the self successfully goes through this progressive retrogression, the self realizes itself to be free from the binding psyche-logical "hang-ups" which have unknowingly framed its affective style, its attitude towards the external living ambiance, for it has witnessed the *primordial* ground of its being by entering into the dimension of being totally different from the dimension of experience with which the self is most familiar, that is, the everyday mode of existence. What this means to the self is that the alleged "incorrigibility" of the self as an epistemological subject in its negotiation with the external world is *shattered*. Along with this, the individually configured affective style is freed from its individuality, and thereby the personal body embodies a sense of "universal man." We may be careful to understand what this "universal" means. It is more of a recognition of commonality in all the sentient being qua life phenomena and it is not achieved through intellectual abstraction, but through a existential, practical de-tentional modality. The self then realizes that it is no longer a contingent being, but is a necessary being when it is contrasted with the individuality and contingency of its earlier mode of existence. Thus freed from the individuality, it also loses the salient mark of mineness which the self has claimed in respect of all the experience it has undergone in the everyday mode of existence.

In the final analysis, the self is fundamentally transformed into un-self or no-self, for it has witnessed the primordial ground of its groundlessness by entering via the process of progressive retrogression into the dimension which has been denied prior to this existential, practical undertaking. This may be alternatively stated as follows. If the self is *grounded* in groundlessness, there is no point of claiming its self-hood other than to say that it is no-self. When no-self is experienced and fully appropriated, the self as an epistemological subject disappears, and becomes incorporated qua no-self within the personal body. In this instance, there is no differentiation between the no-self and the personal body, which gives a basis for extending beyond the materiality of an physical object, providing such a self with the capacity of obtaining a felt inter-resonance, for example. It means, among other things, that the self as an epistemological subject is transformed into the personal body as an epistemological-actional apparatus, for the latter is a locus for both knowing and acting. "Knowing" here includes both "explicit" and "implicit" orders of knowing, since there has occurred in the process of progressive retrogression an appropriation of the self in the form of no-self within the personal body. Accordingly, the personal body is fully equipped to presence itself to a shaped thing in the external living ambiance when it decides to engage it.

This dimension into which the self has entered is a *subtle* dimension impervious to external sensory perception, which comes into a purview through a heightened awareness of affectivity. This is the fruit of achieving a higher degree of psychophysical integration. Insofar as the personal body in this modality of engagement achieves a higher degree of psychophysical integration, his or her being is neither psychical nor physical, but stands in the primordial ground out of which the psychical and the physical merge. Epistemologically, this implies that what is considered to be an implicit order of knowing, when the self as an epistemological subject engages itself in knowing, is brought into an explicit order of knowing. Due to a subtle, yet, crystal clear function of samadhic awareness, therefore, there is no bifurcation between the explicit and the implicit orders of knowing, because the latter is appropriated within the personal body. More specifically, the negative affectivity is purged to the point that it destroys the proto-doubt which characterizes the tensional modality of engagement.

This point may be restated in terms of the concept of feeling-judgement as follows: the gap, which existed in the tensional modality of engagement between knowing-that and feeling-that, is sealed. There is an increasing sense of balanced harmony between knowing-that and feeling-that in the de-tensional modality. For this reason, the balanced harmony between knowing-that and feeling-that is an experience foreign to the tensional modality of existence, but becomes increasingly an integral part of the personal body in the de-tensional modality, as he/she make progress in going out of the tensional modality of engagement.

Needless to say, insofar as the de-tensional modality of engagement is an existential, practice *process*, it admits of an infinite degree of this balanced harmony between knowing-that and feeling-that. When this process is not complete, that is, when the ideal is not achieved, a relative predominance of the one over the other is bound to occur, each asserting its "right" of knowledge, since the de-tensional modality carries its "memory" sedimented in the mode of tensional modality. In the course of de-tensional modality of engagement, when the feeling-that predominates knowing-that, which is a reversal of the feeling-judgment operative in the tensional modality of engagement, the personal body will be victimized by its negative affectivity as well as by the mental pollution infesting the society and living environments. Care must be taken in this instance to restore, by means of various physical exercises, a provisional balance appropriate to the affective style of each person.

Although the precise "mechanism" is not known yet, one of the salient contributing factors that leads the personal body into this subtle dimension in the course of self-cultivating meditation is attributable to an acquisition of a technique for rhythmic, balanced breathing. Breathing is not simply an inhalation and an exhalation of "air" as chemistry analyzes it, but in the de-tensional modality it is a harmonization of psychophysical energy (*ki*-energy) or (*spiritus*) which is *pervasively* present in the living nature, as its invigorating activities. Since this psychophysical energy manifests various degrees of subtlety, the deeper the process of sedimentational process, the more radical the transformation of the personal body. In this process, the self becomes transformed into the dimension that unfolds in proportion to the depth of the samadhic awareness, into the dimension higher than psychophysical energy. In light of the theory of attunement, this suggests that the personal body realizes itself fully to be an epistemological-actional apparatus, instead of the self merely as an epistemological subject, for the self has been transformed into no-self. When this occurs, the self is no longer an inherent limiting condition for negotiating the object other than itself. This is for example what Dōgen meant by "casting off the mind."

NON-TENSIONALITY

If the personal body who has achieved a higher degree of his/her psychophysical integration remains in the de-tensional modality of engagement, that is, in the essential sedimentational process which puts the personal body into a journey to discover itself within its interiority vis-à-vis a progressive retrogression, it is more than likely that we will receive a criticism to the effect that whatever transpires during the course of the essential sedimentational process is *subjective* without having any bearing upon how the personal body relates itself actionally as well as epistemologically to the external living ambiance. In order to dispel this kind of criticism, we must now take the personal body out of the conceptual context of the de-tensional modality of engagement, and bring it back, albeit theoretically, to the disclosed world of everyday mode of existence. By situating it there, we must then examine how it can be instantiated within the conceptual framework of the theory of attunement. For this reason, a new and another modality of engagement has yet to be introduced.

To designate this new modality of engagement, the efficacies of which the personal body has appropriated within itself through the essential sedimentational process, and the manner through which it relates itself to the external living ambiance, we shall employ the term non-tensionality. The use of this term is introduced so as to demarcate it from the previous two modalities of engagements, namely tensionality and de-tensionality without losing its generic and philosophical relationship with the latter two terms. The non-tensional modality of engagement is *neither* tensional *nor* de-tensional. The prefix "non" is attached in order to emphasize this double negation as a way of qualifying this particular modality of engagement. We may characterize the sense of this double negation, while noting its generic relationship with the other two terms, by saying that non-tensional modality of engagement is the *achieved* goal of the de-tensional modality of engagement which is an existential, practical process of going out of the tensional modality of engagement operative in the field of everyday existence.

With this understanding of the term non-tensionality, our next task is to articulate its philosophical meaning within the conceptual framework of the theory of attunement. One of the most essential features of the theory of attunement is its recognition of the fluid bilaterality between the personal body and an object in the living ambiance. In view of this concept of bilaterality, an appropriate question that we might ask is: what kind of attunement obtains when the personal body embodies this non-tensional modality of engagement?

We have observed in the analysis of de-tensional modality of engagement that the personal body becomes an epistemological-actional apparatus, an affective sensorium. This is in marked contrast with the self of the personal body simply as an epistemological subject which overshadows the affective sensorium of the personal body. That the personal body becomes an epistemological-actional apparatus means that it presents itself as a *whole* to an object in contrast to the self presenting itself to an object as an epistemological subject. In the latter case, the object engaged by the self reveals itself to be mostly an epistemological object in the sense that it falls within the natural capacity of the sensory apparatus. On the other hand, when the personal body presents itself to an object as an epistemological-actional subject, the object thus engaged by it acquires an actional status as well. Therefore, the point that we must observe here is that an object which is engaged by the personal body is both actional and epistemological.

For the purpose of analysis, we shall first indicate briefly the change of the meaning of the term epistemological, which occurs when an object is engaged by the personal body as an epistemological-actional apparatus. Up to this point, we have understood the term epistemological to mean knowledge primarily concerned with, and derived from external sensory perception. This corresponds to what we earlier called the explicit order of knowing. However, as we have observed in the analysis of the de-tensional modality of engagement, what is considered to be implicit in regard to the order of knowing is appropriated within the personal body as an affective sensorium. Consequently, when we say

that the personal body in the non-tensional modality of engagement is an epistemological-actional apparatus, the term epistemological includes both explicit and implicit orders of knowing. In
order to avoid misunderstanding, we must point out here that
since the implicit order of knowing is appropriated within the
personal body, what is implicit prior to the essential sedimentational process becomes also explicit. This is the practical consequence of achieving a balanced harmony between knowing-that
and feeling-that as we have examined in the previous section dealing with the de-tensional modality. In this harmonized balance,
there is no bifurcation between the explicit and the implicit orders
of knowing when the personal body is in the non-tensional
modality of engagement.

   This may be explicated again in light of the contrast which we
made between attending self-consciously and attending unself-consciously. When we apply the preceding analysis to attending
unself-consciously, attending is no longer an act of the self primarily interested in the affairs of the external living ambiance, but
rather the person as a whole, as an epistemological-actional, affective sensorium. Consequently, the scope of attending is enlarged
from the self as an epistemological subject to the personal body as
an epistemological-actional, affective sensorium. This follows
from our observation that the self is transformed into no-self in the
process of progressive retrogression which describes the de-tensional modality of engagement. This enlargement of the scope of
attending has a further bearing upon attending unself-consciously.
"Consciousness" which is operative in this instance is no longer a
consciousness associated with the self, that which is divorced from
the body. This consciousness is *an altered state of higher awareness* appropriating the object-body, that is, samadhic awareness.
The alteration in this case is a practical consequence of the progressive retrogression, the essential sedimentational process, and
the evaluative adjective "higher" indicates that consciousness *transcends* the scope of the self where the tensional mode of consciousness is operative, without, however, this transcendence incapaci-
tating the everyday mode of consciousness. This was, for example,
the meaning of appropriation. Therefore, the "higher awareness"
unique to non-tensional modality of engagement includes both the
explicit and implicit orders of knowing.

We must note here a consequence of observing the enlargement of the scope of attending unself-consciously, and apply it to the bilateral feature of the theory of attunement: the physical delineation of both the personal body and a shaped thing in the external living ambiance is no longer a salient mark of obtaining an attunement which is more or less fixed in the case of the tensional modality of engagement, unless it is called upon by the person as its primary concern. This follows from our previous observation of the inoperation of the external sensory apparatus in the essential sedimentational process. That is, the object-body with its definite physical boundary in respect of the personal body is synthesized within its subject-body. By implication, this also applies to the physicality of a shaped thing in the external living ambiance.

What the above observation entails is that the physical delineations of both the personal body and the object engaged by him/her do not present themselves as a barrier to each other when an attunement obtains. Epistemologically, this suggests that an object engaged by the personal body in the non-tensional modality of engagement reveals not only its explicit aspect but also its implicit aspect, because the personal body in this modality has appropriated both the explicit and the implicit orders of knowing. The assumption here is that what is revealed is correlative with the epistemological apparatus of the personal body. In light of this disclosure of both the explicit and the implicit aspect of an object, the kind of attunement which obtains is an attunement by means of the "inter-resonance" between the personal body and an object. The inter-resonance here may be understood to mean a mutual *responding* between the personal body and an object in the external living ambiance in respect of both the explicit and the implicit dimensions of their beings. Figuratively speaking, we can think of an implicit aspect of an object as its "interiority" which cannot be revealed through the external sensory perception.

But what is the interiority of an object? We may think of it as its nature in the sense that that which makes an object what it is as it is revealed to the personal body in the non-tensional modality of engagement. Here, we are on the verge of entering into the domain of parapsychological phenomena. For our purpose of interpretation, we may think of a disclosure of the interiority of an object to be a crystal-clear realization which locates the ontic status of an object within the complex, causal matrix of conditioned generation-extinction. This crystal clear realization enables the person to *play* ("*yuge*") with an object in question (samādhi-at-play).

With this observation, we can now turn our analysis to the actional aspect which has emerged as a consequence of the personal body being fully transformed into an epistemological-actional apparatus, and which also follows from the consequence of the enlargement of the self into no-self. Here, we must distinguish within the theoretical framework of the theory of attunement a class of actions which accompanies the use of a tool (and hence, the tool being an actional object) and a class of actions which does not. In the former case, the appropriation of an actional object is primarily concerned with the nonessential sedimentational process, for it requires a "coordination of the body" in the sense of refinement of the voluntary-nervous system. That is, it calls for a mastery of the technique which a tool demands of its user to the point that the mastery can realize a *life* of an actional object, that is, a tool. When this mastery occurs, the tool becomes "second nature," not essentially distinct from the personal body. In the latter case where the actional object is not extrinsically involved, that is, no tool is involved, an actional *object* is the personal body itself. A surprising consequence in this regard, which follows from the transformation of a self into no-self, is that the personal body as an epistemological-actional apparatus is an actional object itself. There is a curious transformation here. When the self of the person remains as an epistemological subject and therefore is the initiator of action, it encounters resistance from the body, because the body as an object which is a carrier and a bearer of action is not appropriated within the personal body, that is, it is not synthesized within the subject-body where the degree of psychophysical integration remains a natural integration. In sharp contrast to this, when the personal body is an actional object, as an object, it is axiologically the same as the shaped things in the external living ambiance. We witness here an instance of actional "oneness of the body and the mind"—"oneness" in the sense of nonduality. This is because there is no "consciousness of" the action on the part of the personal body as that which is a *subject* opposing its actional object, although this does not mean that there is no awareness of the action on the part of the personal body, either. This awareness is a special kind of awareness which we have called "samadhic awareness" in the sense that it is aware of both its external and internal living ambiances through its affective sensorium without explicitly separating them. When we understand consciousness of as an source of the action performed by the self in the sense of attending self-consciously, we might think of samadhic awareness as that awareness which is performed by the personal body as an affective sensorium in the sense of attending unself-consciously. The action performed in this manner, in other words, achieves the *tao* of action.

When the person which has achieved a tao of action, that is, when it engages itself as an actional object, a verification of the experiential meaning of its action lies in the "beholder" of this action, neither subjective nor objective, that is, only those persons which are in the possession of the action where an inter-corporeality is established among the community of the persons. This is an expression of the inter-subjective world where "nothing is concealed." In this community, insofar as the performance of actions is concerned, it does not matter whether it is "yours" or "mine." Actions in this community, in other words, abolish the boundary of personalization. This should not suggest, however, that both subjective and objective features of the action are not analyzable into salient features of a particular action realized as a *tao* of action. For example, the action performed is *in harmony with* the person, its feeling-judgement being confirmed by both the person itself and the others beholding it. It, in other words, flows with a tao.

With these clarifications of the term epistemological in reference to attending unself-consciously and the actional status of the personal body as achieving a tao of action, the nature of attunement which obtains between the personal body and an object in the external living ambiance go through a radical modification—so radically different from the one which obtains when the person is in the tensional modality of engagement, when it is in the everyday mode of existence.

This may be discussed in terms of the feeling-judgement which is a salient feature of the theory of attunement. We observed earlier that the feeling-judgement is immediate and spontaneous, and the sense of immediacy and spontaneity is in proportion to the degree of psychophysical integration of the personal body, which is cultivated through the sedimentational process. Moreover, we noted that knowing-that and feeling-that are one and the same in feeling-judgement. When we apply this understanding of feeling-judgement to the non-tensional modality of engagement which the personal body has appropriated, the following consequences follow from it.

In the non-tensional modality of engagement in which the personal body has appropriated both the explicit and the implicit orders of knowing, there is no predominance of either knowing-that or feeling-that in its execution of feeling-judgement, unlike the tensional modality of engagement in which, as we have analyzed, the self as an epistemological subject predominates or overshadows its body which is an affective sensorium. In other words, there is a perfect harmony between knowing-that and feeling-that. To speak paradigmatically, the content of knowing-that in this modality of engagement is a crystal clear realization which enables the person to locate an object in question within the complex, causal matrix of the conditioned generation-extinction. The content of feeling-that, on the other hand, is a felt disclosure of an interiority of an object through inter-resonance between the personal body and the object in question. Although we have articulated these two aspects of feeling-judgement, that is, knowing-that and feeling-that, separately for the purpose of analysis, we must point out that the paradigmatic understanding of both knowing-that and feeling-that is a second order enterprise, because they are not two separate *momenta* experientially. Those aspects of knowing-that and feeling-that in feeling-judgement are reached spontaneously and immediately without involving a consciousness of. This is because the personal body has become, to use Dōgen's terminology, *a true human body*. It embodies a samadhic awareness which functions as an epistemological-actional, affective sensorium. In this experience there is an attunement between the mind and body, between I and the other, and finally between human nature qua microcosm and physical nature qua macrocosm. Here we witness the meaning of somatic knowledge in the paramount sense of the term.

CONCLUDING REMARKS

In part 3, we have sketched a theory of attunement as an instance of creative thinking. In this context, the term attunement was used to designate descriptively the nature of engagement that obtains between personal body and things in the living ambiance. In using this term, we have sought to ground it ontologically in the adaptability with which personal body is originally and inherently endowed at the time of its birth, or philosophically, in its radical contingent fact of "thrownness." Moreover, we have introduced the term attunement in order to account for the bilateral relationship obtaining in personal body's engagement with the things in the living ambiance—understanding this engagement to be both epistemological and actional in character.

Consequently, that which is appropriated through attunement we have termed somatic knowledge, and this must be sharply demarcated from "cognitive" or "intellectual" knowledge since the word "somatic" primarily refers to the mode of appropriation that lies in the personal body. Somatic knowledge does not simply mean intellectual "knowledge about the body" but knowledge gained through *the body*. It was contrasted with "cognitive or intellectual knowledge." Intellectual knowledge is that mode of cognition which results from objectifying a given object, taking propositionally a subject predicate form, while divorcing the somaticity of the knower from "the mind" of the knower. For these reasons, intellectual knowledge circumscribes its object, incapable of becoming one with the object. By contrast, somatic knowledge in its immediate, everyday occurrence, lacks this objectification. There is a "feeling-judgment" operative in somatic knowledge. Along this argument, we pointed out that somatic knowledge is closely related to the formation of habit.

We have emphasized the bilateral aspect as a means to acquiring somatic knowledge in order to remedy the one-sidedness from which the Western philosophical tradition suffers. After pointing out the fluid bilaterality operative between the personal body and the things engaged by it, we have specified the structural components of this bilaterality in terms of its formal conditions and have then outlined its corresponding experiential correlate. The experiential momentum for this bilaterality was discussed vis-à-vis a coming-together of the personal body and the things in the living ambiance.

We have then argued that the experiential momentum of coming-together as constitutive of attunement creates its own somatic field, and hence personal body experientially creates its own spatialization and temporalization. The energy responsible for creating the somatic field was found to have its source in the psychophysical energy inherent in personal body, along with its pervasive presence in the invigorating activities that occur in the living ambiance. This recognition of the creation of a somatic field through psychophysical energy which issues from personal body in the experiential momentum of coming-together, has led us to an analysis of affectivity. We have shown that affectivity is an essential component in the experiential momentum, and moreover, that the concept of affectivity logically requires that that which does the affecting and that which is affected must come-together in order for an attunement to obtain in terms of a common quality (or qualities).

This bilaterality in affectivity was further specified, in light of its experiential correlate, by means of feeling-judgement. We have argued that when personal body forms judgement in the experiential momentum of "coming-together," there can be no distinction between knowing-that and feeling-that. This feeling-judgement was contrasted with intellectual judgement where only knowing-that is emphasized. In feeling-judgement, both knowing-that and feeling-that are inseparable momenta constituting the affectivity in the experiential momentum of coming-together, although there is a proportionality of knowing-that and feeling-that depending on the degree of psychophysical integration discernible in the personal body. Feeling-judgement is spontaneous, immediate and pre-predicative, unlike intellectual judgement which takes a subject-predicate form.

In light of the appropriation of somatic knowledge, we have contended that this feeling-judgement must be sedimentational in character, that is, it must be formed through habit, for the proportionality of knowing-that and feeling-that must be integrated within personal body. This has led us to make a distinction between the essential sedimentational process and nonessential sedimentational process. The nonessential sedimentational process is primarily concerned, physiologically speaking, with a refinement and an enhancement of the voluntary nervous system. In contrast, the essential sedimentational process requires a progressive retrogression, via a form of meditation, in the altus of personal body, particularly to what Yuasa refers to as the "emotion-instinct circuit" and the "unconscious quasi-body circuit."

Having made a distinction between the essential and nonessential sedimentational process, we then proceeded to explicate the stratification of the somatic modalities of engagement. This term "stratification" was introduced into the theory of attunement in order to trace the transformation of the somatic modalities of engagement through the process of essential sedimentation.

The assumption here is that personal body is provisionally dualistic in the everyday mode of existence, or that it is endowed only with a natural degree of psychophysical integration. We have argued that the essential sedimentational process enables personal body to achieve a higher degree of psychophysical integration, and eventually, a nondualistic perspective.

We have pointed out three different kinds of somatic modality of engagement when we discussed stratification. The first kind of somatic modality was termed tensionality, and this tensionality characterizes our everyday mode of existence. We have explained that the term tensionality is derived from adding tension, which in turn translates philosophically into attention. We have interpreted this attention experientially to means: to attend to something self-consciously, which has led us to analyze attending self-consciously as a characteristic of our everyday mode of existence. This modality of engagement excludes the sleeping state and the matrix of habits which have already been sedimented in a particular personal body. Through an analysis of attending self-consciously with respect to feeling-judgement, we have demonstrated that there is a predominance of knowing-that over feeling-that when this modality of engagement forms a judgement. In turn, this indicated to us that there is a provisionally dualistic stance at work in the modality of attending self-consciously. Epistemologically interpreted this means that personal body functions only as an epistemological subject, attending only to the explicit order of knowing, and thus failing to incorporate within personal body the implicit order of knowing which is deeply rooted in the somatic modality of personal body.

The second stratum of somatic modality of engagement we have termed de-tensionality. This term was introduced into the theory of attunement in order to describe the essential sedimentational process. We have demonstrated that the de-tensional modality of engagement is that modality of engagement in which personal body existentially and practically goes out of the tensional modality of engagement by progressively retrogressing into the altus of its body. This modality of engagement we have examined in terms of attending unself-consciously, while providing a philosophical derivation from attending self-consciously.

The third stratum of somatic modality of engagement we have termed non-tensionality. This term designates an achieved, ideal goal of de-tensional process of sedimentation, and hence it is conceptually demarcated both from the tensional and the de-tensional modality. We have argued that personal body in this modality of non-tensionality embodies, when it is viewed epistemologically, the explicit and the implicit orders of knowing, and when it is viewed actionally, personal body performs a tao of action. It reaches its goal through feeling-judgement without forming an intellectual judgement.

NOTES

INTRODUCTION

1. For the purpose of the present work, the other topics to which Ichikawa gives a full phenomenological analysis in his book are eliminated. They include "my body for others for me," "the other's body," and the "body as implexes."

2. This comment questions the scope of phenomenological method originally conceived by Husserl, but is not directed to the intrinsic weakness of phenomenological method itself. What we need is a phenomenology of psyche broadening the scope of phenomenological investigation that is confined to everyday consciousness. Husserl, I believe, would not disapprove of such an endeavor.

CHAPTER 1. ICHIKAWA'S VIEW OF THE BODY

1. Ichikawa Hiroshi, *Seishin toshite no shintai* [The Body As the Spirit] (Tokyo: Keisō shobō, 1979). Hereafter it will be abbreviated as *Seishin*.
  Ichikawa Hiroshi, born in 1931, is a graduate of Kyoto University and was the third recipient of the Yamazaki Award for his book, *Seishin toshite no shintai*. He is currently teaching at Meiji University in Japan. His other major work is entitled *Mi no kōzō: shintairon o koete* [The Structure of Incarnate Body: Beyond the Theories of the Body]. He is editor of *Shin tetsugaku nyūmon* [A New Introduction to Philosophy], *Gendai testugaku jiten* [A Contemporary Dictionary of Philosophy] and co-author of *Shintai no genshōgaku* [A Phenomenology of the Body].
  My exposition of Ichikawa's view of the body in chapter 1 and chapter 2 pertains to part 1 of *Seishin*. The translations are all mine.

2. For differences in the phenomenological methods of Husserl and Merleau-Ponty, see Remy C. Kwant's "Merleau-Ponty and Phenomenology" in *Phenomenology*, ed. Joseph J. Kockelmans (New York: Doubleday & Company, Inc., 1967), pp. 365–392.

3. For a discussion of "natural attitude" and "epoché," see Edmund Husserl, *Ideas: General Introduction to Phenomenology*, trans. W. R. Boyce Gibson, (New York: Collier Books, 1967), pp. 45–46. And, for an examination of the various levels of "epoché" and "transcendental reductions," see Maurice Natson's *Edmund Husserl: Philosopher of Infinite Tasks*, (Evanston: Northwestern University Press, 1973), pp. 42–83.

4. The difference between Husserl and Ichikawa on this point comes down to a difference in doxic belief. Husserl believed that there is such a thing as essence and by understanding the essence one comes to understand what reality is. When it is seen from a broad perspective of intellectual history, this belief is an influence from the Greek attitude wherein, for example, the pre-Socratics endeavored to find the basic stuff (*archai*) of the universe. By contrast, Ichikawa believes in the activity of a thing, and by articulating the structure of this activity, one comes to understand what reality is. In Japanese intellectual history, this attitude can be found as far back as in Kukai (774–835) and all the way through Nishida Kitarō (1870–1945).

5. For Kant, the body as a thing-in-itself was unknowable, and the way through which he deals with the body is through "sensations" which requires a further unpacking as Ichikawa shows in the following two chapters.

6. Ichikawa, *Seishin*, p. 3.

7. Ichikawa, *Seishin*, p. 7.

8. Ibid.

9. Ichikawa, *Seishin*, p. 4

10. Ibid.

11. Ibid.

12. Ichikawa, *Seishin*, p. 8.

13. Max Scheler, "Lived, Environment and Ego" in *The Philosophy of the Body*, ed. Stuart F. Spicker (Chicago: Quadrangle Books Inc., 1970), pp. 159–186.

14. Ibid.

15. Ichikawa, *Seishin*, pp. 8–9.

16. It may not be clear at this juncture why Ichikawa claims that the subject-body is a "kind of *cogito*." It will become clearer later when

he discusses vis-à-vis the double sensation the function of "intuition of identity" between the subject-body and the object-body which he thinks constitutes the "lived body scheme." Ichikawa, *Seishin*, p. 9.

17. The reason that Ichikawa accepts the obscure, hazy horizon of consciousness as *cogito* is due to his understanding of "mood" (*kibun*). See p. 37ff for a discussion of mood.

18. This comparison is pointed out to me by Thomas Downey of Temple University. This point will be clarified when Ichikawa deals with the phenemenological analysis of emotion, feeling, perception and thinking in chapter 2.

19. This "intentionality" is analyzed in chapter 2 where Ichikawa deals with the structure of the living body. Particularly, Ichikawa argues that this intentionality is a primary function of the living human body, called "directionality" through which the living body *orients* itself to the external ambiance as well as its internal ambiance. Ichikawa's concept of body's orientation may be parallel with Scheler's idea that the intentionality issuing from the lived body is distinct from the intentionality of perceptual consciousness. See, for example, Max Scheler, "Lived Body, Environment, and Ego" in *The Philosophy of the Body*, ed. Stuart E. Spicker (Chicago: Quandrangle Books, 1970), pp. 159–186.

20. Ichikawa, *Seishin*, p. 9.

21. Yuasa in chapter three refines this observation, and calls it the self-grasping awareness of the body. See the section "Coenesthesis" in Yuasa's body-scheme.

22. This statement is not all that puzzling. For example, Whitehead states in his *Modes of Thought* (p. 161) that the indeterminacy of the boundary exists between the body and nature, when considered "with microscopic accuracy." In contrast to Whitehead's microscopic accuracy, however, Ichikawa's contention must be understood in terms of a *lived* experience of the subject-body.

23. Ichikawa, *Seishin*, p. 10.

24. Ichikawa, *Seishin*, p. 11.

25. Paul Varlery, *Analecta* LII, Œuver Bibliotheque de la Pleiade, p. 72.

26. Ichikawa, *Seishin*, p. 11.

27. Ichikawa quotes Karl Jaspers' *Allegemeine Psychopatholgie*, Springer Verlag, S.75. Ichikawa, *Seishin*, p. 11.

28. Ichikawa, *Seishin*, p. 12.

29. Ichikawa, *Seishin*, p. 13.

30. Merleau-Ponty's concept of "habit-body" (*le corps habituel*) refers to a sedimentation or habit-formation of the lived body, which is neither reducible to the for-itself nor to the in-itself. It casts an invisible arc, or threads of the body's intentionality, toward an object in preparation for an action by the object-body.

Ichikawa seems to incorporate within his concept of subject-body Merleau-Ponty's concept of "habit-body" in terms of the concept of "body-space" as an essential characterization of the subject-body. For Merleau-Ponty's concept of "habit-body," see *Phenomenology of Perception*, trans. Colin Smith (London: Routledge & Kegan Paul, 1961), p. 139.

31. Ichikawa, *Seishin*, p. 14.

32. Ichikawa, *Seishin*, pp. 13–14.

33. Ichikawa, *Seishin*, p. 14.

34. The other "body-space" is called "social body-space" (*shakai-teki shintai kūkan*) and this "social body-space" is said to be generated vis-à-vis "my" relationship with others, that is, my body-space as it is experienced by others. Ichikawa takes note of the fact that there is a range of "fleeing distance" detectable by wild animals; a range of distance that a certain animal flees from in fear of its own life, before its foe sets in. Analogously, Ichikawa argues, there is a territory that he calls my body-space within which a certain displeasure or restlessness can be experienced if, for example, someone else occupies a chair upon which one habitually sits. According to Ichikawa, this is because my social body-space is violated (*Seishin*, pp. 14–15).

35. Ichikawa, *Seishin*, p. 14.

36. In his *Experimental Phenomenology* (New York: Paragon Books, 1979, pp. 140–142), Ihde also notes that tactile perception is a "distance sense" and says that the object of perception "is absorbed into my experiencing as an *extension* of myself." (emphasis added) Generalizing this point, Ihde diagrams the "extension" in the schemata: "(human-machine) —> world," where he says that the parenthesis indicates an "embodiment relation" between a human and a machine or an instrument. The world, then, is experienced *through* this embodiment relation, and this embodiment relation is said to cover tactile, visual, and auditory perceptions whenever there is a mediated experience. We

may note a major difference in the understanding of Ihde and Ichikawa with respect to the concept of extension. In Ihde, the relation that holds between a human and a machine is a *mediated* "embodiment"; a machine or an instrument is not fully *appropriated* into the bodily engagement. On the other hand, Ichikawa thinks that a machine or an instrument is appropriated into the bodily engagement. The difference lies, therefore, in the fact that Ichikawa conceives of the use of a machine or an instrument as involving an achievement of skillfulness so as to make it an "incarnate" machine or instrument.

37. Ichikawa, *Seishin*, p. 16.

38. Ichikawa's concept of "bodily dialogue" is believed to be an elaboration and conceptual development of Merleau-Ponty's "subject-object dialogue" (*le dialogu du sujet avec l'objet*) through which a subject "penetrates" and "assimilates" an object. See Merleau-Ponty, *Phénoménologie de la Perception* (Paris: Librairie Gallimard, 1945), p. 154. Merleau-Ponty's concept of subject-object dialogue is unilateral, that is, the movement of body's intentionality is envisioned only from the subject to an object. As we see shortly, Ichikawa's concept of bodily dialogue is bilateral. For an exposition of Merleau-Ponty's concept of subject-object dialogue, see Nagatomo Shigenori, "Ki-Energy: Underpinning Religion and Ethics" in *Zen Buddhism Today*, November 1990.

39. Ichikawa, *Seishin*, pp. 16–17.

40. Ichikawa, *Seishin*, p. 16.

41. Ichikawa, *Seishin*, p. 17.

42. Ibid.

43. This observation seems an reiteration of Merleau-Ponty's concept of "intentional arc" functioning in the "subject-object dialogue." For a major difference between Merleau-Ponty and Ichikawa on this point, see n. 38.

44. On p. 18 of *Seishin*, Ichikawa cites Gibson's experiment from Edward T. Hall's *The Hidden Dimension* (Garden City, New York: Doubleday, 1959), pp. 80–90.

45. See note 41 above.

46. Ichikawa, *Seishin*, p. 20.

47. Ichikawa, *Seishin*, p. 21.

48. Ibid.

49. Ibid.

50. Ibid.

51. For a more extensive discussion of the ambiguity of "being-in-the-environment," see p. 28 ff.

52. Ichikawa, *Seishin*, p. 22.

53. Ichikawa, *Seishin*, p. 23.

54. Jean-Paul Sartre, *L'Être et Le Néant* (Paris: Gallimard, 1943), pp. 366–67.

55. Ichikawa, *Seishin*, p. 23.

56. Ibid.

57. Ibid.

58. Ichikawa, *Seishin*, p. 24.

59. Ibid.

60. Ibid.

61. Ibid.

62. Ibid.

63. Maurice Merleau-Ponty, *Phénoménologie de la Perception* (Paris: Librairie Gallimard, 1945), p. 109.

64. Ichikawa, *Seishin*, p. 25.

65. Ibid.

66. This distinction is noted in Yuasa Yasuo's *Nihonjin no Shyūkyōishiki* [Japanese Religious Consciousness] (Tokyo: Meicho kankō kai, 1981).

67. Ichikawa, *Seishin*, p. 25.

68. Ibid.

69. Ichikawa, *Seishin*, p. 26.

70. When we deal with Yuasa's concept of "body-scheme" in chapter 3, we learn from Yuasa that this "primitive somatic sensation" is an inner feeling of one's own body, which Yuasa calls "coenesthesis." Ichikawa's primitive somatic sensation is perhaps related to protopathic sensation.

71. See note 69 above.

72. We do not question at this juncture what this "deeper layer" means. When we discuss Yuasa's body-scheme, it will be evident what it means.

73. See note 69 above.

74. I cite Descartes' "unofficial position" here. Ichikawa's concept of "bodily dialogue" may fruitfully be compared, for example, with Aristotle's concept of "*sensus communis*" which seems to function as a synthetic unity for various perceptions, much like Kant's transcendental apperception. Although this synthetic function recognizable in Aristotle's concept must be a preconscious, though still cognitive, operation, Ichikawa's bodily dialogue is based on "somatic knowing" presupposing the bilaterality between an awareness of an object and an object of awareness. His concept of bodily dialogue may further be compared with Merleau-Ponty's "bodily intentionality" where, according to Merleau-Pointy, a subject-object dialogue takes place, through the "intentional arc" between that which is engaging and that which is engaged in our perceptual and bodily action.

75. Ferdinand Aliquie, ed., *Descartes: Œuvre Philosophique* (Paris: Garnier Freres, 1973), Tome 3, p. 119.

76. *Ibid.*, n. 3.

CHAPTER 2. ICHIKAWA'S CONCEPT OF THE BODY QUA STRUCTURE

1. Ichikawa, *Seishin*, p. 56.

2. Yuasa Yasuo, *Shintai: Tōyōteki shinshinron no kokoromi* [The Body: Towards An Eastern Mind-Body Theory] (Tokyo: Sōbun sha, 1976), p. 65.

3. See note 1 above.

4. This position has its phenomenological origin in Ichikawa's notion of the "bodily dialogue" that occurs between the living body and its ambiance. Also, one might argue that it is not the "meaning" but the "value" that the living body finds in its environment. However, a value emerges *after* making a judgement on the meaning of a fact that is presented to the living body. See *Seishin*, p. 17.

5. See note 1 above.

6. Ichikawa, *Seishin*, pp. 56–57.

7. Ichikawa, *Seishin*, p. 57.

8. Ibid.

9. Ibid.

10. Ichikawa, *Seishin*, p. 58.

11. In this regard, Merleau-Ponty's body's intentionality may be thought of as corresponding somewhat to Ichikawa's "orientational structure," ibid.

12. We may note that Merleau-Ponty's treatment of the body's intentionality deals only with the second, namely the directionality which has been cast externally to the ambiances. *Seishin*, p. 58.

13. Ichikawa, *Seishin*, p. 59.

14. Ibid.

15. Ichikawa, *Seishin*, p. 60.

16. Ibid.

17. Ibid.

18. Ichikawa, *Seishin*, p. 62.

19. Ibid.

20. Ibid.

21. Ichikawa, *Seishin*, p. 63.

22. Ibid.

23. Ibid.

24. Ichikawa, *Seishin*, p. 64.

25. Ibid.

26. Ichikawa, *Seishin*, p. 65.

27. Ichikawa, *Seishin*, p. 66.

28. Ibid.

29. Ichikawa, *Seishin*, p. 67.

30. Ibid.

31. Jean-Paul Sartre, *Esquisse d'une theorie des emotions* (Paris: Hermann, 1936), p. 42.

32. Op. cit., p. 43.

33. Ichikawa, *Seishin*, p. 69.

34. Ibid.

35. Hadley Cantril, "Perception and Interpersonal Relations," in *American Journal of Psychology*, vol. 113, p. 123.

36. Ibid.

37. Ichikawa, *Seishin*, pp. 70–71.

38. Ichikawa, *Seishin*, p. 71.

39. Ichikawa, *Seishin*, p. 73.

40. Ibid.

41. Ibid.

42. Ichikawa, *Seishin*, p. 74.

43. Ibid.

44. Ibid.

45. Ibid.

46. Ichikawa, *Seishin*, p. 75.

47. Ibid.

48. Tennesse Williams, *Cat On A Hot Tin Roof*, p. iv.

49. Ichikawa, *Seishin*, p. 77.

50. Ichikawa, *Seishin*, pp. 77–78.

51. Ichikawa, *Seishin*, p. 79.

52. Ibid.

53. Maurice Merleau-Ponty, *The Primacy of Perception*, ed. John Wild (Evanston: Northwestern University Press, 1964), p. 167.

54. Ichikawa, *Seishin*, p. 80.

55. We shall see that it is otherwise when in part 1 we deal with Dōgen's concept of the body, particularly in reference to the practice of "just sitting."

56. For a fuller articulation of this concept, see Yuasa Yasuo, *The Body, Self-Cultivation and Ki-Energy* to be published by SUNY Press, translated by S. Nagatomo and Monte Hull.

CHAPTER 3. YUASA'S BODY-SCHEME

1. Yuasa Yasuo, *Ki Shugyō Shintai* (Tokyo: Hirakawa shuppan, 1986). I have given a brief biographical account of Yuasa Yasuo in David E. Shaner, Nagatomo Shigenori, and Yuasa Yasuo, *Science and Comparative Philosophy* (Leiden, Holland: The Brill Publishing Co., 1989), pp. 1–11. *Ki Shugyō Shintai* will be published by SUNY Press under the title, *The Body, Self-Cultivation and Ki-Energy*, translated by Nagatomo S. and Monte Hull.

2. This chapter was originally presented to the conference "Giving the Body Its Due," held at the University of Oregon, November, 1989. Ms. Ruth Tonner, a friend at Temple University, kindly went over this paper to make sure that my English is intelligible, and Professor Maxine Sheets-Johnstone put a superb finishing touch on the paper. My appreciation goes to their selfless efforts.

3. An historical predecessor to the concept of "body-scheme" was the concept of the lived body (*leib*) which Max Scheler analyzed. See Stuart F. Spicker, ed., *The Philosophy of the Body* (Chicago: Quadrangle Books, Inc., 1970), pp. 159–86. Also in relation to Bergson's concept of "motor-scheme," see Yuasa Yasuo, *The Body: Toward an Eastern Mind-Body Theory*, trans. Nagatomo Shigenori and T.P. Kasulis, ed. T.P. Kasulis (Albany, New York: SUNY Press, 1987).

4. I have given an account of Yuasa's "body-scheme" in relation to the concept of somatic self within the Japanese intellectual tradition in David E. Shaner, Nagatomo Shigenori, and Yuasa Yasuo, *Science and Comparative Philosophy* (Leiden, Holland: The Brill Publishing Co., 1989), pp. 126–192.

5. What follows concerning Yuasa's "body-scheme" is my summary presentation.

6. We are still at a stage where we do not possess a hermeneutical device to understand how energy-phenomena can be transformed either into a perceptual image or into a neuron-firing, or how to correlate the perceptual image with the neuron-firing. Insofar as this issue is not solved, Yuasa's stance in taking the body-scheme as the information circuits remains a philosophical presupposition.

7. Yuasa Yasuo, *Ki Shugyō Shintai* (Tokyo: Hirakawa shuppan, 1986), p. 73.

8. This peripheral ego-consciousness is exemplified by the experience of double sensation which Aristotle (*Metaphysics*) talks about, in which there is an active-passive ambiguity felt between the pointing finger and middle finger. Ichikawa Hiroshi provides a phenomenological description and meaning of this double sensation. See Nagatomo Shigenori, "Ichikawa's View of Body" in *Philosophy East & West*, 36, no. 4, October, 1986. pp. 375–391.

9. Husserl's "passive synthesis" seems to be resurrected as the body's intentionality (*le corps intentionel*) in Merleau-Ponty's *Phenomenology of Perception*, which casts an invisible intentional arc prior to the comportment of the body. Thus, in Merleau-Ponty, it is not a passive function but is an active readiness of the body to comport itself in the world.

10. Yuasa Yasuo, *Ki Shugyō Shintai* (Tokyo: Hirakawa shuppan, 1986), p. 74.

11. In addition to the splanchnic sensation, Yuasa includes in the circuit of somesthesis a dermal sensation, and the sensation of balance, ibid., p. 75.

12. Yuasa Yasuo, *Ki Shugyō Shintai*, p. 77.

13. Yuasa points out a need to study the unconscious in this respect, because memory connects consciousness to unconsciousness, that is, to a storage of the past data of experience, ibid., p. 77.

14. Ibid., p. 78.

15. Ibid.

16. I use the word "usually" here to suggest that there are yogins who can control the function of the autonomic nervous system, for example, the heart beat.

17. Visual perception will be correlated with the eyes and thinking roughly with the frontal lobe of the brain, for example.

18. One may recall in this connection Sartre's characterization of emotion as the power to magically transform the world. See Jean-Paul Sartre, *Esquisee d'une theorie des emotions*, p. 41 ff.

19. Yuasa Yasuo, *Ki Shugyō Shintai*, p. 81.

20. Eliot Deutsch characterizes aptly the ideal of the body cherished in the Western culture as "muscle man." See Eliot Deutsch "De Corps" (unpublished paper). This generalization, I believe, still holds, although recently there have been attempts to incorporate Eastern meditation techniques into a theory of sports. See, for example, James F. Brandi, "A Theory of Moral Development and Competitive Sports." Ph.D. diss., Loyola University, 1989.

21. Yuasa Yasuo, *Ki Shugyō Shintai*, p. 93.

22. The cultivation methods of "*samādhi* through constant motion" and "*samādhi* through continual sitting" were first introduced by T'ien T'ai Master Chih I (538–597) in his *Maho Chih Kuan*. The goal of these methods is to reach the state of *samādhi*, a completely unified state, through either sitting meditation or walking meditation. Yuasa mentions several cultivation methods such as *kaihōgyō* and recitation of mantras such as *daimoku* and *nembutsu*. *Kaihōgyō* is a method of *prāxis*: namely walking through mountains for so many miles a day for a thousand days over a ten year period, while holding in mind an image of a buddha or reciting a mantra.

23. Yuasa Yasuo, *Ki Shugyō Shintai*, pp. 85–84.

24. Robert C. Solomon, in *The Passions: The Myth and Nature of Human Emotion* (South Bend, Indiana: University of Notre Dame Press, 1976), uses aptly the metaphor "hydraulic" to refer to the exercise of conscious will as a way of "controlling emotions."

25. Having made this comparison, I would like to point out that Yuasa's account is advantageous in that he not only specifies the emotion-instinct circuit as that which is habitualized but also how it can be habitualized. Yuasa elaborates on the second point in terms of personal self-cultivation.

26. Yuasa Yasuo, *Ki Shugyō Shintai*, p. 88.

27. Here a relationship between the first external sensory-motor circuit and the third emotion-instinct circuit is indirectly established.

28. De Benedict Spinoza, *Ethics*, trans. R. H. M. Elwes (New York: Harper & Row Publishers, 1966). Part 5, prop. 16, proof.

29. Yuasa Yasuo, *Ki Shugyō Shintai*, pp. 92–93.

30. Ibid., p. 86.

31. Yuasa's "unconscious quasi-body circuit" roughly corresponds to the "subtle body" (*suksma śarīra*) of which Yogic tradition speaks. This "subtle body" is believed to support the gross body (*sthūla śarīra*)

in its psychophysiological function and is the object on which a healer works. Yogic tradition recognizes one more "body" beyond this subtle body, the "causal body" (*kārana śarīra*). This "causal body" probably corresponds to *shên* of Taoist tradition.

32. Yuasa Yasuo, *Ki Shugyō Shintai*, pp. 168–169.

33. Ibid.

34. A question may arise in this connection whether the *ki*-energy is a construct or a real energy. Insofar as its effect is concerned, *ki*-energy is real but not a construct, for it has been proven from its clinical effectiveness in acupuncture medicine. It is known how it functions. This is analogous to a situation where one can hear a sound without knowing who is sounding it. However, it is not yet known *what* this energy is. In this respect, it appears to be a construct if we attempt to find a substance of this energy. Here we need to remind ourselves of the fact that the East Asian tradition has avoided an investigation of "substance," persisting through time, which underlines a phenomenon.

35. Ibid., pp. 167–168.

36. Nagahama Yoshio, *Harikyū no Igaku* [Acupuncture Medicine] (Osaka: Sōgen sha, 1982), pp. 159 ff.

37. For a detailed examination of this point, See David E. Shaner, Nagatomo Shigenori, and Yuasa Yasuo, *Science and Comparative Philosophy* (Leiden, Holland: The Brill Publishing Co., 1989).

38. According to Nagahama, the vibration of *ki*-energy is measured to be 15–50 cm/sec. while nerve-impulses travel 5–80 m/sec. See also Motoyama Horoshi, *Ki no nagare no sokutei shindanto chiryō* [The Treatment, Diagnosis and Measurement of Ki-flow] (Tokyo: Shūkyō shinri shuppan, 1985), pp. 1–23, and "Electrophysiological and Preliminary Biochemical Studies of Skin Properties in relation to the Acupuncture Meridian," in *Research for Religion and Parapsychology*, vol. 6, (2) (June, 1980), pp. 1–36.

39. Yuasa Yasuo, *Ki Shugyō Shintai*, p. 161.

40. Ibid., p. 168.

41. Ibid., p. 161.

42. Ibid.

43. See note 41 above.

44. See note 41 above.

45. This should not suggest that the *ki*-energy is reducible to emotion. Acupuncture medicine maintains that the *ki*-energy "activates the physiological functions in close contact with the object-body while connecting the body to the external world." Although it is not treated in this text, the second point in this quote, namely that the *ki*-energy intermingles with the external world through the body is extremely important. See Yuasa Yasuo, *Ki Shugyō Shintai*, pp. 168–169.

46. To understand how Japanese archery is a form of meditation in motion, see Eugen Herrigel's *Zen in the Art of Archery* (New York: Vintage Books, 1971).

47. *Nembutsu* is a short phrase consisting of *namu amidabutsu* ("to entrust oneself to Amida Buddha"), which is recited by the practitioner of Shin Buddhism.

48. Yuasa Yasuo, *Ki Shugyō Shintai*, p. 120.

49. Ibid.

50. We might compare Aristotle's hierarchical theory of soul as is expressed in *De Anima* where he places the vegetative soul at the bottom and intellectual soul at the summit of his hierarchy. In contrast, Yuasa attempts to see in the vegetative soul and the region below it a source for achieving ideals such as tao, nirvana, and satori—ideals cherished in the Eastern philosophical traditions. Aristotle's theory is an upward-moving transcendence, progressively eliminating the somatic dimensions of a person to reach the active mind in which process we can detect Plato's influence, while Yuasa's theory is a downward-moving transcendence, increasingly appropriating the somatic dimensions of a person. It is a trans-descendence from the perspective of everyday consciousness toward the regions below it. This should not, however, suggest that the experiential correlate to "trans-descendence" is simply a downward movement: there are both ascents and descents of the psyche in this process. I wonder if the Platonic and Aristotelian models, insofar as their theories of the body are concerned, might not be causing people in the West to soar up too high on the wings of reason and speculation when what is needed is first a proper launching pad.

51. I have given an analysis of Dōgen's experience in "An Analysis of Dōgen's Casting off Body and Mind" in *International Philosophical Quarterly*, vol. 27, no. 3, September 1987, pp. 227–247.

52. Here I am excluding Descartes' position advanced in *The Passion of Soul*. The union of the body and soul that was guaranteed by the "sincerity of God" is for now disregarded.

53. Aside from the provisionality suggested by the tentative opposition between the first two and the last two circuits of Yuasa's body-scheme, we can take a few examples for maintaining provisional dualism first by way of citing a broader existential situation of human existence; no historical person can escape sickness, aging and dying. This suggests that the human living body functions independently of the mind. If it were otherwise, for example, one's mind should be capable of preventing him/her from dying. The second one is a modest one of learning a new performative skill or technique, such as playing the violin or karate. When one learns karate, for example, one's mind cannot freely control the movements of the body. If it were otherwise, a new karate learner must be an instant master of self-defense!

54. We may indicate the direction of our investigation while contrasting it with Ichikawa's concept of body-scheme, so that we can easily trace a coherent, thematic thread running in our inquiry. One of the crucial reasons that Ichikawa formulated his concept of synthesis between the subject-body and object-body to be ambiguous and preconscious lies in the fact that he did not concern himself with an articulation of somatic transformation (such as Dōgen's "just sitting") on what Ichikawa called "the obscure, hazy horizon of consciousness," a cogito lurking beneath the alleged transparency of our everyday consciousness. Broadly, a method or procedure to achieve the synthetic oneness according to our interpretation of Dōgen lies in transforming the negative momentum involved in every thetic positing, i.e., the negative power of "I" not being identical with its epistemological object, into a positive one, tracing it back to the *ground* of the obscure, hazy horizon of cogito. This is existentially accompanied by a gradual elimination of mineness, for "just sitting" as a form of meditation has the function of *lowering* the activities of ego-consciousness which has its home in the alleged transparency of our everyday consciousness. We shall witness how the body appears when the center of everyday ego-consciousness is brought back to the ground of the "obscure, hazy, horizon of cogito." In this regard, Dōgen's practice of "just sitting" may be thought of as consciously appropriating what is preconsciously grasped as an ambiguous oneness through which Ichikawa claims that the body is the spirit.

CHAPTER 4. BUDDHISM AND DŌGEN'S CONCEPT OF THE BODY

1. For an extensive treatment of Dōgen's biography in English, see Hee-Jin Kim, *Dōgen Kigen: Mystical Realist* (Tucson, Arizona: The University of Arizona Press, 1975), chapter 2.

2. Tamaki Kōshirō, ed., *Nihon no shishō: Dōgen shū* [Japanese Thought: A Collection of Dōgen's Works] (Tokyo: Chikuma shobō, 1975), vol. 7, p. 30. Hereafter abbreviated as *Dōgen shū*.

3. Tamaki Kōshirō, *Nihon no meicho: Dōgen* [Japanese Master Piece: Dōgen] (Tokyo: Chūōkoron sha, 1974), p. 332.

4. I owe this point to Professor Yuasa Yasuo. See, for example, his *The Body: Toward an Eastern Mind-Body Theory* (Albany, New York: SUNY Press, 1987).

5. "Shukke kudoku" in *Dōgen*, ed., Terada Tōru (Tokyo: Iwanami shoten, 1980), vol. 2, p. 314. Hereafter, all of the quotations from *Shōbōgenzō* are cited from this edition, unless otherwise noted, and only the name of a fascicle will be given in citation along with the volume number.

6. There is a statement in the "Kattō" fascicle of *Shōbōgenzō* to the effect that the four elements are originally empty (*kū*), and the five *skandhas* do not exist. We shall for now disregard the meaning of this statement.

7. When the term "great" is added to these four natural elements such as the great Earth, great Water, and so forth, it suggests that the power which each element carries is greater than the collective power of the humans. If a rain storm with lightning, that is analyzable into wind, water and heat, for example, hits our habitat, it paralyzes our human activities and we cannot but accept its course waiting for it to pass away. In contrast to this adverse situation, the same elements such as heat and water, nurture our life, for example, in the production of food and environmental protection. In either case, we humans are placed under the care of these natural elements, although we have a tendency to become oblivious of this fundamental fact.

8. Although Dōgen does not spell it out, we might note that in these elements of lived experience, there is a working of the psychophysical, vital force (*ki*) in variously modified forms, which are said to be "harmoniously combined."

9. We can perhaps go back historically to Plato for the origin of this kind of dualism, since he understood the body as a prison house for the soul.

10. For example, there is no mention in his writings about the dispositional tendency with potential formative energy.

11. The concept of "Oceanic Reflection" is analogically derived from the great and calm ocean which reflects the appearances of a myriad of things. Tamaki observes that this *samādhi* refers to the *samādhi* of *Mahāvairocara*, which is identified with the universe itself. He states, "The universe itself is Mahāvairocara, and this Buddha is always in the state of samādhi. According to this interpretation, the world we experience is nothing but appearances reflected in the samādhi of this Buddha." See Tamaki, *Meicho: Dōgen*, p. 306.

12. "Kai-in Zanmai," vol. 1, p. 141.

13. Tamaki Kōshirō, *Nihon no Shisō: Dōgen shū* (Tokyo: Chikuma shobō, 1975), vol. 2, p. 20. Hereafter abbreviated as *Dōgenshū*.

14. Nishiari Bokusan, *Shōbōgenzō keiteki* (Tokyo: Daihōrinkaku, 1974), vol. 3, p. 64.

15. Tamaki, *Dōgenshū*, p. 20.

16. Tamaki Kōshirō, *Nihon no Meicho: Dōgen* (Tokyo: Chūōkoron sha, 1975), vol. 7, p. 306. Hereafter abbreviated as *Meicho: Dōgen*.

17. "Kai-in Zanmai," vol. 1, p. 142.

18. Ibid. Dōgen's idea of the human body as a whole of numerous dharmas within a specific temporal situation is consistent with his larger thesis of "being-time" (*uji*), that is, an inseparability between a time and a being. Dōgen argues that whenever we experience a thing (a being), there is also a time corresponding to it. Being cannot announces itself except through its temporalization, that is, "time is a being and a being is a time." See on this point Dōgen's "Uji" fascicle in *Shōbōgenzō*.

19. Ibid.

20. "Shukke kudoku," vol. 2, p. 315.

21. Ibid.

22. "Hostsubodaishin," vol. 2, p. 374. For Dōgen, this position also entails an ethical implication in that "if there is no momentary generation-extinction, the evil of a later moment cannot be left behind, nor can the good of a later moment advance itself forward."

23. See note 17 above.

24. Ibid.

25. This objection doesn't arise in Dōgen or in Zen tradition in general. One of the purposes of Zen training is to lower the activities of our everyday consciousness, including an act of reflection, and eventually to go beyond the workings of everyday consciousness.

26. See note 17 above.

27. Yuasa Yasuo, *Shinshin kankeiron to shugyō no mondai* [Issues in Mind-Body Relationship and Personal Self-Cultivation] in *Shisō*, no. 698, August 1982, pp. 30-34.

28. See note 17 above.

29. This point is also made by phenomenologists such as Sartre when he recognizes that there is a pre-reflective self in any conscious act. See Ichikawa's discussion of this point in the section "Intentional Structure," chapter 1.

30. In spite of Dōgen's claim that an "I" goes through a constant generation-extinction, one may contend that there is a persistent lived feeling that there is an I which distinguishes itself from the others. Why is there this persistent lived feeling? In view of the contemporary philosophical issues, this issue involves two separate problems. One is a problem of memory and the other pertains to the individuality of a particular body. In Dōgen's mind, as I surmise, these two issues are collapsed into one problem, namely an individual "configuration" of *samskāra*. Unfortunately, however, Dōgen does not seem to address himself to this particular issue in his writings at least explicitly.

31. "Kai-in Zanmai," vol. 1, p. 143.

32. Ibid.

33. See note 17 above.

34. See note 31 above.

35. See note 31 above.

36. This process of uncovering, for example, must be distinguished from Heidegger's "releasement" (*Gelassenheit*) achieved through meditative thinking, since the latter does not involve a somatic modification or transformation. See, M. Heidegger, *Discourse on Thinking*, (New York: Harper & Row, 1969).

37. See note 31 above.

38. The use of the term "place" may remind us of Nishida's "Logic of Place" (*basho no ronri*) which identifies three epistemological

perspectives, "place vis-à-vis being," "place vis-à-vis nothing," and "basho vis-à-vis absolute nothing." For a brief explanation of these concepts, see Yuasa Yasuo, *The Body: Toward an Eastern Mind-Body Theory* (New York: SUNY Press, 1987). These three epistemological perspectives reflect three ontological dimensions of reality. See Nishida Kitarō, *Hatarakumono kara mirumonoe* (From Working Reality to Its Seeing) in vol. 4 of the *Complete Works of Nishida Kitarō* (Tokyo: Iwanami shoten, 1979). Those who are familiar with Nishida's work may find his concept of place resurrected in part 3 as the three modalities of the human body.

39. See note 31 above.

40. As will be demonstrated later, a "what" of nondependence and nonopposition designate, generally speaking, a somatic act which is uniquely issued from the appropriated body, and a "what" as a noematic content is an instance of the former. This is derived from the coincidence between thought and action, or to use Dōgen's terminology, "practice and understanding corresponding to each other."

41. Epistemologically, this would translate into seeing "dharmas as they are" (*shohō jissō*). We shall see how this is developed when we deal with Dōgen's experience of "casting off the body and the mind." See, chapter 6.

CHAPTER 5. DŌGEN AND THE BODY IN MEDITATION

1. "Gakudō Yōjin Shū" in *Dōgenshū*, p. 59.

2. Karaki Junzō, *Mujō* [Impermanence] (Tokyo: Chikuma shobō, 1965), p. 284.

3. "Gakudō Yōjin Shū" in *Dōgenshū*, pp. 67–68.

4. Ibid., p. 68.

5. Ibid., p. 86.

6. Ibid., p. 87.

7. Ibid., p. 83.

8. Ibid., p. 70.

9. Ibid., p. 72.

10. Ibid., p. 81.

11. Yuasa Yasuo, *Shintai: Tōyōteki Shinshinron no Kokoromi* [The Body: Toward an Eastern Mind-Body Theory] (Tokyo: Sōbun sha, 1976), pp. 143–147.

12. Ibid., pp. 86–87.

13. Nakamura Hajime, ed., *Bukkyōgo Jiten* [Dictionary of Buddhist Terminology] (Tokyo: Tokyo shoseki, 1983), p. 40.

14. Tamaki, *Dōgenshū*, p. 87.

15. Yuasa Yasuo, *Tōyōbunka no Shinsō* [The Depth of Eastern Cultures] (Tokyo: Meicho kankōkai, 1983), p. 197.

16. "Gakudō Yōjin Shū" in *Dōgenshū*, p. 75.

17. "Zazengi," vol. 1, p. 126.

18. "Fukan Zazengi" in *Dōgenshū*, p. 50.

19. Ibid., p. 50.

20. "Fukan Zazengi," Abe Masao and Norman Waddell trans., *The Eastern Buddhist*, p. 122.

21. For detailed instructions on the method which should be employed in assuming the lotus position, see Abe and Waddell, trans. "Fukan Zazengi," pp. 122–123.

22. Abe and Waddell, trans., "Fukan zazengi," p. 123.

23. Tamaki Kōshirō, "Dōgen no Meisōteki Sekai" ["Dōgen's World of Meditation"] in *Dōgen Shisō no tokuchō*, ed., Kagamishima Genryū (Tokyo: Shunjū sha, 1980), p. 12.

24. If, on the other hand, this statement is given as a *kōan*, a riddle for the aspirant to solve, it would have the function of lowering the activities of his everyday consciousness, thereby allowing him to plunge himself into the deeper region of the consciousness. However, Dōgen did not belong to the tradition in which *kōan* was used for this purpose.

25. "Zazen Shin," vol. 1, p. 128.

26. Akiyama Hanji, *Dōgen no Kenkyū* [A Study of Dōgen] (Tokyo: Iwanami shoten, 1935), p. 256.

27. Ibid.

28. T. P. Kasulis, *Zen Person/Zen Action* (Honolulu: University of Hawaii Press, 1981), p. 73.

29. This "neutralization" may be conceived as corresponding to Husserl's later terminology, "pre-predicative judgement" developed in *Experience and Judgement*.

30. Sawaki Kōdō *Dōgen Zen no Sankyū* [An Investigation into Dōgen Zen] (Tokyo: Chikuma Shobō, 1976), pp. 208–209.

31. Merleau-Ponty takes the "body's intentionality" as basic, and both space and time are subsumed under the concept of "bodily space." He argues that "we must avoid saying that our body is in space or in time. It inhabits space and time." See Maurice Merleau-Ponty, *Phenomenology of Perception* (London: Routledge & Kegan Paul, 1962), p. 139.

32. Sawaki, *Dōgen Zen no Sankyū*, p. 208.

33. Ibid., p. 209.

34. "Zazen Shin," *Dōgen*, vol. 1, p. 128.

35. Tamaki, *Meicho: Dōgen*, p. 291.

36. According to Takazaki, the term "*shin jin*" appears only once in Nyojō's writing in the form of "*shinjin totsuraku*," that is, "casting off the body and the mind." See Takazaki Jikidō, *Bukkyō no Shisō: Kobutsu no Manebi: Dōgen* (Tokyo: Kadokawa shoten, 1974), vol. 11, pp. 50–51.

37. *Saṃskāra* is in fact a tangential concept having a bearing on both mind and body, when we understand the mind broadly to include the unconscious. The (personal) unconscious, when viewed physiologically, refers to the autonomic function of the body, although it is not exhaustive of it. Although various images the personal unconscious creates cannot be identified directly with the autonomic function of the body, it is suspected that the energy responsible for these images is rooted in the unconscious. Yuasa taking this energy to be *ki* argues that the various images created by the unconscious is a transformation of this ki-energy. See Yuasa Yasuo, *The Body, Self-Cultivation and Ki-energy*, trans. Nagatomo Shigenori and Monte Hull, to be published by SUNY Press.

38. "Bendōwa," in *Dōgen*, vol. 1, p. 22.

39. Ibid.

40. Ibid.

41. Ibid., vol. 1, p. 23.

42. Ibid..

43. Ibid., p. 23.

44. Tamura Yoshirō, *Bukkyō no Shisō: Zettai no Shinri—Tendai* [Buddhist Thought: An Absolute Truth: Tendai] (Tokyo: Kadokawa shoten, 1974), vol. 5, p. 51.

45. Ibid.

46. "Bendōwa," in *Dōgen*, vol. 1, p. 20.

47. Ibid., vol. 1, p. 11.

48. Takahashi Masanobu, *Dōgen no Kyōsetsu: Sono Sōgō Kaishaku* [Dōgen's Teachings: Its Comprehensive Interpretation] (Tokyo: Risō sha, 1978), pp. 71–72.

CHAPTER 6. DŌGEN AND THE BODY IN TRANSFORMATION

1. We could translate the term as "casting off the body-mind," as David E. Shaner adopts it in his *BodyMind Experience in Japanese Buddhism: A Phenomenological Study of Kukai and Dōgen* (Albany, New York: SUNY Press, 1985). Although such a rendition is worthy of consideration, especially in view of Dōgen's idea of "immobile sitting," we shall for now disregard it.

2. Takazaki, *Kobustu no manebi: Dōgen*, pp. 49–52. Through a correspondence with Professor Kimura Kiyotaka at Tokyo University who works in the same department with Professor Takazaki, I have been informed that Professor Takazaki no longer cherishes this hypothesis. Even though Dōgen might not have misunderstood "mind-dust" for "body-mind," since it raises an interesting philosophical issue, I shall retain my present account.

3. The alternative five others, basad upon *Kegon kyō* are desires for treasure, sex, food, honor, and sleep. The ones cited in the text are derived from *Hokke kyō*. It is not clear which one was Nyojo's understanding.

4. The five kinds of barrier refer to the covering of the mind inconducive for generating a positive attitude, and include (1) avarice, (2) anger, (3) torpid state, (4) depressive as well as hypersensitive state, and (5) doubt.

5. *Kleśa* is a difficult term to be rendered appropriately into English. Here, it is translated as "covering desire" in view of the philosophical position advanced in the previous chapter. It designates an outflowing desire of the human body with a defiling force of afflicting human mind and body. Buddhism counts three fundamental *kleśas* as (1) avarice, (2) anger and (3) stupidity. Takazaki, ibid., p. 49.

6. According to the entry in *Hokkyoki*, Dōgen, perhaps in dissatisfaction, challenged his teacher, by humbly requesting "Please do not arbitrarily grant me the seal," when the latter granted to Dōgen the seal of transmission, ibid., p. 53.

7. Tazato Yakumu, *Shidōsha o kitaeru Dōgen zen no kenkyū* [Study of Dōgen Zen for the Leaders] (Kyoto: PHP kenkyūjo, 1983), p. 30.

8. This suggests generally that an occasion for satori is pervasively present in our everyday life-world.

9. Generally speaking, satori via the auditory experience suggests a deeper state of samādhic awareness than the one attained through visual heightening. In meditation, auditory hallucination is much rarer than the visual hallucination, and when it is experienced negatively in a pathological case, it accompanies a severe physical pain which is absent in the case of visual hallucination.

10. "Keisei sanshoku," in *Dōgen*, vol. 1, p. 292.

11. For Aristotle's concept of *sensus communis*, see *De Somno et Vigilia*, chap. 2, 455a 32.

12. "Mujō seppō," in *Dōgen*, vol. 2, p. 69.

13. See, for instance, Lawrence E. Marks, "On Colored-Hearing Synesthesis: Cross-Modal Translations of Sensory Dimension," in the *Psychological Bulletin*, May 1975, pp. 303–27.

14. "Mujō seppō," in *Dōgen*, vol. 2, p. 67.

15. Ibid., p. 70.

16. "Ikka myōju," in *Dōgen*, vol. 1, p. 105.

17. For example, a choice of a "quiet" place for sitting is a demonstrating of Zen's wisdom of affectivity.

18. Here *shinjin totsuraku* may be understood either as "casting off the body and the mind," or "casting off the mind-dust." Because of this ambiguity, the phrase is not rendered into English.

19. Nyojō's criterion for *shinjin totsuraku* was to remove at least one of these "barriers." Since there is no indication in the text which one of these barriers Dōgen "cast off" when Nyojō recognized Dōgen's confirmatory experience, we shall treat them generally as a form of negative affectivity.

20. I include "doubt" (tamerai) in this category, because psychologically speaking, it is a vacillation of the indecisive attitude.

21. Akiyama Satoko, *Satori no bunseki* [An Analysis of Satori] (Tokyo: Asahi shuppan sha, 1980), pp. 90–91.

22. Umehara Takeshi, in *Kobutsu no manebi: Dōgen*, p. 272.

23. Takahashi, ibid., p. 68.

24. "Bendōwa" in *Dōgen*, vol. 1, p. 14.

25. Eliot Deutsch, *Personhood, Creativity and Freedom* (Honolulu: University of Hawaii Press, 1982), pp. 35–55.

26. Tamaki, *Meicho: Dōgen*, p. 15.

27. Ibid.

28. "Bendōwa" in *Dōgen*, vol. 1, p. 13.

29. Ibid., vol. 1, p. 14.

30. Ibid.

31. Ibid., vol. 1, p. 15.

32. In *The Body, Self-Cultivation and Ki-Energy*, Yuasa suggests that this vital force *ki* is both psychological and physical in nature. Or it is neither psychological or physical in origin. The psychological and the physical are a manifest expression of this vital energy.

33. See note 29 above.

34. "Yuibutsu yobutsu" in *Shōbōgenzō* ed., Nakamura Sōichi (Tokyo: Seishin shobō, 1976), vol. 4, p. 405.

35. "Hotsubodaishin," in *Dōgen*, vol. 2, p. 212.

36. "Busshō" in *Dōgen* vol. 1, p. 45.

CHAPTER 7. DŌGEN AND THE BODY IN ACTION

1. "Sokushin zebutsu" in *Dōgen*, vol. 1, p. 85.

2. "Shinjin gakudō" in *Dōgen*, vol. 1, pp. 75–76.

3. Ibid., vol. 1, p. 76.

4. Ibid., vol. 1, p. 80.

5. Here we witness a marked contrast between Dōgen and Parmenides in their approaches to knowing things. Parmenides thought that only being is real and its reality lies in thinkability, while rejecting an appearance unworthy of reality. This difference between Dōgen and Parmenides may be explained in terms of the distinction between practical knowledge and theoretical knowledge. Parmenides sought theoretical knowledge in the thinkability of being, while Dōgen sought practical knowledge which delivers humans from suffering.

6. "Shinjin gakudō" in *Dōgen*, vol. 1, p. 74.

7. Ibid.

8. "Sokushin zebutsu" in *Dōgen*, vol 1, p. 85.

9. "Ikka myōju" in *Dōgen*, vol. 1, p. 105.

10. "Busshō" in *Dōgen*, vol. 1, p. 45.

11. See note 9 above.

12. "Ikka myōju" in *Dōgen*, vol. 1, p. 104.

13. "Shinjin gakudō" in *Dōgen*, vol. 1, p. 75.

14. "Inmo" in *Dōgen*, vol. 1, pp. 225–226.

15. Ibid., vol. 1, p. 225.

16. "Mujō Seppō" in *Dōgen*, vol. 2, p. 67.

17. Yuasa Yasuo, *The Body: Toward An Eastern Mind-Body Theory* (Albany, New York: SUNY Press, 1987).

18. See note 13 above.

19. Ibid., vol. 1, p. 76.

20. Ibid., vol. 1, pp. 77–78.

21. "Kai-in Zanmai" in *Dōgen*, vol. 1, p. 143.

22. "Kōmyō" in *Dōgen*, vol. 1, p. 161.

23. "Bukkyō" in *Dōgen*, vol. 1, p. 391.

24. "Ikka myōju" in *Dōgen*, vol. 1, p. 105.

25. "Kai-in Zanmai" in Dōgen, vol. 1, p. 142.

26. "Zenki" in Dōgen, vol. 1, p. 275.

27. "Genjō kōan" in Dōgen, vol. 1, p. 37.

CHAPTER 8. PRELIMINARIES AND A THEORY OF ATTUNEMENT

1. Whenever the term "living ambiance" is used throughout this part, I would like to have it understood as also implying a shaped thing, an object in it. Naturally, one may question why the living ambiance can include the inanimate object, because the inanimate thing is not a living being. The model I have in mind in including the inanimate things in the living ambiance follows an organic nature of our environments, where there are regulated cyclic activities, in the process of which the inanimate thing can decompose into nothing and then is given a new life, although a strict identity between them may not be maintained at this point of our scientific understanding.

2. Tom Downey points out to me that this statement is ambiguous: (1) it seems to assert that the problematic of attunement is concerned with the relationship between a personal body and external ambiance, or (2) it seems that the ambiance is the plenitude out of which a person arises, in which case "ambiance" loses the sense of externality. Although the second alternative is the position toward which the theory of attunement strives, I shall for now takes the first alternative as a starting point to introduce the theory of attunement.

3. This either/or attitude can be traced back to Aristotle who, for example, in his *Metaphysics* upholds that a thing cannot be both being or non-being, or both true and false, thereby justifying the validity of the law of contradiction as a criterion for judgment. According to this model of thinking, the basic particulars are individuals which are frozen within a conceptual field disregarding temporal flow. In view of a dynamic temporal unfolding of life, the method is a conceptual fabrication.

4. This was, for example, a reason that Scheler thought that there is a foundational intentionality of the lived body distinct from the intentionality associated with the perceptual consciousness. See Max Scheler's "Lived body, Environment and Ego," in *The Philosophy of the Body*, ed., Stuart F. Spicker (Chicago: Quadrangle Books, Inc., 1970). It is more clearly stated in Ichikawa when he demonstrated that

cogito is dependent for its function and survival upon the body. See chapter 2 on Ichikawa.

5. For this point, see Yuasa Yasuo, *The Body: Toward An Eastern Mind-Body Theory* (New York: SUNY Press, 1987).

6. Yuasa Yasuo, "Shinshin kankeriron to shugyō no mondai" [The Issues in Mind-Body Relationship and Personal Self-Cultivation] in *Shisō*, no. 698, August, 1982. pp. 30–34.

7. Elsewhere, I have characterized "meditation" within the Japanese intellectual history as a way of effecting both "horizontal" and "vertical" transcendence. See Nagatomo Shigenori, "A Japanese Concept of Self" in *Science and Comparative Philosophy*, co-authored by Yuasa Yasuo and David E. Shaner, (Leiden, Holland: The Brill Publishing Company, 1989), pp. 126–192.

8. This goes in the opposite direction from Aristotle's hierarchical theory of the soul, for example. The active mind as the apex of this hierarchy subsumes the nutritive soul as its bottom, wherein a principle of this nutritive soul is merely a biological growth and decay. See Aristotle's *De Anima*.

9. What I am proposing here is not to belittle the value of theoretical knowledge, but to offer an alternative to it.

10. This seems to follow if we accept Ichikawa's argument that *cogito* is dependent upon the body in its concrete function and survival. The theory of attunement differs from Ichikawa's contention in a crucial way, however. Ichikawa recognized the status of *cogito* in "the obscure hazy horizon of consciousness" that lurks at the bottom of the body *qua* subject. However, since he did not take into account the meditational aspect which effects a somatic transformation as we saw in Dōgen's practice of "just sitting," he failed to elucidate the ground of "intelligibility" in this obscure, hazy horizon of consciousness, a dark *cogito*. See Nagatomo Shigenori's "Ichikawa's View of the Body," in *Philosophy East and West*, vol. 36, no. 4, October, 1981.

11. Eliot Deutsch, *De Corpus*, unpublished paper.

12. I owe the concept of "tensionality" to Merleau-Ponty's "body's intentionality" and Ichikawa's "lived bodily scheme." Even though both Merleau-Ponty and Ichikawa have recognized a oneness of the body and the mind in a certain sense, this oneness is a partial oneness, or potential oneness that is not fully actualized or appropriated in the personal existence *qua* body. In case of the Merleau-Ponty, it is most evident when he

sought the origin of "body's intentionality" in the concept of the third term which is neither body nor mind, suggesting a certain "tension" embedded in Merleau-Ponty's concept of "the third term." In case of Ichikawa, his concept of "oneness" is an ambiguous unity between the "bright" and "hazy and obscure" horizons of *cogito*.

13. Tom Downey points out that one of the implications of this universal fact is that we cannot speak truthfully of a personal body apart from, or outside of, his/her ambiance, for to be embodied is to be within, and act out of, ambiance.

14. This idea of the body functioning as a principle of verification was suggested to me by Professor Eliot Deutsch during the course entitled "The Body" in the fall of 1982.

15. I am trying to identify here the lowest common denominator, and Tom Downey supplements it with the following remark: To be, one must be embodied. To be embodied means an internal ambiance (e.g., disposition) and an external ambiance (e.g., other things). The body embodied in ambiance is a *world*. Yet, body and ambiance constantly shift and change through attunements (physiological, perspectival, etc.) which, in turn, call up the need for further attunement. This is the lowest common denominator; internal ambiance—body—external ambiance (i.e., the world)—attunement. Based on this understanding, I attempt to describe "attunement" later on from the perspective of tensionality, de-tensionality and non-tensionality.

CHAPTER 9. A GENERAL THEORY OF ATTUNEMENT

1. We may take this as a conceptual origin of a school, a tradition, or a culture, which becomes a basis for ethnic consciousness. In fact, it applies to any grouping of people when the group distinguishes itself from the other groupings.

2. See, for example, Yuasa Yasuo's *The Body: Toward an Eastern Mind-Body Theory* (Albany, New York: SUNY Press, 1987), pp. 99–109.

3. For a discussion of various body-spaces, See Nagatomo Shigenori's "Ichikawa's View of the Body" in *Philosophy East and West*, vol. 36, no. 4, October, 1981.

4. Although I cannot go into the details of this observation here, we can cite Dōgen's treatment of physical nature and time as an

instance of this point. Also, Kimura Bin, a contemporary Japanese psychiatrist, points out that time is experienced differently between a neurotic and psychotic patient. See his *Jikan to jiko* [Time and Self] (Tokyo: Chūōkoron sha, 1982).

5. The use of the term "anima" may remind us of C. G. Jung's distinction between anima and animus. His concept of anima or animus ranges from a sexually activated ideal image of an opposite sex to its spiritual consummation vis-à-vis the various processes of individuation, culminating in the concept of "Self" (*Selbst*). What I have in mind here is the energy source which activates the process of individuation.

6. The term "feeling-judgement" was suggested to me by Professor Yuasa of Tskukba University in a private conversation in the Spring of 1982.

7. Ichikawa Hiroshi, *Seishin toshite no shintai* [The Body as Spirit] (Tokyo: Kesisō shobō, 1979), pp. 8–19.

8. For a fuller discussion of this point, see Nagatomo Shigenori, "Ki-Energy: Underpinning Religion and Ethics" in *Zen Buddhism Today*, November 1990.

CHAPTER 10. A STRATIFICATION OF ENGAGEMENT

1. Martin Muller, *Prelude to the New Man: An Introduction to the Science of Being* (Rancho Santa Fe: Santa Fe Associates, 1979), p. 10.

2. Most of dream states on the other hand are indicative of the tensional modality, not in the sense, however, that the person attends self-consciously to the images of dream, since the consciousness in the dream state is a mere observer. The tensionality in most dream states is witnessed when there is a discrepancy between the images of wakening and dream world. Where there is no tensionality, there is a correlativity between the wakening world and dream world, which in the terminology of the theory of attunement, is a nontensional modality of existence.

3. The history of Western philosophy has provided two directions to account for this. Idealism absorbs the object within the self as an epistemological subject, because it leaves the body in the background of the experiential *momentum*, disallowing it full participation. When seen in this manner, idealism cannot but insist upon an meaning bestowing activity on the part of the self as an epistemological subject. On the other hand, empiricism, pretending that the self is an "objec-

tive" observer without any determination, relegated a reality to an object, that is, only to the matter or the physical body. Obviously, neither of them is a sufficient treatment of the experiential momentum.

4. This distinction between the explicit and the implicit is borrowed, although I deviate from his original use, form Yuasa's unpublished paper "Contemporary Science and an Eastern Mind-Body Theory," delivered at Japan-France Joint International Conference held at Tsukuba University, Japan, in November, 1984.

5. Edmund Husserl, *Ideas: A General Introduction to Phenomenology* (New York: Colier Books, 1976), p. 96.

6. Yuasa Yasuo, *Kindai Nihon no Tetsugaku to Jitsuzonshisō* [Modern Japanese Philosophy and Existential Thought] (Tokyo: Sōbun sha, 1970), p. 28 and p. 304. Elsewhere, I have also characterized this "progressive retrogression" as comprising both a horizontal and vertical transcendence. See David E. Shaner, Yuasa Yasuo, and Nagatomo Shigenori, *Science and Comparative Philosophy: Introducing Yuasa Yasuo* (Leiden, Holland: The Brill Publishing Co., 1989).

7. For detailed accounts of what one experiences in the process of meditation, see, for example, Motoyama Hiroshi, *Toward A Superconsciousness: Meditational Theory and Practice*, trans. Nagatomo Shigenori and Clifford R. Ames (Calif.: Asian Humanities Press, 1990).

GLOSSARY
FOR JAPANESE TERMS

Abe Masao　　　　　　　　　　阿部　正雄
Akiyama Hanji　　　　　　　　秋山　範二
Akiyama Satoko　　　　　　　秋山　さと子

banshō　　　　　　　　　　　　万象
Bendōwa　　　　　　　　　　　弁道話
bodaishin　　　　　　　　　　菩提心

chikaku　　　　　　　　　　　知覚
chiken　　　　　　　　　　　　知見

daishi　　　　　　　　　　　　大死
Dōgen　　　　　　　　　　　　道元
dōitsusei no chokkan　　　　同一性の直観

dōshin dōki　　　　　　　　　同身同機
dōshin dōmei　　　　　　　　同心同命
dōsei　　　　　　　　　　　　　同棲
dōtoku　　　　　　　　　　　　道得
Dōzan　　　　　　　　　　　　道山

Eisai　　　　　　　　　　　　　栄西
fudō　　　　　　　　　　　　　不道
fugen naru gaki nari　　　　不言なる我起なり

fukakuteiteki　　　　　　　不確定的不可変的身体空間
　　kahentekishintai kūkan

gaikai kankaku undō kairo	外界感覚運動回路
Gakudō Yōjinshū	学道用心集
genshō toshite no shintai	現象としての身体
gogai	五蓋
gōitsu	合一
gyō	行
Hakuin	白隠
hikari	光り
hi shiryō	非思量
heijōshin	平常心
henshin	遍身
Hōkyoki	宝慶記
hō no nen	法の念
hotsubodaishin	発菩提心
ichi gōsō	一合相
ichinyo	一如
Ichikawa Hiroshi	市川　弘
ikeru shintai zushiki	生ける身体図式
ikkamyōju	一顆明珠
ikari	いかり
ikon	意根
ikon zadan	意根坐断
jiko	自己
jinkai	尽界
jisetsu	時節
jōdō hōnno kairo	情動本能回路
jōshikiteki nigeron	常識的二元論
ju	受
junkoteiteki shintai kūkan	準固定的身体空間
junsui shii	純粋思惟

Ki Shugyō Shintai	気修行身体
kai in zanmai	海印三昧
kage	影
kaku jin	客塵
kankyōnai sonzai	環境内存在
kannō dōkō	感応同交
Karaki Junzō	唐木　順三
Kyashata	伽耶舎多
kegon	華厳
ki	気
kibun	気分
kitai	基体
kobutsushin	古仏心
kōdōkanōsei	行動可能性
koga	吾我
kokoro	こころ
kōseiteki kōzō	向性的構造
kōzōtoshite no shintai	構造としての身体
kū	空
kūmu	空無
kyakutai toshiteno shintai	客体としての身体
meiryō ishiki	明瞭意識
mono	もの
Motoyama Hiroshi	本山　博
muishikiteki junshintai	無意識的準身体
mujō	無常
musabori	貪り
mushin	無身
Myōe	明恵
Nagahama Yoshio	長浜　善夫
Nakamura Hajime	中村　元
Nandai	難提

ningen tekina	人間的な
nen	念
nenbutsu	念仏
Nyojō	如浄
ooi shishin tokudo sha	応似比身得度者
ryōgiteki ichigensei	両義的一元性
sanzen	参禅
Sawaki Kōdō	沢木　興道
seishin	精神
Seishin toshiteno shintai	精神としての身体
seitokutecki shintai kūkan	生得的身体空間
seizon kanōsei	生存可能性
shaku shin	赤心
shikan taza	只管打坐
shiki	色
shiki	識
shikōsei	指向性
shikōsei	志向性
shikōteki kōzō	指向的構造
shin	身
shin	心
shin ishiki	心意識
shinjin	身心
shinjin ichnyo	身心一如
shinjin dotsuraku	身心脱落
shinjitsu nintai	真実人体
shinki icchi	心気一致
shinshin gyōnen	身心凝念
shintai kūkan	身体空間
shintaiteki taiwa	身体的対話

shintai to shite no jiko	身体としての自己
shiryō	思量
shō	証
shōbō	正法
Shōbōgenzō	正法眼蔵
sō	相
sokugen shinjin	即現身心
shukan shintai	主観身体
shutai toshite no shintai	主体としての身体
shutai	主体
shutaika	主体化
taitatsu	体達
Takahashi Yoshinobu	高橋　賢陳
Takazaki Jikidō	高崎　直道
Tamaki Kōshirō	玉城　康四郎
tamerai	ためらい
Tamura Yoshirō	田村　芳朗
taisei naibu kankaku kairo	体性内部感覚回路
tōgō	統合
tōkai	悼悔
toraware	とらわれ
Tōyōbunka no Shinsō	東洋文化の深層
tsuge shiraseru	告げ知らせる
tsūshin	通身
u shin	有心
Umehara Takeshi	梅原　猛
ware	われ
yakushin kainō	翻身回脳
Yuasa Yasuo	湯浅　泰雄

Yakuzan Kūkō	薬山　弘道
yugō	融合
zazen	坐禅
zenshin	全身
zenshin	全心
zenshin naibu kankaku	
kairo	全身内部感覚回路
zenki	全機

BIBLIOGRAPHY

Akiyama, Hanji. *Dōgen no Kenkyu* (A Study of Dōgen). Tokyo: Iwanami shoten, 1935.

Akiyama, Satoko. *Satori no Bunseki* (An Analysis of Satori). Tokyo: Asahi shuppansha, 1980.

Aristotle. *Nichomachean Ethics*. Ed. Richard McKeon, in *The Basic Works of Aristotle*. New York: Random House, 1949.

———. *De Anima.*

———. *De Somno et Vigilia.*

———. *Posterior Analectics.*

Brandi, James F. "A Theory of Moral Development and Competitive Sports." Ph.D. diss., Loyola University, 1989.

Cantril, Hadley. "Perception and Interpersonal Relations" in *American Journal of Psychology*. Vol. 113, p. 123

Chih I. *Maho Chih Kuan.*

Descartes, René. *Descartes: Œuvre Philosophique*. Ed. Ferdinand Aliquié. Paris: Barnier Freres, 1973.

Deutsch, Eliot. *Personhood, Creativity, and Freedom*. Honolulu: The University Press of Hawaii, 1982.

———. *De Corpus.* (Unpublished paper).

Dōgen, Kigen. *Shōbōgenzō*. Ed. Terada Tōru. Tokyo: Iwanami shoten, 1980. Vol. 1 and 2.

———. *Shōbōgenzō*. Ed. Nakamura, Sōichi. Tokyo: Sheishin shōbō, 1976. Vol. 4.

———. "Fukan Zazengi." Trans. Abe Masao and Norman Waddell in *Eastern Buddhist.*

Hall, Edward, T. *The Hidden Dimension*. Garden City, New York: Doubleday, 1959.

Heidegger, Martin. *Discourse on Thinking*. Trans. John M. Anderson and E. Hans Freund. New York: Harper & Row, 1969.

Herrigel, Eugen. *Zen in the Art of Archery*. New York: Vintage Books, 1971.

Husserl, Edmund. *Ideas: A General Introduction to Phenomenology*. Trans. W. R. Boyce Gibson. New York: Collier Books, 1976.

———. *Experience and Judgement: Investigations in A Genealogy of Logic*. Trans. James S. Churchill and Karl Ameriks. Evanston: Northwestern University Press, 1973.

Ichikawa, Hiroshi. *Seishin toshite no Shintai* (The Body as the Spirit). Tokyo: Keisō shōbō, 1979.

Ihde, Don. *Experimental Phenomenology*. New York: Paragon Books, 1979.

Kant, Immanuel. *Critique of Pure Reason*. Trans. Norman E Smith. New York: St. Martin's Press, 1965.

Karaki, Junzō. *Mujō* (Impermanance). Tokyo: Chikuma shobō, 1965.

Kasulis, T. P. *Zen Person/Zen Action*. Honolulu: The University of Hawaii Press, 1981.

Kawai, Hayao. *Kage no genshōgaku* (A Phenomenology of Shadows). Tokyo Shisaku sha, 1976.

Kim, Hee-Jin, *Dōgen Kigen: Mystical Realist*. (Tucson, Arizona: The University of Arizona Press, 1975).

Kimura, Bin. *Jikan to jiko* (Time and Self), Tokyo: Chūōkōron sha, 1982.

Kwant, Remy C. "Merleau-Ponty and Phenomenology" in *Phenomenology*, ed. Joseph J. Kockelmans. New York: Doubleday & Company, Inc., 1967.

Marks, Lawrence E. "On Colored-Hearing Synesthesis: Cross-Modal translations of Sensory Dimension" in *Psychological Bulletin*, May 1975, pp. 303–328.

Merleau-Ponty, Maurice. *Phenomenology of Perception*. Trans. Colin Smith. London: Routledge & Kegan Paul, 1962.

———. *Phénoménologie de la Perception*. Paris: Gallimard, 1945.

———. *The Visible and The Invisible*. Trans. Alphonso Lingis. Evanston: Northwestern University Press, 1968.

———. *The Primacy of Perception*. Ed. John Wild. Evanston: Northwestern University Press, 1964.

Motoyama, Hiroshi. *Ki no nagare no sokutei shindanto chiryō* (The Treatment, Diagnosis and Measurement of Ki-flow). Tokyo: Shūkyō shinri shuppan, 1985.

———. "Electrophysiological and Preliminary Biochemical Studies of Skin Properties in Relation to the Acupuncture Meridian" in *Research for Religion and Parapsychology*, vol. 6, June 1980.

———. *Toward A Super-consciousness: Meditational Theory and Practice*. Trans. Nagatomo Shigenori and Clifford R. Ames, (Calif.: Asian Humanities Press, 1990).

Nagahama, Yoshio. *Harikyū no igaku* (Acupuncture Medicine). (Osaka: Sōgen sha, 1982).

Nagatomo, Shigenori. *Science and Comparative Philosophy*. Leiden, Holland: The Brill Publishing Company, 1989.

———. "Ichikawa's View of the Body" in *Philosophy East & West*, vol. 36, no. 4, October 1986.

————. "An Analysis of Dōgen's Casting off Body and Mind" in *International Philosophical Quarterly*. Vol. 27, no. 3, September 1987.

————. "*Ki*-Energy: Underpinning Religion and Ethics" in *Zen Buddhism Today*, November 1990.

Nakamura, Hajime, ed. *Bukkyōgo Jiten* (Dictionary of Buddhist Terminology). Tokyo: Tokyo Shoseki, 1983.

Natson, Maurice. *Edmund Husserl: Philosopher of Infinite Task*. Evanston: Northwestern University Press, 1973.

Nishiari, Bokusan. *Shōbōgenzō Keiteki* (Commentary on Shōbōgenzō). Tokyo: Daihōrinkaku, 1974.

Nishida, Kitarō. *Hatarakumono kara mirumonoe* (From Working Reality to Its Seeing) in vol. 4 of the *Complete Works of Nishida Kitarō*. (Tokyo: Iwanami shoten, 1979.)

Rahula, Walpoha. *What The Buddha Taught*. New York: Grove Press, Inc. 1959.

Ross, David. *Aristotle*. London: Methuen & Co. Ltd., 1974.

Sartre, Jean-Paul. *L'Être et Le Néant*. Paris: Gallimard, 1943.

————. *Esquisee d'une theorie des emotions*. Paris: Hermann, 1936.

Sawaki, Kōdō. *Dōgen Zen no Sankyū* (An Investigation into Dogen Zen). Tokyo: Chikuma shobō, 1976.

Scheler, Max. "Lived Body, Environment, and Ego" in *The Philosophy of the Body*. Ed. Stuart F. Spicker. Chicago: Quadrangle Books Inc., 1970.

Shaner, David E. *The BodyMind Experience in Japanese Buddhism: A Phenomenological Study of Kūkai and Dōgen*. Albany, New York: SUNY Press, 1985.

Solomon, Robert C. *The Passions: The Myth and Nature of Human Emotions*. South Bend, Indiana: University of Notre Dame Press, 1976.

Spinoza, Benedict. *Ethics*. Trans. R. H. M. Elwes. New York: Harper & Row Publishers, 1966.

Takahasi, Masanobu. *Dōgen no Kyōsetsu: Sono Sōgō Kaishaku* (Dōgen's Teachings: Its Systematic Interpretation). Tokyo: Risō sha, 1978.

Takazaki, Jikidō. *Bukkyō no Shisō: Kobutsu no Manebi: Dōgen* (Buddhist Thought: Imitatio De Old Buddhas—Dōgen). Tokyo: Kadokawa shoten, 1974.

Tamaki, Kōshirō. *Nihon no Shisō: Dōgen Shū* (Japanese Thought: An Anthology of Dōgen). Tokyo: Chikuma shobō, 1975.

————. *Nihon no Meicho: Dōgen* (Japanese Masterpiece: Dōgen). Tokyo: Chīōkōron sha, 1974.

————. "Dōgen no Meisōteki Sekai" (Dōgen's World of Meditation) in

Dōgen Shisō no Tokuchō (Characteristics of Dōgen's Thought). Ed. Kagamishima Genryū. Tokyo: Shunju sha, 1980.

Tamura Yoshirō. *Bukkyō no Shishō: Zettai no Shinri—Tendai* (Buddhist Thought: An Absolute Truth: Tendai). Tokyo: Kadogawa shoten, 1974.

Tazato, Yakumu. *Shidōsha o Kitaeru Dōgen Zen no Kenkyū* (Study of Dōgen Zen for the Leaders). Kyoto: PHP Kenkyūjo, 1983.

Thomas, Edward J. *The History of Buddhist Thought*. London: Routledge and Kegan Paul, 1933.

Umehara, Takeshi. *Bukkyō no Shisō: Kobutsu no Manebi:Dōgen* (Buddhist Thought: Imitatio De Old Buddhas—Dōgen). Tokyo: Kadokawa shoten, 1974.

Yuasa, Yasuo. *Ki Shugyō Shintai* (Ki-Energy, Self-Cultivation and the Body). Tokyo: Hirakawa shuppan, 1986.

———. *Shintai: Tōyōteki Shinshinron no Kokoromi* (The Body: Toward an Eastern Mind-Body Theory). Tokyo: Sōbun sha, 1976.

———. "Contemporary Science and an Eastern MindBody Theory". A paper delivered in the Japan-France Joint International Conference at Tsukuba University, Japan, in November, 1984.

———. "Shinshin kankeiron to Shugyō no Mondai" (Issues in Mind-Body Relationship and Personal Self-Cultivation) in *Shisō*, no. 698, August 1982.

———. *Tōyōbunka no Shinsō* (The Depth of Eastern Cultures). Tokyo: Meicho kankokai, 1983.

———. *Nihonjin no shūkyōishiki* (Japanese Religious Consciousness). Tokyo: Meicho kankōkai, 1081.

——— and Sadataka, trans. *Ōgon no Hanano Himitsu* (The Secret of the Golden Flower). Tokyo: Jinbun shoin, 1980.

———. *Kindai Nihon no Tetsugaku to Jitsuzonshisō* (Modern Japanese Philosophy and Existential Thought). Tokyo: Sōbun sha, 1970.

Whitehead, Alfred North. *Modes of Thought*. New York: The Free Press, 1968.

Williams, Tennessee. *Cat On A Hot Tin Roof*.

INDEX